T0269867

swimming with the
BLOWFISH

swimming with the
BLOWFISH

HOOTIE, HEALING, AND ONE HELL OF A RIDE

JIM SONEFELD

DIVERSION
BOOKS

Diversion Books
A division of Diversion Publishing Corp.
www.diversionbooks.com

First Diversion Books edition, June 2022
Hardcover ISBN: 9781635767674
eBook ISBN: 9781635767681

Printed in The United States of America
1 3 5 7 9 10 8 6 4 2

Library of Congress cataloging-in-publication data is available on file

To my family

CONTENTS

The eye sees only what the mind
is prepared to comprehend.

—ROBERTSON DAVIES

FOREWORD

MY INITIAL ENCOUNTER with the name "Soni" was during my first semester at the University of South Carolina. A girl I had a major crush on invited me to her dorm room, so I excitedly walked all the way across campus to Bates House to see her. But, when I got there, she instantly grabbed her camera and said, "Let's go."

We then walked to the sand volleyball courts nearby and she gave me the camera, saying, "Go get on the bridge over there and take this picture for me." When I got to the bridge I looked down and written in the sand I saw in very big letters, "I LOVE SONI!"

I took the picture, gave her back the camera, and decided *I hate this Soni!*

Well, little did I know that I was going to spend the rest of my life chasing dreams and living them out, right by his side.

We went from driving around in a van, sleeping on the floor with the smell of foot and ass everywhere, to touring Europe in a jet. We loved, fought, cried, laughed a lot, and did whatever it took to play the music that we knew was very distinctly ours.

Jim "Soni" Sonefeld has lived a life that is rife with fun and pain, light and darkness, but always with an amazing amount of love. The way he sees the world is one of a kind and his story is one for the ages.

We have done many things together we are proud of, and some, not so much. He is my brother and always will be.

Darius Rucker
2022

Darius Rucker is a singer-songwriter, three-time Grammy Award winner, and member of the Grand Ole Opry

PROLOGUE

I HAVE BECOME fully detached.

I may be the king of my castle, but I am the only one in it. Over the months and years, I've become separated from my own family. Every day I tell them I love them, yet my actions don't match my words. Just one example: I've spent tens of thousands of dollars building this immaculate space at the back of our long, narrow, neighborhood lot so I can spend time writing music apart from them, yet still *technically* be home. I've spared no expense with architects, builders, designers, and home audio specialists, but no matter how much I've invested in creating this fortress, a space where I can rule without interruption, there's no escaping the real problem in my life: me.

This two-story garage/apartment we call "The Back House" is the perfect space for entertaining, but I mostly just entertain myself. The room is painted in reds and golds, browns and dark greens. There's a flat-screen TV, a couch, my piano, and a multi-track recording device I struggle to understand. There are plenty of stools next to a bar fully stocked with rum, tequila, Jägermeister, and a variety of bourbons—all of these, my favorites—along with a separate fridge that holds a small wine collection. There is also a full bathroom with a shower. If this place had a stove, I could live out here.

~

At approximately 10:30 a.m. on Sunday, November 14, 2004, I'm lying on the expensive corduroy couch, but my mind is not at rest. I had treated myself to a late-night session of songwriting, but it had turned into another bout of misery and substance abuse. After a solid eight to ten hours watering my body with bourbon and ginger ales, now my mouth is dry and my lips gummy. Hidden on top of the highest stereo component, where only my 6'2" body can reach, is a little baggie full of white powder and a partially smoked joint in a makeshift ashtray.

Through my agitated rest I hear the downstairs door open and then close. My daughter Cameron runs up the carpeted stairs. When she gets to the top, she happily skips over like the bubbly, unfiltered 4-year-old she is, and plops down on my chest.

Though her words are few, they land heavy on me.

"Dad, what are you doing?" Cameron doesn't seem hurt by my absence from the main house; she just seems curious. She's asked me similar questions before, like, "Daddy, why does your breath smell funny?" or "Daddy, why do you keeping falling asleep in the middle of our bedtime story?"

This morning though, I'm struggling to come up with an answer. My lips are stuck together—not from dehydration, but by some other power I can't describe.

Again she says, "Dad, what are you doing?"

I say nothing.

Frustrated, she hops off of me and scurries back down the stairs. I manage to sit up, and when I do, all I can hear is Cameron's question ringing over and over and over again in my hazy head. It's like there's a needle skipping on a scratchy old vinyl record.

Dad, what are you doing? What are you doing?

The only way to shut off the incessant question now is to answer it.

What *am* I doing? Why *am* I out here sleeping, while my family is in the house watching "The Wiggles" and having a blast? Why *aren't* I participating in the joys of bacon, eggs, pajamas, and general silliness?

The answer is suddenly clear: "I'm no longer in control." Something else is controlling me. I am pretty sure it's drugs and alcohol, and I'm sick and tired of getting my butt kicked daily by them. I want to be free of the pain and suffering, yet I can't imagine my life without these chemical crutches.

At this moment, though, something stronger is pulling me to make a move. Should I take a leap of faith by following the small voice inside me that is saying, "If you'd just reach out and ask someone for help, this confusion and enslavement can be over right now"?

I begin the walk down the long flight of stairs, holding the rail. I tell myself I don't *need* the rail. I'm not hung over. *I* don't get hangovers. To admit to being hung over is to admit failure. (The truth is, I'm probably still drunk.)

Descending toward the bottom, I take in the images displayed on the wall as they slowly pass by. I gaze at a set of colorful, 11x14 photos of the band, some of my favorites ever, taken for a *Time* magazine article back at the height of our fame. Our faces are gleeful and fresh, smiling back at me. There's a gold record plaque from Australia, commemorating the sales of our second album *Fairweather Johnson*—a reminder of the extensive reach our music once had. And next to it, for our contribution to the million-selling *Friends* soundtrack (our huge radio hit "I Go Blind"), hangs a shiny, silver platinum record. *Friends*, I think. I'm thankful none of mine are here to witness me in this condition.

As I reach the landing, I catch a blurry glimpse of myself in the bathroom mirror. I stop and stare. My long, blond hair is tangled and dirty. My shirt is badly wrinkled and has a spill stain across the shoulder.

I despise the figure in the mirror.

one

NAPERVILLE VIA EVERYWHERE

IN THE SUMMER of 1973 I was eight years old, and that was the year our family's Oldsmobile station wagon rolled into Naperville, Illinois.

My parents Otto and Mary Lou Sonefeld loved the heck out of us kids and provided us with the best opportunities they could manage, even though we had to uproot often. We arrived in Naperville from Vienna, Virginia, where we'd moved to from Winnetka, Illinois, where we'd moved to from Vienna, Virginia, where we'd moved to from Alexandria, Virginia, where we'd moved to from Lansing, Michigan, where all four boys had been born. It was our fifth move in as many years—my dad was continually searching for better job opportunities—and I had grown accustomed to the changes of scenery and how to quietly fit in as the new kid. All these moves, though, probably explained why my mom colored her hair, and why dad was going bald.

I was really hoping I could make friends again this time. My two older brothers Mike and Dave, who were eleven and thirteen, must have been fretting about finding new buddies; my quiet little brother and roommate Steve, only six years old, was probably hoping to find an appropriately aged friend for himself, too. And if three-year-olds can conceive of friendships, then my sister Katie was likely also dreaming of a playmate.

The new house on Hercules Lane was a modest split-level with a sloping, curved driveway leading up to a garage and a basketball net. And right next to the house was a swarm of kids gathering in the adjoining yard.

"What have we here?" Mom said, always the encourager. "Looks like you kids will fit right in that group. Oh, Katie, there's even a girl!" It didn't matter that the girl she was referring to was three times Katie's age. I think Mom was just relieved there was at least one female in the group.

Within minutes there was a scrum of kids playing football—we ran, we chased, we tackled, and on that side yard we began building friendships in just the way that suited me: with a ball.

~

Dad went to work, a long forty hours a week, so Mom was the one in charge of wrangling our little posse from town to town and taking care of us as we settled into each new place. We four Sonefeld boys were not always reserved little bundles of joy, either—Mom would usually refer to us using that age-old phrase, a "handful."

We learned about life through trial and error, but mostly, error. Our discoveries often began with well-intentioned questions like, "If we light this cardboard on fire in the bedroom, will it create smoke?" or "I wonder if Steve, minding his own business in his stroller, will float if I push him off the dock into the lake?"

Luckily it was a pretty shallow lake.

My dad was reserved, and had been raised by hard-working Michiganders where nothing came for free, even though he occasionally would show us he believed that life should also be spontaneous and fun. Once, when we'd been living close to Lake Michigan in northern

Illinois, he let all four young boys sit unbuckled in the rear-facing seat of his station wagon with the window completely down, and he pulled right up to the edge of the lake during a fierce storm—it was both thrilling and terrifying.

Mom was naturally playful, always trying to get us to dance, or sing, or play sports with her. She had been a cheerleader, and tennis player, and singer herself, but now she was burdened with the day-to-day running of the house, so she taught caution as well as fun. When Katie was born in 1971, it helped balance the family ship that was listing heavily with males.

~

My folks believed their middle child, Jimmy (that would be me), would best thrive at a small neighborhood Catholic school in Naperville. I didn't have any major problem getting along in school as a pre-teen—my grades were solid, but my report cards often featured the comment, "does not apply himself." The truth was, I was easily distracted by girls, sports, and music, and was generally annoyed by the many books I was forced to read, most notably, the Bible.

My religious education, which I believed was meant to help me better navigate the whole "right from wrong" thing, only ended up setting me back further in my already inadequate, scrambled thinking. Frankly, the whole *God* thing scared me. Though I was being told about a risen Jesus Christ who loved me deeply, the nuns were also intimidating me with talk of a wrathful god, hellfire, and the idea that I should suffer, just like our Lord and Savior had suffered for me. This gave me a massive dose of guilt that I carried around as a child. The Old Testament violence and vengeance not only shocked me, it also felt like the opposite of the whole *Jesus loves you* stuff. Unable to reconcile the confusing theology taught in my religion classes, I would keep my head down to avoid locking eyes with Sister Helen, Sister Judith, or Sister Barbara, fearing their judgmental words, "Jesus loves you, but you are a sinner, not worthy in God's eyes—AND A FIERY PIT IN HELL AWAITS YOU IF YOU KEEP IT UP, MISTER SONEFELD!"

Just how was I supposed to digest that? It seemed unfair that I would have to face the punishment of an angry god for actions as innocuous as putting my arm around some girl.

There was more: could my personal salvation really be hinged on my believing an array of bizarre stories from the book of Genesis that didn't seem to align with basic, modern science? The story of a man who lured all the world's animals two at a time onto a giant boat in preparation for a worldwide flood was hard for me to fathom. Also, when the nuns went on about Adam and Eve wandering naked in a garden and its direct connection to my sinful life, I couldn't stop thinking about a cute girl wandering around naked in a garden with only a few leaves covering her.

It wasn't all the nuns' fault. I was selfish. (I was also eleven years old.) I pushed back on everything from having to attend confession, to repeating prayers I didn't comprehend, to having to wear my dumb school uniform. None of this was worthy of my time.

To my short list of local authorities for whom I already held a distaste or suspicion—teachers, principals—I added the blurrier, trickier, harder-to-comprehend party-killer called God.

~

We were fortunate that our parents showed us the virtues of compassion and empathy. My mom was always standing up for someone who'd been excluded from a group for one reason or another, and Dad continually showed us the value of speaking up for what is right instead of ignoring injustice. Between the two of them we had an up-close view of putting others first rather than putting yourself at the front of the line. They helped create the first youth soccer league in Naperville, even though neither had ever played the sport, and they sponsored an inner-city Chicago family at Christmas by becoming their Santa Claus. Considering that they already had five of us to feed, clothe, and play Santa for, this was a huge deal. Dad, a child of the Depression/WWII years, thought gift-giving was for practical items like socks or underwear, but Mom, who was seven years younger, chose to see the *fun* in functional, and thought Christmas was for toys and more creative giving.

Mom stayed up half the night wrapping the presents for the inner-city family as if the gifts were for her own children, and she insisted that we kids take part in it, too. Then, Dad, Dave, Mike, and I loaded up the station wagon to deliver. But the joy and excitement turned to sadness as, within half an hour of our safe little subdivision, we found ourselves in drab, concrete projects that resembled a war zone. Seeing for the first time the vast cultural, racial, and economic differences proved to be a profound experience for me. My dad—having only the apartment number and three of his kids holding a half-dozen giant bags of Christmas gifts—did what came naturally: he was friendly and acted like he was supposed to be there (he surely never met a stranger), leading his little crew to the family's home.

This was *his* unconditional love, and it made a great impression on me. Many years later, when I asked Dad about that Christmas, he admitted he wasn't so sure that it had been smart to roll into what was known to be a dangerous neighborhood with nothing but his three boys, a bunch of gifts, and good intentions. But he also never regretted showing us firsthand what love looks like.

I really wanted to emulate my parents, but I fought a strong, self-serving nature. I had a good deal of love in my own heart; it just seemed to face a roadblock with my love of deviance.

two

KICK BALL, KICK DRUM

SPORTS WERE THE main outlet for my prepubescent energy and quickly became the lens through which I viewed life; for a start, I would instinctively chase after anything you threw in front of me, over and over again, like a loyal golden retriever.

I was a natural at throwing and catching and had a strong competitive streak. In our neighborhood, sports revealed what season it was: baseball and its many derivatives like "pickle," "home run derby," and "500," meant it was summer; when the footballs came out, real or nerf, it was fall. We pulled out the hockey sticks and pucks as the snow turned into nicely hard-packed layers each winter; and when the snow melted in the spring, the basketballs, soccer balls, and skateboards all showed themselves and wouldn't be put away again until winter came back around.

Soccer was my greatest passion, though. Besides loving the touch of the ball at my feet, I loved the international group of parents and their kids who came together for their mutual love of soccer—there were Germans, Yugoslavians, Brits, Australians, Iranians, and Asians all happily mixed together. I thought it was so cool that this thread of soccer ran all the way around the world, connecting Africa to Asia, to Europe, to South America, and right through my own little town. I was happy spending hours alone juggling the ball in the driveway, firing low passes off the front porch concrete wall, or shooting into our backyard goal. But I also enjoyed the camaraderie of being on a team, and a strong friendship with two of my best buddies, Will and John, crossed over from soccer to school to our social life. The three of us spent hours playing soccer, listening to music, talking about girls, and complaining about the cruel world ruled by overbearing grownups.

~

There was another source of inspiration fighting for a place in my heart: music.

Music gave me a different sort of buzz, one that had nothing to do with competition. Music spurred my imagination, painting pictures in my mind. I drifted off to faraway places—scenes of musicians playing their instruments, or me on stage, or lovers loving, or even the smile of a girl I had a crush on. The combination of notes, chords, harmonies, words, and textures mesmerized me. Perhaps the music was just a soundtrack to feelings that already existed?

I remember first feeling drawn to contemporary music simply because it was catchy. I begged my mom to purchase an unabashedly unhealthy breakfast cereal called Super Sugar Crisp in the late 1960s because it contained a super-flimsy but workable 45-rpm record—a single by The Archies, a fictional band featured in their own animated TV series. It was bubble gum pop rock at its finest and I ate it up like the sweetened flakes inside the box.

The Archies aside, the first song that really moved me was "Love Her Madly" by The Doors. It wasn't the most intricate song ever written, but the clarity was profound, as if I were standing right next to the musicians as they were playing their instruments. Jim Morrison's voice was riveting and intimidating. Combined with the unique keyboard sound, it sent me to somewhere I can only describe as a dark carnival. I didn't understand the lyrics, all those seven horses and blue dreams, yet it was taking me somewhere wonderful, pulling me into the unknown. Hearing that song for the first time—me and my dad were driving somewhere, and it came on the radio—well, something in me was transformed.

My parents, like a lot of hip, middle-class parents in the early 1970s, had a big old stereo unit: a huge piece of mahogany furniture with a turntable, a radio, an 8-track player, and somewhere to store your records. Their record collection gave me an eclectic set of music to choose from—Motown to rock to country to instrumental. There was The Beatles, of course, but also Creedence Clearwater Revival, Stevie Wonder, Marvin Gaye, The Who, and Led Zeppelin; there was classic country and blues like Glen Campbell, Willie Nelson, Jim Reeves, and Muddy Waters; and some stuff I'd never touch, like Dave Brubeck and the Boston Pops.

But there was one record that set me on the journey to becoming a musician: Elton John's *Goodbye Yellow Brick Road*. I remember sitting in our living room at Christmastime listening in complete awe to that album. Elton's deep mystical ballads like "Sweet Painted Lady" and "Candle in the Wind" intrigued me with their sexual imagery. The monumental, eleven-minute "Funeral for a Friend/ Love Lies Bleeding" fascinated me. . . . But it was "Saturday Night's Alright (for Fighting)" that set me on the percussive path that would last me a lifetime.

As that song blared out of the speakers that Christmas, I picked up two drumstick-shaped pieces of a discarded Christmas toy called "Super Toe," which featured a plastic kicker and a field goal, and started to drum along. Even then I was right in time with the beat; it was totally natural and involuntary. I was mimicking Nigel Olsson's drum fills—this meant I was drumming along with Elton John! I was a DRUMMER! It was magical!

At that moment, a tiny musical spark inside me became a flame.

There weren't many opportunities for a young boy like me in the 1970s to hear and *see* drummers drumming. The few I took advantage of were thrilling moments that became engrained in my memory, such as the school night when my parents excitedly woke me up just so I could watch the famous big band drumming legend Buddy Rich thrashing and sweating on The Tonight Show. Or, while up late on a sleepover with my buddies Will and John, finding a TV show with a psychedelic drum/percussion performance by The Edgar Winter Group of their instrumental hit, "Frankenstein." Or finding myself staring entranced in a Holiday Inn during an out-of-state eighth-grade basketball trip as a live band performed in the bar. I couldn't take my eyes off the drummer even though I was obviously breaking curfew and not supposed to be in a bar in the first place. (Based on these experiences I assumed that professional drummers only drummed *late* at night . . .)

~

The constant tapping of my toes and endless pattering of my knuckles and fingertips were met with disapproval by my teachers, and often by my parents, but it was difficult to get my hands and fingers to stop.

So I devised a way to temporarily avoid annoying people around me by covertly tapping certain teeth together. It was almost like having a little drum kit in my mouth. Tapping the top edge of my smaller front bottom teeth to the backside of my thicker front teeth sounded like a kick-drum; tapping my bottom cuspids against my eye teeth on the top sounded like a snare drum; rubbing my bottom teeth backward and forward was my hi-hat cymbals or shaker. Sometimes I played along to songs I had memorized and sometimes I just made stuff up and just noodled around with new patterns. (I still do this *dental drumming* to this day.)

All the rhythms that started in my brain and manifested into pounded-out patterns were like breathing to me; they came continuously and without thinking. And, perhaps deciding it would be less expensive than sending me to a doctor or psychologist to see if I had mental problems, my folks suggested drum lessons.

I was starting seventh grade when I had my first lesson at Naper Music on Ogden Avenue. My instructor Ron immediately spoke to me like I was a drummer, not some lowly student. He was hip, too. He wore a pair of zip-up leather boots with a slightly elevated heel and a smooth, silky, button-down shirt.

To start with, at home I practiced the single drum patterns from a beginner's manual by hitting a thick, hard-covered book, proudly holding the new drumsticks just as Ron had showed me. About a month later—waiting to see my progress and perhaps also balancing a tight budget—my parents upgraded me to a more official drum pad with a stable, wooden base. Then, on my thirteenth birthday, I wondered why my mom was following me up the stairs to my bedroom. . . . She just wanted to see my face when I opened my door to find a brand new, sparkly CB-700 three-piece drum kit. A gold Camber ride cymbal sat like royalty on a silver stand; a hi-hat stand with cymbals stood to the left; a perfect drum throne awaited me.

"They weren't cheap," Mom said, "so we'd prefer that you use them. A lot."

She wouldn't have to tell me twice.

~

I did all of the drum exercises my fancy-booted drum instructor Ron gave me, and eventually I moved my kit down to the basement where I could keep the growing volume farther away from the rest of the family.

With sports still taking up much of my free time, I didn't have time to join up with other kids who were forming bands in garages throughout Naperville, so I spent most of my drumming time alone in the basement. My mom, my biggest supporter, would occasionally come through on her way to and from the laundry room and shout out something encouraging like, "That sounds great!" or "Is that CCR you're playing along with? I like that!"

With my big, padded headphones plugged into my Panasonic portable cassette player, I'd pound away, mimicking Doug Clifford of Creedence Clearwater Revival, Don Henley of The Eagles, Led Zeppelin's John Bonham, Boston's Sib Hashian, and Stan Lynch of Tom Petty and The Heartbreakers, to name just a few.

Ron must've really believed in my progress over the first year, because he convinced me I was good enough to sign up for an upcoming drumming contest in Chicago. I worked hard to learn the piece we picked out, but by the time I was in the car with Mom and Dad heading to the contest, I was plagued with self-doubt and negative thinking. In fact, I narrowly avoided throwing up from nerves.

When we arrived, I was terrified, but one of the judges opened things up by telling the story of a girl who'd competed years earlier. "She wasn't intimidated by being in a big competition," he said, "or the fact she was the only girl. Instead, she stepped right up and dazzled the judges with her smooth skills and easygoing smile, and won first place. Her name? Karen Carpenter."

For some reason this story really calmed me down, and that day I—just like Karen before me—knocked it out of the park, taking home my own first-place trophy. Drumming never looked or felt the same after that. A big dream was growing in my heart.

three

AN OUNCE

FROM CATHOLIC SCHOOL I went to a public high school, which was great for me because I got to leave religion behind, besides being forced to attend church most Sundays. It would be a long time before I willingly picked up another Bible.

Like a lot of kids hitting high school, I carried with me approximately one ounce of confidence. For a start, I wasn't exactly graced with good looks. I could make the girls laugh, but my teeth had been a mess most of my childhood from running into lampposts, chairs, and baseballs with my face—hence the braces. If having hair that could not be moved was your thing, then you would have loved me; it was permanently straight and flat, no matter how many strokes of a hairbrush I put through it in an attempt to make it feather or part. Then there were the long, toothpick legs; honestly, it was as if there were a competition going on between my thighs and calves to see which could be skinnier. I also boasted clunky, bony knees that stood out like little planets.

As for friends, well, before I would ever set foot in Naperville Central High School, I was introduced to one particular friend who would turn out to be a foe: alcohol.

The summer of 1979 was the first time I found myself in the company of peers who were drinking. I reached right out to join in. I was fourteen, so I quickly rationalized that somehow *I* would avoid any consequences, even though I'd spent years overhearing the conversations my parents were having with my brothers—Dad saying to my oldest brother Dave, "Had you boys been drinking when the cops pulled you over?" or Mom to my other older brother Mike, "If the marijuana wasn't yours, then what was it doing in *your* car?" I was more than willing to look past the fact that what I was doing was wrong, and illegal, because I badly wanted to see how the alcohol would make me feel. It didn't even matter that the taste of the beer was vile. Twelve ounces of it made me forget for a moment that I had bad hair and braced teeth. A few swigs from a bottle of Seagram's 7 and several tokes from a joint sent me to a place of peace. It made me laugh more easily than usual and made the new people around me seem like old friends.

I discovered I liked the escape from normalcy alcohol produced in me. I was certainly no math expert, but I was smart enough to work out that if one beer gave me a feeling of euphoria, then I could double that feeling by drinking two beers, and double *that* high again by drinking four. Of course, this flawed equation ended with me on my knees vomiting by the side of our house that night. The score at the end of my first bout with partying was Alcohol 1, Jim 0, but I knew I would give it another try.

~

One of the advantages of having two older brothers was the trickle-down system of stuff like key chains, bandanas, boots, and clothing. By 1979, Dave was already attending Illinois State University; Mike, though still in high school, lived much of his life away from our house, rebuilding old cars with friends. This left their closet open to me, and I was eager to speed up the hand-me-down process.

One day I found a perfectly faded denim jacket that looked just my size. I went to the kitchen to show Mom just how great it looked on me. Regrettably, a shiny something popping up out of one of the pockets caught her eye.

"Hmmm," Mom said, "what do we have here?" It was a miniature, silver pipe, reeking of something strong. "Well, that will be mine," she said, and I watched as she threw it into the garbage.

Later, with the coast clear, I got the pipe out of the garbage, and my friend Will and I soon found something to put in it. Buzzed, we adventured out on our bikes to feel the wind in our hair and grab some munchies at the nearby drugstore, then walked home in a daze, laughing loudly and bingeing on cheap candy bars.

Yes, we walked home. In our afternoon haze, it seems we had forgotten we rode there on our bikes. The following day Dad noticed they were gone and called the police, who discovered that the bikes had been *abandoned* up at the drugstore. "Those darned kids must have stolen our bikes, gone joy riding, and then dumped the bikes in the parking lot behind the drugstore where no one would see them," I said, convincing myself of this scenario off the top of my head.

Unfortunately, the bikes were sitting in the racks directly in front of the drugstore, and had been there since, oh, Friday afternoon, said the store manager. It looked for all the world as if someone had forgotten them.

~

That was bad enough, and kinda funny, but I was to do worse, and less funny.

When I was about fifteen, I convinced a friend of mine to let me take his parents' Chevy Suburban from the party he was throwing to go buy more beer at a 7-Eleven with my shoddy fake ID. Unfortunately, I thought a few donuts in the grass would be fun on the way to the store, until the dewy evening caused the vehicle to careen wildly into a pine tree or two. Not wanting to stick around the scene of the crime, I immediately swung the vehicle back into the street, leaving a fresh patch of rubber in the process, and headed back to the party.

I had hit a tree so hard that a branch had sheared completely off and was now jammed into the rear quarter panel and fender of the truck. I was in big trouble. Kids immediately started gravitating toward the huge dent and were trying desperately to remove the tree limb sticking out of the truck. Others just stood around pointing and laughing.

When I saw a police car coming toward the party, I went into full panic mode and ran like hell. If I could just make it back home into my bedroom and under my covers, I somehow thought I would be safe. If I could shut my eyes and slow down my racing heart and fall asleep, maybe it would all just go away.

That was how I often dealt with fear as a child. I'd run and hidden in the bushes at age four when I'd about lopped off my neighbor's ear while wildly swinging a golf club without paying attention; my parents thought I'd been abducted when they couldn't find me. Then, in first grade, I'd run from the approaching police at the downtown Winnetka drugstore when I thought I would get in trouble because our bikes were laying all about the sidewalk. (Mike had forced me to stand outside the store to watch over the bikes while he and his friends went inside.) No one, including my mom, could find me, and the police were eventually alerted I had gone missing. (I was at home under my bed.)

Now, at fifteen, I had the covers pulled up tight against my cheekbones once again, hoping against hope that no consequence would come for my horrendous driving blunder. The peace lasted for about thirty minutes, followed by a knock on the front door. Both of my parents answered.

"Otto, Mary Lou, I hope the two of you are doing well."

"What brings you here, officer?" my mom said. "Or should I say, *who* brings you here?"

"We received information that your son may have been involved with a traffic incident this evening, and we need to ask him a few questions."

"I think Michael is upstairs. Should we get him?"

"Actually, it's Jim I need to speak to. Is he home?"

Mom and Dad looked at each other, about as confused as two people could be with this surprising news that it was not Mike, the recidivist, who was needed for questioning by the Naperville Police Department.

Seconds later, the lights in my bedroom were on. I was busted.

It took me half a summer of community service to pay my debt to the City of Naperville, which was ironic, as I was already working for the Park District. Now, instead of $3.50 an hour, I was working for free.

four

THE BEAUTIFUL (COLLEGE) GAME

MY DAD'S ENTHUSIASM for refereeing soccer in Aurora, a largely Mexican community nearby, gave me the opportunity to see a bigger, more vivid picture of life beyond Naperville.

Seeing Dad hustling up and down the field yelling "*Cambio!*" to the sidelines, whistling for "*entretiempo*," and communicating in Spanish to the field players, was inspiring to me, and his willingness to jump into a new culture showed me that great discoveries await those who bravely seek out new experiences. (Plus, it made him cool.) Within the year, I was not only on the roster of one of those Mexican teams, but also invited to join a club team called the Aurora Kickers, who were about to embark on a fourteen-day soccer exhibition tour in Germany in 1982.

It was a trip that would change my soccer trajectory and my life.

~

The Kickers, like most of the soccer community flowing from the huge melting pot of Chicago, were a blend of Mexican, Eastern and Western European, British, and American players, and they had exactly one slot available on their roster when the offer came.

Playing against real German teams was a thrill. Walking through the streets of Frankfurt in our matching, blue satin team jackets emboldened with red and white USA lettering gave me a feeling of immense pride. Traveling south, I noticed a familiar sign: Darmstadt. It was the town that harbored the base where my father had been sent as a young soldier, maybe just a few years older than I was then, to train during the Korean War in the early 1950s.

The World Cup happened to be taking place in the summer of 1982, in Spain, and for the first time my eyes widened to a wonderful picture of what football means to the rest of world outside the United States. I'd seen professional soccer played with the North American Soccer League's Chicago Sting, but the World Cup was next level. Imagine the intensity and cultural obsession of our Super Bowl, but one that only takes place every four years and includes countries that span the globe. Since the United States had not qualified for this tournament in over thirty years, it remained pretty much unknown stateside. The rest of the world, though, had been eagerly awaiting it for those long four years. Life in German towns simply stopped if there was a German match being played; one day at an Italian restaurant, we couldn't get a single waiter to serve us because they were all huddled in front of a small radio in the kitchen anxiously listening to their Italian side playing against Argentina. I'd never seen anything like this focus and energy toward soccer, and it was thrilling.

Returning to Naperville, something inside me had changed. Traveling abroad made me feel I was capable of doing more, of going further, of thinking bigger. It was matched also by a physical self-assurance. A growth spurt had left my shoulders a little broader and my walk a little taller; and my braces were gone, so I now had a smile I was proud of, too.

~

Some of the kids I called friends were labeled by many parents as the *wrong crowd*—teenagers who didn't have a mom or dad home regularly, who smoked dope and cigarettes unabashedly, stayed out late, ditched classes, and generally defied authority. I was thought of as one of the *good kids* in the group; I had two parents at home, made decent enough grades, played on a sports team, and didn't appear as though I'd just been in a gang fight. But the distinction was a cruel one between *wrong crowd* and *good kid*, and I found myself regularly defending the character of my friends, who didn't have the benefit of the things I had. I knew on the inside I wasn't much different from them. Yes, I might wear a soccer shirt or letter jacket and be dating a pom-pom-shaking cheerleader (the braces and the acne were gone!), but behind the veneer I was smoking dope, drinking alcohol, and skipping school, too.

With high school coming to an end, I needed to figure out where I would attend college. Finding a Division One soccer program was what I cared about most. I wanted deeply to prove I could compete at the highest college level, so I passed up a few offers from smaller colleges, and took a big risk in doing so.

I chose the University of South Carolina. My grandparents on my mom's side, George and Eleanor Hornberger, had retired near the university, and my mom's sister Janet and family also lived in the area. With no guarantee of a soccer future, other than a fair tryout promised to me by the head soccer coach, Mark Berson, I decided to roll the dice and commit my efforts to South Carolina.

Though school was not due to begin at the university until mid-August, my instinct told me it would be best to cut the umbilical cord from my high school group, from our parties, and from Naperville, sooner rather than later. Lucky for me, my older brother Mike, who had just driven back to Naperville for a brief respite from his job in South Carolina working for our Aunt Janet, was about to go back to the Palmetto State. Two days later, I placed a few bags of clothes, my stereo, and my drum kit in the bed of my brother's 1969 aqua green Ford F-150 pickup truck and hopped happily into the small cab. With Kilo, my brother's German shepherd puppy, sleeping at my feet, I was pumped to get started on my journey south with my cooler older brother.

Prior to this trip, the two of us hadn't been particularly close. I'd already gotten him busted with the pipe from his denim jacket, and I'd also managed to blow an entire bowl of pot embers the wrong way all over the backseat on the way to an REO Speedwagon concert in Chicago. Not only had I failed the cool test that night, but my presence had also ruined his chance to be alone with his girlfriend. Then there was the night I "threw a rod" on the engine of his super-bad 1966 Thunderbird, probably from all my revving around town in anger when I was trying to catch up with my then-date, who'd ditched me at a dance.

Rolling out onto the highway leaving Naperville though, Mike had either had a major change of heart, a faulty memory, or a willingness to forgive, because he and I spent that trip and our first weeks in Columbia rebuilding our friendship, hanging out at the river drinking cheap beer, and driving around the city celebrating our newfound independence together. He had his own apartment, and I stayed at my Aunt Janet's house and got a temporary job lifeguarding.

But my true purpose was to play NCAA Division I soccer, and the success, or failure, of that soccer dream rested on a couple of short walk-on tryouts that August. I trained as best as I could on my own in the July heat—think a "Rocky"-type figure sweating and working against all odds, in slow motion, of course.

(It may not have been that badass.)

As early August arrived, I went to watch a practice and see what I was up against. I stared with envy at the new freshman recruits brought in from Miami, St. Louis, Atlanta, Chicago. Most of them were on big scholarships, they all had matching boots and practice uniforms, and the grizzled, mustachioed veterans on the team looked like grown men.

What I'd give to be part of that team.

Ten days later, my tryout arrived. I was alongside maybe a dozen other unaffiliated, mismatched soccer scrubs like myself, and I wondered if any of their dreams were resting on two short tryout sessions. Did they have backup plans in case the coach chose not to keep *any* walk-ons? I guess *my* only backup plan was to just be a regular college student, but that was not at all what I had come eight hundred miles to do.

After the second hard day of tryouts, head coach Mark Berson and his fiery Irish assistant Trevor Adair asked me to stay behind for a conversation. Maybe they had noticed just enough skill, or had an intuition I was at least teachable.

"Be here for practice with the team tomorrow morning at 8:00 a.m. sharp," Trevor said. "The locker room is down the hill if you need any tape or treatment."

I was the only walk-on who'd made it, but I stayed composed and acted like I was meant to be there. "Thanks, Coach," I said, like it was normal, and walked away. Deep down though, I was jumping for joy.

~

At the end of my freshman year, I found myself trudging back to Naperville with a dismal 1.1 grade point average—oh, and I'd also lost my freshman-year playing eligibility after suffering a broken foot during my first match midway through the season. I saw myself as just another local loser whose big college sports dreams had collapsed, and now I was back home . . . until a letter arrived from South Carolina saying that if I came back and got Bs in two summer school classes, I could be reinstated on probation for the fall semester.

Within hours I was making plans to head back to South Carolina.

~

Back at school, I worked my ass off to get on the team, and by my third year I was a season-long starter. We went all the way to the Final Eight in the NCAA tournament. I still couldn't concentrate on the books and the reading (the only exception being all the album lyrics I consumed by Rush drummer Neil Peart). I was probably undiagnosed ADD to be honest—and an inner urge for individuality made being on a team tough. I would push the envelope by wearing long, dangly earrings, especially if they were going to raise an eyebrow from the authority figures in the athletic department. I would cut my hair, or not cut it, to see if the coaches were paying attention. I would also partake in some excessive drug and alcohol use during our off-season, then pull it back considerably during our regular season so it wouldn't affect my performance on the field.

I wanted to have the best of two worlds: to participate on a team, but make up my own rules along the way. It was becoming apparent that my coach's idea of a good use of time and my idea of the same were at opposite ends of a spectrum.

It all came to a head when I found out that The Grateful Dead were going to play a Halloween show in 1985 in Columbia. Now, going to a Dead show can mean anything from drinking a few beers to smoking some weed to taking a hit or two of acid, depending on what you're into.

I knew what I was interested in, and it was the trifecta.

This was a Thursday night; the team's last regular season soccer match was two days later in Fairfax, Virginia, against George Mason University.

But my college coaches weren't stupid. When they caught wind of our desire to attend the concert, they countered by having the team leave Columbia Thursday afternoon. I, of course, was outraged and took it as a personal affront, sulking all the way.

That Saturday, I scored the first goal for our team against GMU, a long-range header from the edge of the box that looped over the backpedaling goalkeeper and into the net. As my hands rose into the air and my teammates swarmed me in celebration, deep down, I was still mad.

five

BACHELORS OF ART

WINTER IN COLUMBIA left me feeling blue. January and February were cold, wet, and gray. I felt lost and decided I needed a big change. So, with barely even a discussion with another person, and less than a month into my sixth semester of college, I withdrew from school.

Though my dad had changed majors, changed colleges, and even tried the Army before finally earning his degree, and my mom never finished college, they weren't too happy about my decision. What I didn't know then was that my parents were also facing the most difficult period in their twenty-five-year marriage, a union that would end later that year.

~

Since I was renting a house near campus with friends, I decided to remain in Columbia after my withdrawal from the university. I found a job at the South Carolina State Mental Hospital in the adolescent ward, and was given the slightly overstated title of Mental Health Specialist, working with kids who were only a few years younger than me. It was an entry-level position, paid pretty decently, and mostly required that I let kids in and out of different spaces and made sure they stayed out of trouble. I was affectionately given the nickname "Keyman." The experience made me realize how fortunate my home life had been, as many of the kids from the ward were products of broken families. After a period in the ward with the kids, I was transferred to adult "Recreation Therapy," where we got to host a weekly dance for the adult patients. It amazed me that some of the sickest adults in that hospital, whose severe illnesses ranged from dementia to bipolar disorder, could jump right into a smooth, eloquently grooving dance step upon hearing the right Marvin Gaye song. I learned a lot working with those patients every day, and I was sure glad to be away from textbooks for the first time in my life.

But I didn't quit school just to get a paycheck, and a job was not going to fill the void I was feeling, so I scoured newspapers, music stores, and bulletin boards around town to see if anyone was looking for a drummer. I'd been missing a creative outlet in my life—now, without soccer and school filling up my time, I had room to concentrate on making music.

The options weren't endless in a mid-sized, southern city like Columbia, but they sure were amusing:

Bass player needed for Southern style, psychedelic, prog-rock band. Janis Joplin meets Rush, but with cowboy boots. Serious inquiries only.

Indie/college rock band needs female singer with cool hair. Must be willing to travel.

Looking for drummer/bass player for edgy, greasy, alternative country/rock band. Glitter-neck meets glamour-billy. Must wear leather

Lacking experience, I couldn't be picky. At twenty-one I was a late bloomer to be joining my first band. I knew how to keep rhythm, to stay on beat, but I had zero experience with creating original drum patterns while interacting with other musicians.

Eventually, I joined an alternative band named Bachelors of Art. We wrote and played originals and also covered a collection of contemporary alternative songs by bands like Souixsie and the Banshees, U2, The Cult, that kind of thing. Along the way my bandmates turned me on to stuff I'd never heard before, like Echo and the Bunnymen, Cabaret Voltaire, Simple Minds, and Kate Bush.

I played my first live gig ever (not counting the drum competition in Chicago) at The Golden Spur, a bar on the South Carolina college campus. The show had lasted sixty nervous minutes, but once I finished I realized I'd relished every second of it.

We were making original music and traveling out of town to do gigs. I finally got to wear dangly earrings and moussed, spiked hair, too. And, as 1986 rolled by, I learned, very willingly, to party like a rock star. Just because you don't have a lot of fans or a lot of money, it does not prohibit you from partying like you do, so we did. (We had easy access to recreational drugs, since someone was dealing drugs out of the place where we practiced.)

I noticed there wasn't much moral judgment regarding the use of mind-altering substances in the rock music circles I was in, and it was refreshing. I was no rookie when it came to using acid, shrooms, coke, or weed (I had been experimenting with them since I was fourteen), but now having convenient access to them seemed like a big plus.

It was all fun and games until one day, while we were practicing, undercover agents burst into our rehearsal. Being the drummer, I was the last one to hear the fuzz.

"Freeze! Put down the drumsticks!" would be funny in most situations, but not in this one—in fact, I peed a little. Fortunately, I avoided spending the night in jail, but the whole thing definitely shook me up. Just not enough to find another band.

~

I enjoyed working at the hospital, but I noticed there was a clear correlation between wages and education. Most of the upper-echelon employees earned salaries, drove decent cars, and seemed to work steadier hours, while the hourly employees like me, who didn't have college degrees, earned less, worked crappy shifts, and often rode the city bus to and from work. I knew if I was going to end up in the workforce, I would be wise to earn a college degree while I still could. So, much to the relief of my parents, I reentered USC at the start of 1987.

This time, instead of the drudgery of math, science, and business classes, I discovered an academic focus that would nourish my creative side: Media Arts, which combined photography, audio/video production, scriptwriting, and animation.

I continued writing and playing gigs with BOA—even getting my first songwriting credit by contributing the lyrics to a song named, "The Desert." We recorded and released a low-budget album called *This Tribal Courthouse*, which excited all of us—but I really needed to focus on school. I quit and earned Dean's List grades my first semester back, an achievement I had never dreamed possible.

It was a huge relief to finally have confidence in my academic abilities, coupled with motivation for the coursework. But a big question still loomed regarding my unresolved soccer life: could I use my remaining year of eligibility and finally put some closure on my University of South Carolina soccer career? Soccer still held a big place in my heart. I just needed a chance to prove my value.

Good timing was again at work in my life. During the summer, I signed up to play in an amateur soccer tournament with some guys I knew from the Columbia soccer community. One of my teammates turned out to be the South Carolina assistant coach, Trevor Adair. I seized the opportunity, playing my ass off the entire tournament, hustling for every ball and being a vocal team leader like it was another team tryout. At the same time, one of the Gamecocks' top midfielders became ineligible for the fall season because of bad grades, and I was drafted back into the team.

It was a thrill to represent my university for one final season. We dominated a tough schedule. But at the end-of-season NCAA invitational tournament, even though we were the #1 ranked team in the country, we'd been decimated by injuries. I barely touched the field in my final two matches, as I sat out with a stress fracture in my shin bone. Hardly needing a shower after the last match, I stripped off my Gamecock jersey one last time. I looked into the mirror and knew a long and important chapter in my life was ending. That meant only one thing: I would need to start writing the next one.

six

FIRE

BY THE FALL of 1988 I was living in a $150-per-month, third-floor apartment with two roommates. Since the end of the soccer season, I'd been playing in a popular rock 'n' roll cover band called Tootie and the Jones, formed by a group of former South Carolina students. My friend and lead guitarist, Murray "Tootie" Baroody, was super helpful in showing me around the neck of my cheap Hondo acoustic guitar, on which I started to write original songs. My musical influences were all over the map—'60s classic rock, '70s soft rock, disco, hard rock, alternative, classic country, progressive rock, even jazz. None of my early songs worked out, but I was writing, and learning to write, and that's what mattered.

~

One weekday morning in February of 1989, I rolled into my apartment around 7:00 a.m. after partying late with friends. After freshening up as best I could, and needing to be at work in an hour, I pulled on my sweater and jeans and heard what sounded like two people arguing from the apartment directly below. I figured it was an early morning spat, though a serious one, judging from the volume. I then heard someone running across the same apartment, followed by frantic yelling. I went out to our wooden, interior stairwell to listen. Silence—they must have figured it out.

Within a minute there were more loud noises, this time followed by wild rapping on the stairwell door I had just closed. Standing in front of me was a sweating, disheveled, and screaming man.

"Call the fire department, now! There's a fire downstairs and I can't put it out! Wake up the girls upstairs and get out!" (I would find out later that what started out as a late-night, time-lapse photography project filming 30 or 40 lit candles became compromised by a fair amount of hallucinogenic mushrooms, and had—by the time the man banged on my door—become a fully-involved fire, directly under my bedroom.)

I scrambled to find the cordless phone to call 911, while at the same time checking my roommates' bedrooms to alert whoever was home. While ranting to the 911 operator, I quickly shoved an acoustic guitar I'd borrowed from a friend into its case, knowing I could never afford to replace it if I had to (panic does strange things to a person).

As I was on my second lap racing around the apartment, still talking with the emergency operator, I opened our interior stairwell door again so I could run upstairs and wake the girls in the attic apartment. Though less than thirty seconds had passed since I stood at that same door, I could no longer see five feet in front of me as the thick smoke was billowing up the stairwell. As I ran back through our living room, there were already thin sheets of smoke rising from every seam in our hardwood floors. The room was now completely filled with smoke; I was trying to get hold of our kitten, but she wouldn't be corralled, and it was time to get out. (Sadly, the kitten died in the blaze.)

Up at the attic apartment, the girls from upstairs and I jumped onto the fire escape and scurried down—me with the borrowed guitar in hand. As we stood in shock and disbelief, watching from the street, fire burst out of the windows and balconies of the second, third, and fourth floors. While staring at the building, we began to hear muffled sounds of a dog barking madly from inside.

"Did anyone check the first-floor apartment?"

Within seconds, I was knocking on the front door, behind which a large dog was frantically yelping. No one was answering. The door was unlocked, and when I opened it the only noise I could hear in between the barks of the backpedaling black lab was a running shower. The thought entered my mind: how am I going to approach the female tenant who is having her morning shower without having her immediately assume I am either a burglar/rapist, or at a minimum, the biggest creeper in the world? I barely knew this woman and I'd never been in her apartment. God, please guide my words!

The woman apparently didn't hear the floor creaking as I got close to the partially opened bathroom door. With my heart still pounding out of my chest I tried to collect myself before I spoke. Her cheery singing from behind the curtain calmed me. "Hey there, it's Jim from upstairs," I said. "Sorry for barging in, but there is a little fire currently raging upstairs, and I think you're gonna want to get outside rather quickly."

If she was startled, she did well to hide her surprise.

"Oh, shit," she said, "I guess you're right. Thanks!"

I backed up slowly and tried to encourage her seventy-pound pooch to follow me out the front door, but the growling told me he/ she was more interested in eating me than following me. "Come on, buddy! Who wants to go outside!" As I pranced out the door clapping my hands and looking back at the dog—who seemed to have zero intention of exiting without its owner—I forgot there were a couple of steps off the porch. I completely busted my ass, tumbling down the stairs and into the street. The other tenants quickly helped me up, as a blaring fire engine arrived. The tear in my jeans and my freshly bloodied knee and wrist seemed insignificant compared to the mayhem around me.

It's a bizarre feeling to lose almost everything you own in a fire. After returning the guitar to its very thankful owner, I ended up with a t-shirt, a sweater, a pair of boxers, and my ripped jeans— basically, all the things I was dressed in. I don't even remember if I was wearing shoes.

~

I crashed with friends for a short time while I figured out where I would go next. I was able to take one last walk through our burnt-out apartment with my brother Mike, who had become a local firefighter, to see if there was anything to salvage. I walked timidly through the charred frame that previously held our front door. To the right was the small balcony where I would sit strumming my acoustic guitar in the afternoon sun; all that remained were some scorched threads of our hammock , hanging from two blackened hooks. The smell of the interior was overwhelming. A barely recog- nizable heap of burned-up clothing was in the spot that used to be my closet. With the tip of my boot I kicked the top of the pile off, revealing the remains of a garnet Adidas sweat jacket from winning a prestigious NCAA soccer tournament in Indiana in 1987. On my stereo turntable, whose plastic dust cover had shriveled up into a wad from the extreme heat, sat Rush's *Hemispheres* album, melted into smooth, vinyl waves. A dozen darkened drumsticks, which I kept in a glass beer pitcher I'd inherited from my brother Dave, looked like stems from a dozen roses that someone had torched with a flamethrower. A set of blue-sparkle Reuther drums I was borrowing from a friend sat dull and grey in the corner, badly smoke-damaged. I would spend months taking it apart piece by piece, scrubbing and polishing everything back to its original state, and then returning it to the owner.

I recovered one meaningful keepsake that somehow avoided the destruction: my family photo album, which held the fading pictures of the first twenty-five years of my life.

Otherwise, I was homeless.

Since I'd hopped into Mike's pickup truck to chase my soccer dream five and a half years earlier, the idea of home had changed. Dave had married and moved away. Mike was living in South Carolina. Mom and Dad's divorce led to the sale of our childhood home. Within only a year or two of the divorce, Mom had headed to Atlanta with Katie and Steve, and Dad would find work in Florida. With nowhere to go back to, I could only look forward. But, if home is where you lay your head, then I currently had a serious problem defining *home*.

I was overwhelmed by the outpouring of donations of clothing, blankets, and other odds and ends by friends and other college students I'd never even met. But it was a spontaneous passing of the hat by a local rock band that became the thread that would connect my current state of homelessness to my future home.

~

That band was called Hootie & the Blowfish.

I'd seen their posters around campus—Mark Bryan, their blond, curly-haired guitarist, was a fellow student who had sat near me in an audio production class. One night, just a day or two after the fire, onstage at a local dive called Rockafellas, Mark took his hat off his head and rallied the crowd to help fill it. "Come on, y'all! As many of you may have heard, there was a big fire on campus, and our friend Soni here was one of the tenants who was displaced. Please put whatever you can spare in the hat as it's going around. This guy doesn't even have a kitchen to cook in, so he could use a few bucks."

I was humbled by the gesture. Though they barely knew me, this simple yet powerful act of charity—love, really—was my introduction to the band. I would not forget the act, as it would become an important lesson in years to come. By the time Mark poured the donations out of his sweaty ball cap into my grateful hands on the side of the stage, there was $32 and a condom, thankfully still in its wrapper. That was a lot of cash in 1989, especially for a guy with nowhere to live (and probably one more condom than I actually needed). These were good guys, and I knew it immediately that night. What I didn't know was that Brantley Smith, the talented drummer for Hootie who was sitting at the back of the stage that night, was then mulling over his future with the band.

seven

FROM TOOTIE TO HOOTIE

IN MAY 1989 I finally put my hands on the coveted University of South Carolina scroll, somehow managing to squeeze a four-year Bachelor of Media Arts degree into a six-year period. In September, I auditioned for Hootie.

I was still playing for Tootie and the Jones, and had also started drumming for a roots/rock/reggae outfit called Calvin & Friends back in the spring—not to mention I'd scored a full-time job with the university, which included videotaping South Carolina football games on the weekends. But when I heard Brantley was leaving the band and Hootie were now writing their own stuff, my interest was immediately piqued, and I went to audition with them in a 10' x 20' self-storage unit where many local bands rehearsed.

The band back then was already set, minus the drummer: Mark Bryan, Dean Felber, and Darius Rucker. Lead guitarist Mark was the easiest to talk to on the day I auditioned; we bonded over the similar class schedules we'd had and the success of the NFL team we both worshipped, the Washington Redskins. I noticed he wasn't dressed to impress anybody, either; he looked like a poster child for distressed clothing (torn and tattered) years before it became fashionable. But his excitement level for learning songs and playing them was higher than anyone else's in the deafening metal-and-concrete box in which we now found ourselves.

Dean Felber played bass. His family had grown up close friends with Mark's family in Maryland, and he and Mark had played in a high school band together, but they'd only ended up at South Carolina by coincidence. He was a more difficult personality to read. He was quiet, though he seemed comfortable in his own skin, and I would have to pay close attention to his every word, because he didn't use many of them to express his feelings.

Darius Rucker, the lead singer of the band, dressed like a more dapper version of Mark Bryan, in a typical late '80s collegiate uniform: khaki shorts, t-shirt emblazoned with the name of his favorite bar, Monterey Jacks, and untied, tannish work boots. He didn't come off as someone who wanted to be in charge of the band, but when he did speak, he was confident and self-assured. Both his spoken voice and his singing voice commanded attention. Together, these three musicians seemed to be peas in a pod, with a singlemindedness that said, "Let's write. Let's practice. Let's play gigs."

I quickly found out they had a serious obsession with R.E.M., which meant I had to learn more than a dozen R.E.M. tunes. Other songs we covered came from Joe Jackson, The Police, Don Dixon, The Clash, The Ramones, and The Smithereens; and we also worked on a handful of originals they'd already recorded with their former drummer. The Hootie set list required physicality—they played faster than I was used to. Rehearsing speedy songs back-to-back-to-back like "In the City" by The Jam, "Radio Free Europe" by R.E.M., and "Freedom Bound" by the Rave-Ups, made my wrists feel like flimsy rags. I was in top physical form after spending years playing soccer, but now after a few fast songs in quick succession I was gasping for air. All I could think was,

"What's all the rushing for? Anyone up for a mid-tempo Pink Floyd medley for a respite?"

It took me only one or two long rehearsal sessions and a few nights out drinking with the guys to get the thumbs-up to take the next step with Hootie & the Blowfish: playing a real gig.

~

On Friday night, September 29, 1989, I played with Calvin & Friends at The Cockpit, a smelly dive bar at USC. The next morning, I dragged myself up early, packed my drums into my Pontiac Phoenix, and prepared for my first gig with Hootie & the Blowfish.

The show was in Clinton, South Carolina, but first I had to work all day on the Sparky Woods Football Show in Athens, Georgia, a two-hour-and-forty-minute drive from home. After the game (a Gamecock victory!), I hauled ass the two hours to Clinton to meet the rest of the band at the gig, a fraternity/sorority mixer at Presbyterian College.

When I arrived, I noticed that the band had brought two ROTC friends to the gig as *security* for the show. "Is Hootie *that* popular?" I asked the husky guy with a marine crew cut.

In a thick New York accent he leaned in and whispered, "Soni, you just do your drumming and we'll watch Darius's back, okay? We're not gonna put up with any fucking racist bullshit here tonight."

With that, he opened his jacket to reveal a black handgun holstered to his ribcage.

"We're all good here," he said, "all good here."

This warning about racist frat boys was news to me; I knew little or nothing about Southern Greek life. The other security guy told me that the this particular fraternity was rooted in its "Southern-ness," obsessed with Civil War-era leaders and antebellum culture. They held some twisted belief that the South would one day rise again, apparently separate from the rest of the United States.

Sure enough, when one of the fraternity brothers was unloading a few kegs from a pickup truck, I noticed a bumper sticker that read, "Heritage—Not Hate," a phrase used to counter arguments that continuing to fly the Confederate battle flag was hurtful and racist. At the time, I just wanted to concentrate on being a drummer and get through three hours of music I was barely familiar with. But if it came down to brawling, I already knew I would defend Darius.

On stage, my inaugural gig with Hootie & the Blowfish went by in a rush. Seeing Mark releasing all of his pent-up energy in front of a crowd, jumping, spinning, looking back to me with his head thrashing up and down, unapologetically missing chords along the way, was joyful to watch. If a mosh pit had broken out in front of the stage, Mark would have been the first one to fling off his guitar and throw himself into the middle of it. His love of bands like The Replacements, Scruffy the Cat, and The Red Hot Chili Peppers was apparent, and his hyper-adolescent spirit came alive on stage.

Seeing the girls go wild as Darius, in his red and black flannel shirt, sauntered through the first verse of "I Melt With You," a song by Modern English, revealed a charisma I hadn't seen in practice. He played a crappy brown Ovation acoustic, but he was still learning, and Mark was his teacher. When anything went wrong with his guitar, he would quickly consult Mark for help—whether it was with tuning, capos, even where to plug it in.

Dean plucked along self-sufficiently, never drawing attention to himself, shyly glancing at me only a few times when we would successfully lock into a solid groove.

None of us wore any special attire, or outfit, or sexy shirt for the gig. In fact, all of us were wearing nearly the same clothes we'd been rehearsing in a few nights prior. Image and persona were unimportant. If we were communicating anything by our pedestrian appearance it was "what you see is what you get." We weren't *portraying* anything; we were simply being ourselves.

As for me, well, my adrenalin kicked in as I smashed away at the drums, a poorly constructed 6-inch drum riser beneath me shaking and shifting. The crowd went crazy for all the R.E.M. songs, and we didn't even run them off when we played a few of our originals, "After You," "Calendar Girl," "JCP (Needs A Fake I.D.)," and "George Harrison," all written while Brantley was still the drummer. I accomplished playing the mass of new material and kept the train on the tracks, while Darius called out songs for the set spontaneously, one after another.

Sadly, though, it turned out we did need those Marines.

As we hung out after the show ended, one of our bodyguards overheard someone from the crowd say, "That n***** best watch his ass if he wants to get back to Columbia without any scratches," and a brief skirmish ensued. Maybe some of these white fraternity guys thought the Black guy was getting a little too much attention from the girls in the crowd; maybe they were jealous of Darius up there on stage, shaking his ass—though really, from what I could see, he barely has an ass at all. Maybe they were simply your garden-variety racists? This was all new to me.

I quickly hopped down from the stage in case I was needed, but one of the Marines blocked my way and said, "Don't ask any questions, Soni. Just pack up your shit. We are getting the fuck out of here!"

Driving off the campus back to Columbia, I thought about what had happened at the end of the gig. I was pleased we got paid, and I had solidified my position as the new drummer for Hootie & the Blowfish, without even having to throw a single punch. But to say the least, it was deeply upsetting to know racism was so close to us, and revealed so unapologetically. I just couldn't for the life of me understand or accept attitudes like that.

~

From the start, Hootie & the Blowfish were a high-energy band, desperate to make a deep connection between themselves and their audience. Playing exact replica versions of cover songs was far less important than emitting zeal and spirit. In our first few rehearsals, I quickly realized there were some incorrect chords being played and great liberties being taken in song arrangements, but it didn't seem to matter, because none of it got in the way of communicating the music and the emotion. Hootie may have been rough around the edges, but we made up for it with youthful exuberance.

Early attempts at original rhythm and rhymes grew from our collective social and musical experiences growing up, as well as what we were each involved with living in a Southern college town in the mid-to-late '80s. We were interested in the youthful ideology of "change," and we had the unique perspective of being an interracial band—"three white guys in an all-Black band," as I would joke years later.

That said, I never gave much thought to the band's interracial makeup when I first got the opportunity to audition. And when I joined the band, Darius, Dean, and Mark didn't appear concerned or obsessed by the Black/white meaning, either. We bonded on creating and performing, meeting chicks, and catching buzzes, but I couldn't help but notice the different lens through which Darius was experiencing the world. The first lyrics I heard from him indicated some of his frustrations.

> I pledge allegiance to the flag
> That's what they taught me in school.
> But, you walk down the street saying
> Where's their allegiance to me?
> Then they treat you like a fool.
> —From "Let My People Go"

and,

> Oh, wipe your eyes little girl

No, don't you cry

The government said they'd help

But we know that they lie

You're a derelict they say

As they raise their fist

I wish they would realize

You didn't ask to be born like this

Yeah, this country's so great

We got money to pay for the president's hate

—From "Little Girl"

As Darius sang these lines over and over, I found myself becoming more invested in them. I sympathized with him and the prejudices he was writing about. I had so many questions and doubts about the world in which I lived. I, too, wondered why government didn't run more efficiently. I wondered why there was war and hatred and poverty.

But I also wondered how I could get another shot of Jägermeister and that cute girl's phone number across the bar.

I was still learning to play guitar and shape my underdeveloped, squirrelly thoughts into decipherable lyrics, and though I was *technically* limited, it didn't affect my proclivity to express myself through music. I kept a notebook full of poems and verses I had been writing since I started college. They were earnest attempts, but none of it matched the music that was coming out of my acoustic guitar, and some of the thoughts could only be described as, well . . . hideous.

Jesus drowning

Do you know the devil's clowning?

Do you know I caught you frowning?

While you lay in sleep

or,

If there were no morals,

The people all would turn their backs

Distorting all the former facts

Melting minds to balls of wax

or,

All this proclaimed notoriety

is perceived through insecurity

All these cars, these bars

A hell-house for the meek

Outcasts shriek, visions are bleak

Sure, the lyrics were frightful, at best. But, like my yearning to get better at soccer through my youth and early twenties, I just kept working at it because I loved the process. In songwriting, I had no teacher, no instructor. The only measure of passing or failing was how a song made my heart feel.

I kept creating what felt like interesting, original chord progressions with my coltish fingers, and continued scribbling rhyme schemes for my innermost thoughts. None of it seemed to work, until one day, it did.

For the life of me, I could not learn the proper way to form the B bar chord. I tried and tried, but I just could not bend my left ring finger to the necessary angle. Eventually, necessity proved to be the mother of invention, and I altered the configuration of my fingers to include a more easily reached C# note instead of a D#. This B add 9 chord had a different vibe altogether; it was subtle and graceful, and I immediately fell in love with the feeling it gave me.

Finally comfortable with the B9, I moved my hand to an E chord, and then played the two chords back and forth and back and forth in an easy, swaying tempo. A drum pattern simultaneously formed in my head—hell, there was always a drum pattern playing in my head!—and it synced to the flow of the two chords. I became lost in a rapture and played the chords over and over. It felt wonderful. I stopped having to think about what I was doing with my hands and fingers, the exercise and the motion, and they began to move by themselves. Now I was free to conjure a story—"With a little love and some tenderness, we can walk upon the water, rise above the mess." It was one of those magical moments that every songwriter hopes for, when the chords, lyrics, and melody are all flowing out together. I wasn't wondering which direction to take the song; it simply propelled itself. More words came: "With a little peace and some harmony, we can take the words / world around us, take 'em by the hand."

Songwriting seemed very Zen, suddenly. Problem was, B major is a tough key for a beginner guitarist, and now the music needed to go somewhere new. The natural place my ears were telling me to go was an F# major, a bar chord that was almost as unmanageable to me then as the regular B chord. It didn't come easy, but I formed my hand to make the F# as the words kept coming: "I got a hand for you, I wanna run with you."

"Holy shit! This is it! This is working!"

The final three-word mantra came: "Hooooooold my hand," and I repeated it three times, before resolving to the E and ending with, "Cause I wanna love you the best I can."

I can see now where the song came from. The world around me seemed divisive and filled with prejudice, hurt, and suffering. I was just singing out a frustration that had been brewing for years. The outpouring of hopeful lyrics in "Hold My Hand" was in response to the unfairness and ugliness in life. It spoke to the brokenness I noticed while delivering Christmas presents in the ghetto as a child. It spoke to the hopelessness I witnessed among the mentally ill I saw while working in the State Hospital, and to the racial strife I was noticing more and more around me. I wanted to lift people up and erase the hurt. I wanted people to treat each other better. I wanted folks to get along and be happy, not be held back or held down. It just didn't seem right that there were segments of society that were voiceless, and I desperately wanted them to have a voice.

In that moment of creation, I wasn't imagining millions of fans singing this song in unison across the globe. I was merely wondering whether my band would like it. It was a groovier, mid-tempo song that went against the grain of the more hurried songs we were playing.

I made a plan to bring it to them at our next practice.

~

The Hootie life was fairly simple in the early days.

We'd all work our day jobs, then write and rehearse later in the day or evening, usually ending up at a bar in Five Points, near USC, drinking together. The band was self-managed. We booked our own gigs, made and hung up our own posters around town, and committed to saving enough money to record some new songs in a better studio so we could have a product to sell at gigs. Though the long-range goal was to get the attention of a record company, we were happy just writing songs and booking as many gigs as we could.

We didn't have room to be picky, so we basically took any gig we could get. Party gigs paid us the best, guaranteed us a flat fee, and usually had a built-in audience. They could take place anywhere from a frat house to a flatbed truck to a field. The only problem with a built-in audience is that you quickly realize they are mostly there to drink cheap draft beer and socialize. We got *paid*, but folks *paid* us little attention.

So, we had to learn how to win over an audience with our music. Given that these gigs were often two to three hours long, we'd play a ton of covers and sprinkle in our original music where we could. The first set usually saw us at one end of the room, courtyard, or parking lot, and the built-in audience hovering around the bar or kegs in the distance. As they loosened up a bit, the awkward space between us would shrink a little, but still there seemed to be an invisible magnet that was pulling them away from us no matter how big the crowd grew. From the stage, we would try to lure them closer with our fancy moves and swagger. (Mark occasionally resorted to screaming at them point-blank, demanding they come forward.)

In the end, we were always thankful for the one brave soul who got hammered off his or her first two drinks and decided to christen the empty dance floor. You could see the brave soul's coworkers or fellow students stare with embarrassment from the fringe and whisper judgmentally, but it was just the icebreaker needed to allow the bigger crowd to plunge in.

During the last thirty minutes of the night, with the booze starting to have its full effect, a cohesion could be achieved between performer and audience. The crowd, hopefully including a gaggle of cute girls, would be pressed up to the front of the stage. Hair would be let down, shirts no longer neatly tucked in, and shoes at last kicked off. The music would grow in volume, loud enough for the organizer to give our slightly buzzed sound man a little look that said, "turn it down a bit before the cops show up." When the last Violent Femmes song, "Add It Up," had finished—always a good closer—we would walk off the side of the stage as the crowd went back to the bar. We'd make anywhere from $500 to $800, not bad for the early '90s. But, since the gear wouldn't load itself, that was the band's job, too.

Money from gigs like these funded a bunch of other gigs where we would get paid next to nothing but could play all of our original music. We'd open for more established bands such as Scruffy the Cat, Johnny Quest, Waxing Poetics, Homeboy Madhouse, No Reason to Hate, Alex Chilton, Egypt, Dillon Fence, and Storm Orphans. We probably never received more than $100 for any of these gigs, but it covered gas, a fast-food stop, and a few beers, and we got to play a set of original music and proudly announce to some other band's fans that we were Hootie & the Blowfish from Columbia, South Carolina!

eight

ON THE ROAD

BY MARCH OF 1990, we had saved enough dough to book time at a studio in Raleigh, North Carolina, with a real producer/manager named Dick Hodgin.

It was a big step up for us. Dick himself was a foul-mouthed, fired-up, trash-talking Tarheel who was not only a respected regional producer, but also a guy who was willing to tell us the truth about ourselves. All we had were dreams and desires and a strong work ethic at this point; what we didn't have were music industry connections.

On the first day of recording, I pulled out my tambourine, anxious to use it. Dick noticed.

"What the hell is that thing?" he squawked in my face. "You ain't gonna use no motherf#@%ing tambourine in my studio, you little sissy!"

I was mortified, especially when I noticed my bandmates laughing, but I'm sure they were just grateful not to be in my shoes.

Over the next few days in the studio, we learned that Dick may have had a loud bark, but he was never gonna bite us. We recorded five songs—"I Don't Understand," "Little Girl," "Look Away," "Let

My People Go," and "Hold My Hand"—and it all went smoothly with one exception: I lost my voice after a late night of Jäger shots. I couldn't hit my high harmony on "Hold My Hand," and one of Dick's other artists, a guy named Gerald Duncan, had to come in and sing my part. It was my first big fail as a Hootie member, but it would not be my last.

As we sat and listened back to the music, we thought it was the right moment to ask Dick if he'd give us some honest feedback on our career status AND consider managing us.

"So boys, ya wanna be in the record business, do ya?" he said. We all inched forward in our seats.

"Well, the music business is like a big superhighway, and you need to take certain roads that will bring you to that big superhighway. So there's all these roads, and many detours, too, but if you work hard, get good directions, have patience, and, of course, make great music, you can get on that superhighway."

"You guys," he said, "are still sitting in the goddam kitchen looking for your fucking car keys!" With that, he burst out laughing and shook his keys at us.

It had been a hard thing to hear, but we needed the lesson. We had barely begun, and there could be no guarantees. He liked our songs, but he also felt they needed to get better. And though he flat out rejected the idea of managing us, he gave us a big gift when he suggested we call a guy in Raleigh named Rusty Harmon, who might just be interested in working in such a role. Physically, we soon learned, Rusty was indeed a big gift, standing 6'7". But more importantly than fitting into the fifth spot on the Hootie basketball squad, he fit the role to manage a small band like us perfectly. He was young, green, and hungry, and willing to help us with booking and promotion and representation.

Immediately, Rusty began making phone calls on our behalf, brainstorming ideas for promotions, and taking over some of the organizing so we could concentrate on writing and performing. We sent out tons of our demo cassette with its simple red artwork, together with our band bio, 8" x 10" black-and-white photos, and a cover letter signed "Russell Harmon - Fishco Management."

We knew it was a long shot, and so it proved. A few companies replied, but mostly it was silence, or a brief reply encouraging us to keep trying. One letter suggested we should pitch our music to Neil Diamond. Another company, Sire Records, won my vote for the most arrogant reply: their response was an unsigned form letter apologizing for returning our unopened tape, and telling us their roster was filled with great bands already. At least we could resell the tape.

$\sim$

With Rusty's help, we extended our touring area to North Carolina, Virginia, West Virginia, and DC. We also played the tourist spots in South Carolina like Hilton Head, Pawley's Island, and Myrtle Beach during the late spring and summer. In the fall, westward expansion led us to Greenville, Spartanburg, Augusta, Athens, Atlanta, and Knoxville.

We navigated these road trips fairly well, considering the long hours traveling, playing, and drinking. Occasionally, too much alcohol would lead us to a point of diminishing returns, and a simple disagreement would turn into a full-blown argument, with yelling, screaming, and even a few punches thrown.

Sometimes, it just made us act silly.

On New Year's Eve at the Grog & Tankard in DC, we played a long set, and as midnight crept closer we were trying to time the midnight countdown correctly so the New Year didn't arrive in the middle of a song. For some reason, Mark decided it was a good idea to invite Steve, a friend of his, onto his shoulders midway through "Hold My Hand," but as Steve got most of the way onto Mark's shoulders, Mark began tilting backward. Before I even had the chance to do anything to stop them, Mark and Steve came careening right into Mark's amp and my drum set, halting not only Mark's playing, but leaving my drums partially collapsed. Dean and Darius just looked at the two of them there, tangled in a heap.

After a brief assessment of the damage, the only thing left to say was, "Good night, everybody. We're Hootie & the Blowfish from Columbia, SC! Drive safely and have a Happy New Year!"

~

Touring was an imperfect science. One time, we drove three hours to Greensboro, North Carolina, to headline a new club that promised a big turnout.

Two people showed up.

Worse was to come. One day, leaving Columbia for an out-of-town gig, Darius and I were proudly packing up our gear into our first trailer when one of us didn't latch the back of it properly. We drove off, unaware, and picked up Dean. As the three of us headed through town to grab Mark at work, beaming with satisfaction that that we were *a band with a trailer* (this was the big time in our eyes), we realized Mark's brand-new Gibson guitar, still in its case, had rattled its way out of the back of the unfastened trailer. Before we could react, it was scooped up and stolen by a passerby.

Beyond the odd disaster, we traveled contentedly and frugally, sharing cramped, smelly spaces. Times were lean, but it strengthened our bond. Eventually, we began bringing a skillful, local soundman, Charlie Merritt, to help us get a more consistent "live mix" on the road, and an old friend, Jeff Poland, to help manage us while we traveled from town to town. We couldn't afford fancy hotels, or even shitty ones sometimes, and often we wouldn't begin looking for housing until we were at the venue; folks would offer us a couch, or floor, or bed, and sometimes we were lucky enough to get a bed with someone in it.

I was dating a woman named Alissa, but our relationship was kinda crazy, and the more we toured, the more I kept finding myself in compromising positions with other women. Late, drunken nights trying to find places to crash were leading to poor decision-making. I can't blame the touring life though—it was my own fault, my own weakness. When I finally got back to Alissa, I would stuff the guilt and shame down deep, hoping it would eventually disappear.

~

With some new audience-tested material, we returned to Jag Studios in Raleigh with Dick Hodgin in February 1991 to produce a new EP, recording "Running From an Angel," "Time," "Drowning," and "Short Blond Hair." The session was great, but not long after returning to Columbia we began having our doubts about whether we had picked the best four songs for the EP. After finally deciding to drop "Short Blond Hair," we used Strawberry Sky's studio in West Columbia and adept producer Gary Bolton to record a song Darius had only recently brought to the band, "Let Her Cry." For a new song, it was surprising to see the warm embrace the audiences were giving it. People responded as if they were hearing a song they already knew, and whether male or female they seemed to instantly relate to it on a personal level.

The song "Time" held a special meaning for me. I was on the front porch of the Greene Street apartment that Mark and I were subletting when I showed him the intro guitar riff I'd come up with, a little arpeggio of notes on an open D chord. Similar to my experience writing "Hold My Hand," the chords, lyrics, and melodies all flowed out together.

> Time . . . why do ya punish me?
> Like the waves rushing over the shore
> You walk all over me

Time . . . why do ya walk away
With a friend of mine
That I call freedom
Can you teach me 'bout tomorrow
And all the pain and sorrow I'll have to face?

Mark thought it was catchy and encouraged me to bring it to the rest of the band at our next rehearsal.

By this point, I was getting a better feel for writing lyrics and melodies with Darius in mind. I wouldn't say I wrote songs *for* him, but I was beginning to write songs *toward* him. We both liked big choruses and mushy love songs. Dean, Mark, and I would usually end up doing three-part harmonies on the choruses, and Darius would wind and weave his way around us and over us. He liked a melodic vocal guide, but he also needed freedom to diverge from it.

The lyrics I'd written for "Time" captured my struggle with some big questions I had in my life. "Why are my intimate relationships so hard to navigate?" "Why can't I see my troubles coming at me sooner?" I was moving forward in my relationship with Alissa, yet I was brimming with a strange mixture of doubt and passion. I loved her, but I feared where we were headed (marriage) and how that future would only become more complicated (by my self-serving desires). My philosophical plea to time itself was in earnest, even if it was just a little self-pitying.

Once Darius sang it, with the lyrics to the verses that he'd revised, the song came alive. Adding his own perspective and dynamics to a song always did that. Mark wrote a glorious guitar solo to go over the bridge section and Dean added a great bass line that made the song thump along.

The creation of the songs was sometimes masterminded by Mark, sometimes Darius or myself, and, less often in the early days, by Dean. It was rarely the same formula twice. Mark was like a machine though, spitting out a great quantity of catchy guitar licks, interesting chord arrangements, and lyrics. Darius was not always a fan of Mark's lyrics, but it was hard to deny the overall wealth of Mark's contributions that stemmed from his tireless songwriting. He didn't put his guitar down much, even when the band wasn't gigging or rehearsing.

We were all willing on some level to give and receive ideas. Everyone checked their egos at the door before sitting down to share song ideas, because there was no guarantee your touching verse or heartfelt chorus would be embraced every time. Someone's idea of amazing was someone else's idea of a cheesy, sappy mess. One thing I learned was that *intention* does not always equal *achievement* in songwriting. We spent hours writing and performing songs like "You Gotta Run," "Brand New Land," "I Don't Think So," and many others, only to ditch them after underwhelming responses from our audiences. It always hurt a little to say goodbye to a song after investing so much time and heart into it. But if we were having trouble detaching from some tired song in our set, our future full-time soundman Billy Huelin, who in 1991 was running sound at The Old Post Office, in Hilton Head, South Carolina, was usually willing to assist us. Sometimes it was just a helpful hint like, "I don't think the kids are diggin' that one"—and other times it came in the form of a direct plea: "I will pay you fifty dollars if you *never* play [name of song] again!"

My confidence increased greatly after "Hold My Hand" was accepted not only by the band, but by audiences. The hard truth was that if a song didn't cause some sort of positive ripple in the fans, then it would eventually fall off of our set list. We diligently kept writing, knowing that when toes began tapping, or hips started swaying, or heads commenced bobbing up and down, it was a great sign.

nine

CAROLYN

BY THE SUMMER of 1991, the band was on solid ground, but my relationship with Alissa was on thin ice. I liked to claim aloud that I was madly in love with her, but after the words faded away, the truth of my actions revealed a shallow, inadequate version of love. I was an immature, career-driven young man who struggled with monogamy, and our increasingly busy band schedule was only going to continue to drive a wedge between us. After her graduation from USC, she decided to move back to New Jersey.

Instead of facing the facts about our relationship and accepting our fate, I did what was becoming a more customary alternative for me: I began writing about it. Plunking away on a slightly out-of-tune, upright piano in a spare room at the university production studio where I had been working since graduation, I penned a song I would call "Goodbye."

> I never thought the day would come
> When I would see his hand, not mine
> Holding on to yours because I could not find the time

And now I can't deny

Nothing lasts forever

But I don't want to leave and see the teardrops in your eyes

I don't want to live to see the day we say goodbye

I'd been noodling around on piano since taking a beginner piano/ keyboard class my final semester in school, and this song was my best attempt so far. In it, I rationalized why Alissa and I should stay together, which in part was the noble idea that "I couldn't imagine my life without her." This was heartfelt and honest. The other attempt at sincerity, though, the idea that "I couldn't imagine her ending up with some other dude," was not the stuff real love is made of.

The most logical path for the two of us would have been for us to continue to go our separate ways, but my stubborn pride and the warped lens through which I viewed love wouldn't allow me to let her go and admit it was over. I couldn't help but beg her, and beg her again to come back, and sure enough, she ended up back in Columbia.

Darius immediately loved "Goodbye," but since it was strictly a piano/vocal song, we had no means to perform it regularly. (We didn't even own a keyboard.) Rather than push the issue and demand we find some way to incorporate it into our set, I calmly let it go. Something inside told me it would be an important song for us one day.

Our live show was still developing. We kept an open mind for trying songs that not only *we* loved, but that we thought the audience would vibe with. We played Led Zeppelin's "D'yer Ma'ker)" for a while. A couple of Bob Marley tunes became regulars in the set. The Rolling Stones's "Waiting on a Friend" had a brief appearance. For a time we even did an acoustic version of KISS's "Beth," and it was my first ever opportunity to come from behind the drums and stand up in front strumming a guitar. I was insecure, but I loved it! Sometimes the crowd would enjoy the weird mixture of songs, and sometimes not so much, but we were brave in trying a wide variety of stuff. Sometimes we'd all just look at each other thinking, "Well, that was a bad idea," or "Let's not do *that one* again."

Darius's ability to sing this mixed bag of songs never ceased to amaze me. He had not only the range but the appetite. He took great pleasure moving from KISS's "Calling Dr Love," to New Grass Revival's "You Plant Your Fields," to the Little River Band's "Cool Change." And if something was too high, he would just look back at me and say, "Soni, you gotta sing that part!" His proud moment came when we would return to the stage for an encore and he would sing part of Barry Manilow's "Even Now." I loved it, because I loved Barry, but Mark and Dean would just stand aside, unimpressed.

Fans were steadily buying our modestly priced $5 tapes with originals on them, so we started to include more of those songs in our sets. It wasn't long before we noticed that more and more fans were beginning to sing along with *our* tunes.

～

Even though we'd heard nothing positive back from the massive second round of tapes we'd sent out to record companies, publishers, and radio stations, we were able to play in front of some industry people at a series of regional showcases. We got some positive signs from a label called JRS; we even drove a van all the way to Los Angeles for another showcase that included them. We didn't leave LA with a signed contract, but we felt confident that JRS would soon be offering us our first recording deal.

Meanwhile, we continued touring, doing what we loved to do most: making music, making friends, and making out (not with each other). Our tour schedule stretched out to Blacksburg, Virginia; Greenville, North Carolina; Tuscaloosa, Alabama; Nags Head, North Carolina; Johnson City and Chattanooga, Tennessee. After playing almost a hundred shows in 1990, we topped that by playing more than 120 shows in 1991. Crowds were growing, even though we didn't fit the image of trendsetting bands that were dominating the rock charts in the early '90s. We weren't grunge or alternative, and we certainly were not what you'd call *cool*, or even trying to look cool—heck, for years you would have had to pay us extra to put on long pants on stage.

But all signs were pointing toward finalizing a record deal with JRS, and in our excitement we drove to Charlotte, North Carolina, and found some cool, affordable apartments for what was supposed to be a one-month recording session. We blocked out dates for February at a premier studio called Reflections. Each day, I woke up envisioning our future with a legitimate record company and conjuring pictures of us visiting radio stations to promote our music. I was walking on air! . . . until JRS slammed on the brakes. We blocked out more days in April and they canceled us again. We scheduled a new date for a few months later, only to be canceled a few days before heading out the door. Were my visions of success just a mirage? The whole circus of contracts and promises and obstacles during this period was an ongoing nightmare. Eventually, we had to accept that our big investment of time, money, and heart had been a failure.

The deal was dead.

~

Shattered would not sufficiently describe our feelings as the end of 1992 beckoned. Looking back, though, I'm not surprised it all took place the way it did. The music industry back then, and still today, is filled with deception, ego, greed, and backstabbing. Money and the love of it will do that.

We still managed to hammer out almost 130 shows during the course of the year, and we were still writing new songs. Desperate to end the nineteen-month drought since our previous recording, we made a decision, rightly or wrongly, to record what would become our third EP, again without the help of a record label. Some thought we should hold out for another offer, but we felt we had to take the matter into our own hands, so that's what we did.

A tragedy intervened.

On November 1, 1992, Darius's mother Carolyn suffered a fatal heart attack. It was the first time any of us had been confronted with a major death in the family, and back then Darius was much like the rest of us in that he was unprepared to digest something so devastating.

Carolyn had been a single, working parent, and they had been very close. We, of course, suggested canceling all our upcoming shows, but that's not how Darius wanted to deal with it. He chose to keep pushing on, trying desperately to keep the rest of his life normal while his heart grieved. I felt ill-equipped to discuss his pain with him; I only knew how to write songs about stuff like this. We knew he was hurting, but since he asked us to plow through each day with work, or writing, or drinking, or whatever seemed routine, we followed his lead.

The funeral was incredible. Watching the intense outpouring of emotion in a predominantly African American church was a new experience for me. I'd only ever gone to Catholic masses and funerals, which tend to be solemn and formal—but here, as people "fell out" in grief, I saw just how a Southern Black funeral works.

As the funeral progressed, I thought about the love Carolyn had shared with the rest of us. Our stops in Charleston to see her helped momentarily balance out our lifestyle of hotels and fast-food meals on the go. Even when you are having a lot of fun traveling from town to town, partying with your mates, the disconnect from a home life can be really hard.

Visiting Darius's mom, aunts, and cousins, the Ruckers and the Middletons, was always a balm. They lived in a neighborhood off Highway 17 South on the other side of the Ashley River outside of Charleston. To see the smiles as our van pulled up and as they joyfully welcomed Darius, and us, back home, was a wonderful feeling; and then to smell the home cooking was like nothing else. Ribs, mac 'n' cheese, black-eyed peas, and collard greens, were not like anything I'd feasted on growing up. Darius's mom—whom he described as his biggest musical influence—would be in the small kitchen with his aunts pleading for us to eat, and then eat more, then we'd have to head to our gig for sound check. I remember wishing we could just take the night off and go straight to bed in our food-induced comas.

We would miss Carolyn dearly.

~

My parents had been as supportive of me as Carolyn had been of Darius, but my dad was beginning to put some subtle pressure on me to consider a more legitimate line of work than playing music in clubs.

Dad knew about the importance of back-up plans. After almost fifteen years of working his way up the ladder as an executive with a thriving railroad company, and walking into what he thought was going to be a big promotion, he was let go unexpectedly. He landed on his feet eventually, but it hurt like hell. Even his and Mom's divorce was something he hadn't seen coming, but he managed to figure out how to move on, broken heart and all. His point to me was to make sure to have options, if possible, because sometimes you don't control your own destiny. He had every right to ask me questions about my future, being the one who funded a good bit of my prolonged college career. It was a question any loving parent might ask of their child who has a bachelor's degree rolled up in a tube under his bed, but who is driving around in a van with three other dudes looking for paying rock 'n' roll gigs.

ten

KOOTCHYPOP

WE DECIDED TO grieve Carolyn's death the only way we knew, and with a spirit we thought would also honor her memory: by making music. We recorded five songs—"The Old Man and Me," "Hold My Hand," "If You're Going My Way," "Sorry's Not Enough," and "Only Wanna Be With You"—with Mark Williams at Reflections Studios in Charlotte, and with some help from Don Dixon, the former producer of R.E.M. among others, and one of our idols.

We named the EP *Kootchypop*—a term Darius had heard from a female comedian when referring to her vagina. One of the joys of being independent artists was the freedom to express ourselves however we pleased, including using an obscure sexual reference as the title to our new CD.

By the time *Kootchypop* was available, our bookings were piled high. We were on our way to playing almost 160 shows for the year. New markets were opening up for us all the time, like Gainesville, Florida; Newport News, Charlottesville, and Virginia Beach, Virginia; Nashville, Tennessee; Baltimore, Maryland; and Lancaster, Pennsylvania.

Dick Hodgin once warned us there are three things that are so powerful they could break up your band: women, drugs, and money. Luckily, we couldn't afford any hard drugs during the early '90s, so drugs weren't an issue. And, when it came to money, there just wasn't much around to argue about and we'd decided long ago to split everything equally.

When it came to women though, it was tricky. The daily tasks of *being* in love, *staying* in love, and occasionally *falling out* of love can get right in the way of a group of guys who have all chosen music and traveling as their number-one companions. There is always an underlying fear, accurate or inaccurate, that a woman could negatively influence a band member or restrict him in some way, and therefore become an obstacle to the band's success.

We all had steady girlfriends at some point, but my relationship with Alissa seemed to cause the most trouble. The first real sign of a problem was when I brought her along for a long weekend of gigs on the Maryland coast, driving a separate car for the two of us. I tried to make the excuse that there was a *family reunion* since we would indeed be meeting some of my family during the weekend, but that was just an attempt to justify my actions. I knew the band would take it as an affront, believing I was making my girlfriend a higher priority than our band. But I did it anyway.

Things got really bad at the end of a show in Myrtle Beach. Alissa had shown up in the dressing room in between encores, and as the band stood dripping with sweat, about to have a quick discussion to decide the night's closing songs, Darius wondered out loud what my girl was doing in the dressing room. We'd all had a few drinks, and I took offense to his question, storming out of the dressing room to my car after a brief but explosive argument, dragging Alissa with me. In my rage I found just enough time to angrily kick over a stack of the opening band's instruments on the way out the door.

Alissa and I hopped right into our Honda Civic and peeled out of the parking lot, fuming all the way back to Columbia, forcing the band to finish the show without me. It happened so quickly that I didn't even bother to grab a shirt. About halfway home, chilly and with my buzz wearing off, I realized there would be a price to pay for this astounding, unnecessary reaction.

A few days later, Rusty, our manager, invited me to our band office to confront me about my relationship with Alissa. I was insulted and angry. While he had a right to share his and the band's concerns, especially after the most recent Myrtle Beach incident, I was pissed that he or anyone in my band would have the nerve to judge me about this. No one in our small, dysfunctional group, except maybe Dean, had any room to question or chide the other on relational matters. During the intervention, I vowed my allegiance to the band, even though on the way out I told Rusty where I thought he should put his advice.

~

Kootchypop was flying off the shelves from the moment we released it in the summer of 1993.

We sold a ton at our shows, and we also had a regional distribution deal, so our CDs were in record stores in many of the markets we were playing. It was hard to imagine there was a band that was more ready than us to be *discovered*. On top of our radio-friendly music and healthy fan base, we had solid management, owned an insured vehicle and trailer, were paid up on taxes, had health insurance, and sold our own merchandise. None of us were strung out on drugs or hiding from the law.

All we needed was a label to get behind us—to believe in us.

Finally, the music industry responded. Tim Sommer, an A&R representative from Atlantic Records, heard we were selling an impressive number of CDs in the South and decided we would be worth seeing in person, so in September he made a trip to Myskyns, a big club in Charleston, South Carolina, and came again the next night to a smaller, scrappier place called Rockafellas, in Columbia.

Tim Sommer was not your regular record company guy, at least not like the kind we'd seen before. For starters, he seemed comfortable in a loud, stinky bar, and looked like he wouldn't be too upset if a beer or Jäger shot spilled on his jacket. Also, he was a musician and had played in bands (he was a member of the art rock band Hugo Largo—we forgave him for being in a band that had two bass players).

After the Rockafellas gig, it took Tim about three minutes to convince us to trust moving forward with him and Atlantic Records. He believed in our music and in us, and he promised that he wouldn't fuck up our already well-oiled machine. Plus, he promised us we wouldn't be asked to wear matching outfits or use synthesizers or hair gel.

"You can wear shorts, or cut-up shirts, or no shirts at all," Tim said. "I don't give a shit. This is about the music."

Dean looked at Darius and said, "I'm keeping my shirt on."

~

On day three of a twelve-day run of shows up the East Coast, I sat down in my hotel room in Blacksburg, Virginia, to make my drunken 2:00 a.m. call to Alissa to say goodnight. I quickly discovered that, earlier in the evening, some girlfriends of hers back in Columbia had dutifully announced to Alissa that I was cheating on her. The short call ended with the loud slamming of the phone on the other end.

In the years Alissa and I had dated each other, I could almost always be found late at night either on the phone, or looking for a phone to call her. My bandmates, who knew me only as "Soni", nicknamed me "Phoney," because when they couldn't find me anywhere else it was likely I was on a pay phone somewhere. I hated the nickname because it always made me feel like I was some obsessive, clingy boyfriend.

Now I hated it because it perfectly described my fraudulent character. I was indeed phony.

eleven

EARTHQUAKES

IN EARLY 1994, we emptied our touring schedule so that we could decamp to a Los Angeles studio to record. But on January 17, a magnitude-6.7 earthquake rocked the San Fernando Valley, where we were supposed live and work for a couple of months. The region was devastated—sixty people died and almost nine thousand were injured, and there were billions of dollars in damages.

The session was pushed to March, and we took a financial beating, even though we were able to scrape together fifteen shows in February. In the meantime, I was still consumed by my failed relationship with Alissa, and I nursed that pain by consuming bottle after bottle of cheap red wine, while the puppy the two of us had taken in together, named Risa, rested at my feet, staring curiously back at me.

~

The band finally reached Los Angeles on Friday, March 11, 1994. Our first thrill after landing was seeing O. J. Simpson rushing through baggage claim. As he reenacted his famous Hertz commercial from the 1970s, I thought, *What's his big hurry?* (Ninety-three days later, he would really have something to run from . . .)

Being in Los Angeles officially changed our status from being big fish in a small pond to being small fish in a big pond. But big ponds like Los Angeles can be very intoxicating, especially to a band coming from sleepy South Carolina. As we drove from the airport to the San Fernando Valley, I stared out the car window in awe. Sunset Boulevard. Warner Brothers Studios. The Hollywood Bowl. This was the place where dreams were made. I wondered if ours would be made here, too.

Soon we unlocked the door to our two-bedroom apartment, Room #433 at the Academy Village Apartments in North Hollywood. In our eyes the place was pretty swanky, because a) it didn't smell like the rancid touring van we'd been spending most of our days in, b) it didn't include the state bug of South Carolina, the roach, crawling all over the place, and c) it didn't have furniture that looked like it was recently pulled from a college dorm. In reality, it was a modest, 900-square foot apartment, barely big enough to squeeze our four big bodies into comfortably. Perception is everything, though, and to us we'd just been handed keys to a castle.

We plopped our bags into our new rooms, instinctively splitting up the same way we always did: Dean and Darius in one room and Mark and me in the other.

Tim Sommer and our Atlantic Records production coordinator, Gena Rankin, warmly welcomed us to our new digs at the Academy Village, immediately becoming the foundational building blocks in our West Coast Hootie family as hosts, business partners, musical friends, and confidantes.

Compared to the menial job of unloading our little duffle bags into #433, we soon had to face the more engrossing proposition of unpacking the thirty to forty songs we'd brought with us, and narrowing them down to a refined dozen. This was done in a long and intense session, with the counsel of Tim and our new producer, Don Gehman, at a funky rehearsal space called The Alley. At a glance the space looked just like one of the many graffiti-riddled clubs we'd spent so much time in back East, but in fact, The Alley was an LA treasure, famous for having hosted rehearsals for the likes of Bonnie Raitt, Dwight Yoakum, and Crosby, Stills, and Nash, to name just a few.

We played down the entire list, foregoing the usual beers and Jägers for lattes and fresh, Southern California health food. As we let go of more than half of those songs, some of which I still had a great fondness for, it was like walking away from a significant other after a tough breakup. I was left wondering if I would ever see them again. There was a positive flip side to this parting of ways—a few of the songs we kissed goodbye to, including one or two that I had penned, made me feel more like I had finally escaped from a bad date. I was honestly quite pleased to be rid of them.

Tracking at NRG Studios, which was within walking distance from the apartment, began slowly as we acclimated to our new environment. One immediate hurdle we faced in the spacious studio was getting over the nervousness of working with such a big-name producer as Don Gehman. We had met with him at a dinner back East to formally break the ice, and though he was about as laid-back a guy as you could ever dream of working with, it was still intimidating knowing we were about to record an entire album with *THE* DON GEHMAN! His impeccable resume was a mile long, and for the four of us it most notably included his impressive work with R.E.M. and John Mellencamp. For me, though, as a drummer, Don sat particularly high on a pedestal. After all, he'd created the loudest, clearest, greatest snare drum sound of the entire '80s: Kenny Aronoff's rattling snare on Mellencamp's *Scarecrow* album.

While Don and I were setting up his pink-sparkle Drum Workshop drum set to use for our session, I asked, "Where did you ever get that amazing snare sound with Kenny Aronoff? It is seriously my favorite of all time. So explosive and so commanding!"

Don looked straight into my eyes and said, "You really want to know?"

"Hell yeah, I wanna know!"

"Then turn around and open that road case behind you."

I wrestled the case open and stared at about a half-dozen snares before he could finish his sentence.

"It's the Ludwig Student Accusonic Aluminum five-by-fourteen."

"Can I touch it?"

"Be my guest."

Like any worthwhile snare drum that has had the hell beat out of it for a number of years, the metallic, silver drum I held in my hands had a lot of what we call character—nicks, scratches, and dings from, well, being a drum. They looked like beauty marks to me, though. After Don took a few whacks on it with a drumstick to let me hear the *magic*, I gently put it back into its resting place, and my heartbeat returned to its regular rhythm.

Dean and Mark set up their instruments about twenty to thirty feet away from me, and the three of us curiously watched as Don's assistant engineer Wade Norton placed dozens of microphones around the room, each connected to what seemed like a million miles of entwined cords and cables. They all led to a giant mixing console in a separate control room behind thick, double-paned, sound-proof glass. It was in that room that Don and Tim would soon begin shaping and sculpting our major label debut.

We got our feet wet with the live recording by attempting the newest song in our scaled-down batch, and I wondered why Don and Tim would have us begin with the song we were least familiar with. This would hardly boost our playing confidence. I decided to shut up and trust their process. Simply referred to as "Dean's Song" because it was so new that it had yet to be properly titled, we spent at least five hours arranging and playing, rearranging and replaying, before any of us were remotely comfortable with it. The song centered around a distinctive bass line Dean had only recently written, and Don and Tim seemed insistent on getting us to finish it. By dinner we had still not gotten it right, so in frustration we decided to put it off for another day.

After dinner we put our best effort into "Go Away," which would later be renamed "Where Were You." It was another relatively new idea, and though the groovy bass and drum tracks came to us more easily than the previous song, its title would foretell its destiny—"Where Were You" would not be found on the final album. At 12:30 a.m., slightly drained and ready for a nightcap, we took the short walk back to #433.

Day two of tracking offered more comfortable musical territory. We blazed through the familiar "Sha-La-La," which had been in our live set for a while. I began hitting the drums with more confidence on each and every take, but Dean, Mark, and I were still getting used to not having Darius in the same room with us, as he was in an isolation booth behind a closed door. This song would be retitled "I'm Goin' Home," and become track #6 on the record.

On day three we all finally hit a stride from which we would not falter. Playing "Hannah Jane," which became the opening track on the record, was like driving a car you know is both fast *and* sturdy. You can push it hard. From the moment the 1-2-3-BOOM, BWAP-BOOM dropped at the top of the song, we all put the figurative pedal to the metal. It was a relief to let it all out—to emphatically reestablish with full confidence that *we are a rock 'n' roll band*. The nerves and anticipation that held us back the first few days finally melted away, leaving only joyful musical satisfaction. For the rest of the night Mark would overdub guitar after guitar after guitar to create the thick layer of rock ecstasy this song had always begged for. We were finally off to the races.

We soon began to understand Don's unique process of recording. Some producers seek perfection; Don was different. Greatness didn't mean flawless or precise to him. He looked for spontaneous, special moments, not necessarily unerring ones. He wanted personality, *our* personality. And sometimes he found it in a lyric enunciated incorrectly or slightly out of time. It made sense that he appreciated these sorts of moments, especially vocally, if you consider all the years he'd spent producing John Mellencamp in the '80s. Mellencamp crammed a lot of lyrics into tight spaces, doing cartwheels that weren't necessarily *rhythmic*. But it worked, because it had personality.

And it wasn't just singing. Don delighted in an occasional weird guitar feedback that would cause the ear to take notice. He thought that if hitting a drum a certain way gave it a strange *ring* or *wonk*, there was a chance it would stand out over a more normal roll. Imperfection, he felt, was a great gift to art. To that measure, he was fine with some of the pushing and pulling—the speed-ups and slow-downs—that were occurring among the four of us while recording. As long as we all slowed down and sped up at the same places, he was satisfied. And he was smart about how pop songs work, too—"a catchy song" he would say, "is a series of important, but short sections, giving the listener something fresh or captivating every five seconds or so."

~

Aside from the recording, we were making some great new friends in Southern California, and most of them liked to party, enabling me to keep to my regular nightly pattern of drinking. On one particular Monday, I was feeling some aftereffects from a rather intense weekend of partying when I nearly passed out doing my morning workout and then vomited up some greenish goop, but I was willing to plow through some occasional physical sickness and mental mushiness and accept it as a small price to pay for the joys of alcohol consumption.

Drinking too much didn't seem to have any effect on the work at hand, anyway. In the studio, we continued soberly and successfully, pushing through "Let Her Cry" and "Drowning" until we got versions that were perfectly imperfect enough for Don. In the days before smartphones and laptops, I spent most of my downtime in the studio writing postcards, reading John Irving's *A Prayer for Owen Meany*, and losing what little money I had to Darius at the pool table. He was virtually unbeatable.

We took a detour from our rock music to try the much softer "Goodbye," the piano-based tune I had written at my day job a couple years earlier. We had never played it live, and after a bunch of attempts recording the piano with my rudimentary skills, I wasn't sure the song was ever going to work with me at the keys. Don assured me that my style of playing was perfect for our purposes, though I knew there must be dozens of more skilled pianists within a few miles who would be better suited for the job. Unable to get a good enough take, we left it for another day.

We continued grinding through the lengthy sessions, getting basic tracks for "I Go Blind," "Look Away," "Only Wanna Be With You," and "Time."

It felt good getting back to #433 each evening after an eight- or ten-hour day in the studio. Arriving there to an occasional care package from back home consisting of homemade cookies, or 100-proof Schnapps, or a letter from family, was glorious. Our ritual on most nights was to gather around the living room phone the four of us shared, for what came to be known as our "Message Party." Drinks in hand, one of us would hit "Replay Messages," hoping to hear the sweet voice of a family member or some good news from Rusty.

One night, after the messages ended, Mark pulled out a sheet of paper we'd been using to list possible album titles and started reading. After several weeks of recording, the label was pressuring us to give the art department something to work with, an image, or theme, or anything, so they could start developing the artwork.

"'Involuntary Abstinence,'" he read, then, "'Message Party,' 'Memoirs from a Dysfunctional Life.' Anyone?"

"How about 'Monica's Reluctance to Lob'?" Darius said. He was obsessed with a comment tennis commentator Bud Collins had made regarding Monica Seles's recent performance in a big tournament we were watching. Collins claimed, "It was Monica's reluctance to lob that cost her the match." We ended up using the comment as the name for our publishing company.

Nothing seemed right. Random titles continued to be thrown up for suggestion, and even a few song lyrics. As one of our favorite old songs, "Learning How to Love You," by John Hiatt, was playing on our jam box in the background, a lyric suddenly jumped out at me. Out loud I said, "Cracked Rear View?"

Heads moved up and down in agreement. No disapproving looks. Darius said, "That's not bad." And, just like that, we had a title for our record. Atlantic Records was now able to start working on the record cover, which coincidentally they assigned to a young art department woman and former University of South Carolina student named Jean Cronin—a nice Gamecock synergy was born.

~

Our relationship with Don continued to flourish. The more we trusted him, the more success he had in leading us, teaching us, and discovering a lot about us in the process. I have a feeling Don found us refreshing as he began to understand our peculiarities. Within our little democracy, he was cultivating an atmosphere that was loose and mystical, naturally ebbing and flowing—yet always purposeful. He filled the studio with specifically scented candles and incense. He showed us how to read Icelandic runes, an ancient lettering system meant to provide insight to your life, or a "mirror to your subconscious process," as Don would say. I was at a major crossroads in life and lacking spiritual direction, so I was especially hopeful that these runes could help me learn from my past and/or nurture new beginnings. As a result of this ambience he created, the pressure and nerves of recording began to lift, without blurring our focus or motivation. The language he used about music constantly had our heads turning in the studio—words like "flappy," "pitchy," and "pushy," and phrases like "digging for trombone." (He even knew how to deal with my ego when I started to get sulky after he chose Darius over me to play percussion on "Drowning.") Being a great producer requires skill not only in *sound*, but in *mind*.

Since Don liked his weekends as much as we did, we all took Saturday and Sunday off, and we filled those days by attending major league baseball games, visiting amusement parks, catching local concerts, and even playing some pickup basketball.

To some extent it was like we were back in college. There was always one person trying to convince everyone else to keep drinking. Often, we would just hang out in #433 with our friends Tina, Stu, Emma, Jill, Gena, Chris, and Rich, staying up late singing Toad the Wet Sprocket and Bruce Springsteen songs. I don't think the neighbors were big fans.

Though I considered myself a celebratory drinker, I would some-times stay up alone after everyone had gone to bed so I could drink a little vodka, strum guitar, and have a little cry. I thought I'd left all my tears over Alissa back in the apartment in Columbia, but I seem to have dragged some of those feelings all the way to California. I didn't know if it was alcoholism, or if I was just feeling sorry for myself. I was slightly embarrassed one night when Mark came out to console me after my whimpering woke him up.

Perhaps this was just a phase? If I wasn't so busy making the biggest record of my life, I might have dug a little deeper to look at the true source of my problems.

Our attempts at recording "Hold My Hand," a song we had played together no less than five hundred times since 1990, served us a challenge we did not see coming. Sitting in the brightly lit, air-conditioned studio at 1:00 p.m. on a Monday was nothing like the atmosphere in which we typically performed this song. For us, this song always came late at night, amidst a swinging and swaying crowd, and that energy was now desperately missing; the anthemic glory we thrived on was nowhere to be found in this sterile, empty room. We tried take after take after take, hoping to summon the magical mood we were familiar with from The Bayou in DC, The Music Farm in Charleston, or Ziggy's in Winston-Salem. In those places, drumming away sweaty and shirtless, my eyes could feast on the raucous crowd singing in unison, hands held high, momentarily causing me to forget I was even playing an instrument. That state of not having to "think too hard about playing your instrument" was exactly what we were searching for. Finally, after three times as many attempts as it should have taken, we nailed a keeper that felt right.

We were in the home stretch now, a well-oiled machine humming along without any foreseeable obstacles. With this self-assured focus we finished "Running From an Angel" and then took another swing at our Day 1 failure, "Dean's Song," putting in three to four more hours of attempts. Our hard work finally paid off and we came away with a tight track, the newly named "Not Even the Trees." Don then gave me one last opportunity to make my debut on piano with "Goodbye." Perhaps he had noticed that I had been earnestly practicing, since my first attempts to get a solid performance had come up short. Miraculously, we got a keeper on only the second take. I breathed a huge sigh of relief.

A collective smile came over the four of us band members as hired keyboardist John Nau slathered piano and Hammond B3 organ all over each of the dozen tracks we'd finished. For years we'd been hoping to hear our songs with some added instrumentation, some sounds that would act as a binding agent for all of our existing guitars, percussion, and vocals. John's soulful touch turned out to be just the effect we'd wished for. Years later we would discover the seasoned keyboardist had done more than just play his parts impeccably. Too shy to admit he had lost the demo tape Don had sent him, which left him unable to rehearse *any* of the songs before walking into the studio, he showed up anyhow. Completely unrehearsed, he sat down and played all of the keyboard parts for the entire album.

~

Atlantic Records, Don, and Tim all convinced us that having a well-known singer on our record would give radio stations and magazines something to talk and write about. Don said that he knew David Crosby, founding member of the Byrds and Crosby, Stills & Nash, from their partying days, but more importantly that he'd kept up with him after they had both gotten sober.

Much to our surprise, and with absolutely zero fanfare, the man himself strolled into the control room one day near the end of our overdubbing sessions. It was an amazing moment for us. After brief hellos, Crosby got situated in the vocal isolation booth. Instead of the typical formalities of "Check, one-two, check, one-two," Crosby slid right into a barrage of funny impersonations and satirical references to drug use that left us all in stitches. He said, "I'm feeling a little perky today, could somebody bring me some smack and a few Quaaludes?" I knew he was clean and sober, but I was still surprised at how freely he discussed drugs and alcohol. It was invigorating.

Jokes aside, Don guided Crosby through "Hold My Hand" as Crosby sang along with the group harmony we had already recorded.

Don then gave him the liberty to go off script in hopes of capturing a few signature moments, and it didn't take long before he did just that. A few minutes later, he sauntered out of the booth as though he'd done nothing more difficult than reciting the ABCs.

Wanting to make the most of the presence of a guy who was a real rock icon, someone asked if he would give us a little advice on something, *anything*, like songwriting or record labels or heroin or what it felt like playing Woodstock. I would remember his words years later as my attitude, my career, and my life were colliding and collapsing around me.

"Pay special attention to this monstrous operation you are now entering called the music business," he said, "and remember you must make the important distinction between the *music*, and the *business*."

"The music," Crosby said, "is the reason the four of you are sitting in this lovely studio in Los Angeles today. The music is the relentless, emotional sensation you guys experience while strumming your guitar or singing on stage or sitting at a piano tinkering away. The music originates deep in each of your hearts, and it's a beautiful, precious gift to be cherished every fucking day."

This was Crosby reciting the indescribable feelings I had held for music since I first began writing songs.

"But," he said, "you need always to be able to clearly differentiate that wonderfully fuzzy feeling you get from the *music* from the evil shit storm that is the music *business*. Because it can drag you down under the water and hold you there breathless until you drown in your own vomit. It will erode your soul quicker than the amount of time it took you to cum when you got laid for the first time. If you can't separate it from the music, the music business can make you wonder why in the hell you ever picked up a guitar in the first place..."

I suddenly felt a little dirty, as though the scum he was describing was now on my fingers.

All the while Crosby had been calm, as if he were a fortune-teller showing us what he saw in our future if we didn't prepare with the right attitude.

"Be careful, gents," he said, "and don't forget, it can also be the time of your fucking lives, and ya wouldn't wanna miss that, would ya?"

And with a smirk of someone who not only knew the bitterness of heartbreak and disappointment, but who had also tasted sweet victory, he walked right out the door and on his merry way.

～

On our final night of recording at NRG, with an excitable energy abounding, we gathered in the control room to briefly strategize which B-sides we would record with our final few hours of studio time remaining. Don walked in and surveyed the haze that was emanating from a joint making its way around the room. Most everyone in the room was now holding a fresh beer, with the exception of assistant engineer Wade and Don. This moment was a first. Of the previous eighteen days and seventeen nights of recording, we never once partied *while* working. Don is no rookie, though. He knew this session could quickly disintegrate into a messy, unorganized Hootie party if he didn't lay down some rules quickly. He firmly stated, "We have two hours to record B-sides, so use your time wisely. No going back to fix any mistakes on these songs, so you better get it right the first time."

Within two hours we had finished seven B-sides—"Almost Home," "All That I Believe," "Araby," "Before The Heartache Rolls In," "Fine Line," "I'm Over You," and "Renaissance Eyes."

～

After eighteen days of recording at NRG, we were officially done with the basic tracks and most of the overdubs for the album. I could see the gratification in my bandmates' eyes. We had just finished making the record WE wanted to make. The record WE dreamed of, without having to rush, without having to worry about a limited budget or resources, and with the perfect leadership

The days ahead, while Don mixed the record and we stopped by to listen and comment, would not call for nearly the same amount of studio hours for each of us band members, so we had some time to discover LA culture. I spent a ton of time cruising around in Tina's car—she was one of our new LA friends and worked in the publishing sector of the music industry, and we'd spend time listening to music, getting stoned and hanging out at her house. It was a healthy relationship for both of us. I was still a mess trying to make sense out of my failure with Alissa, and Tina allowed room for me to be imperfect and broken as I got back to my feet emotionally. I felt like I didn't need to hide anything from her, and that was a huge relief.

It was also fun to see what successful careers in music could bring. We visited Don Gehman's enchanting home and several times hung out at Tina's mom and dad's charming abode off of Laurel Canyon. Her dad was renowned songwriter Tom Snow, and their home was once lived in by The Mamas & the Papas, and later David Bowie. As I walked through sprawling, sunlit rooms and elaborately tiled decks, and dove into shimmering swimming pools with heavenly views of the canyons below, I thought, "All of this came from writing and producing songs?" I couldn't fathom what it would take to end up with such riches.

One day, as we rode back down the canyon to the valley after one of these visits, all crammed into one back seat, it hit me that for now we were still just four guys with big dreams. I was about broke, for a start—but the excitement that we would soon have a CD available in stores nationwide made the reality of being almost broke pretty bearable.

I didn't want our time in LA to end. But eventually we said our goodbyes, and headed east once again.

Having a rough day at age three, after a run-in with a wooden armchair. October, 1967.

Little brother Steve, sister Katie, and first grade me, the nosepicker, in the back of our station wagon in Winnetka, Illinois.

Getting four out of seven of us to smile was probably a minor miracle. 1971.

Outwardly shy, but inwardly beaming over my first drum set on my thirteenth birthday.
Naperville, Illinois, October 1977.

(Above left) Somewhere in the middle of my ten-year dork phase. Naperville, Illinois.
(Above right) Feeling a little confidence my junior year with braces off, hair feathering, and another button undone on my shirt. Naperville, Illinois, 1982.

Sonefeld kids at our Uncle Joe's wedding reception. Saginaw, Michigan, 1974.

HOLD MY HAND

Original lyrics to "Hold My Hand," scribbled on a piece of paper from my university job. 1989.

At home on an extended lunch break from work to write songs and work on my tan. Columbia, South Carolina, 1989.

A muddy NCAA quarterfinal defeat for my Gamecock soccer team in 1985 at The Graveyard, Columbia, South Carolina. (Photo by Andy Lavalley)

A scary apartment fire reduced my stereo and most of my belongings to a melted mess. Columbia, South Carolina.

Iconic Columbia, South Carolina, rock club Rockafellas's February 1989 calendar listing Bachelors of Art, Tootie, and Hootie (my former, current, and future bands) all in action.

A proud father and son moment at my May 1989 college graduation.

First photo session with my new band, in front of Mark's rental house. Columbia, South Carolina, 1989. (Photo by Doug Johnson)

Sweat, glory, and goofiness backstage at the club Greenstreets in Columbia, South Carolina. (Photo by Suzy McGrane)

Dean and Darius, two very happy campers with our first band van, 1990.

In my natural habitat, playfully performing. 1990.

Me in shorts, Mark in pajamas, making Darius look like he's overdressed.

(Above and right). For *Cracked Rear View*, preproduction at The Alley, and recording at NRG Studios, North Hollywood, California, 1994.

A relieved band with producer Don Gehman on the final night of tracking for *Cracked Rear View*, at NRG Studios, 1994. (And I'm wearing a Hootie shirt, haha!)

twelve

EARNIE STEWART, BILL CLINTON, DAVE LETTERMAN

BESIDES THE BLATANT buzz I was feeling for our band, the summer of 1994 was special for another reason: the United States was hosting the soccer World Cup.

Making plans when you are only one part of a four-way partnership is always dicey, but I sold my desire to go to World Cup games by telling the guys that it was a vacation they *all* needed. Obviously, if a Hootie opportunity came up I would have to change my plans; we weren't established enough to say no thanks to a gig that would get us some good exposure.

Sure enough, as the World Cup drew closer, we got a unique offer to play a show in Washington, DC. The press secretary for First Lady Hillary Clinton had seen us playing clubs in DC area and was a fan, and the invitation was for the band to entertain a huge group at a Democratic National Committee party. So, after spending two days in soccer heaven with friends in Chicago, I flew to the nation's capital to play in front of President of the United

States Bill Clinton, First Lady Hillary Clinton, and a large group of supporters.

Unfortunately, the party we were scheduled to play was happening at the exact time the US team would be playing Colombia. This was a huge match, but much to my surprise, they had erected a giant TV screen at the venue and they would show the match live while we played. During the speeches, they had the game turned off, so I was frantically pacing around with my Walkman radio listening to the broadcast in Spanish (I was suddenly very thankful for my combined seven years of Spanish classes in high school and college).

Eventually the gig started, and I could finally watch the big TV in the distance as we played. The tight game went back and forth in front of me; I could barely concentrate. As we approached the second chorus of "Not Even the Trees," Earnie Stewart scored the unlikely second goal for the United States to put us up 2-0. I tried to keep my composure, but I couldn't. I was screaming with joy while at the same time trying to keep the rhythm—and I sped up uncontrollably. My screaming, combined with the massive tempo swing, caused the entire band to whip their heads around in unison.

"We scored! We scored!" I yelled while trying to point to the game with my sticks, still continuing the song. Honestly, they were lucky I didn't stop the song altogether for a spirited sprint through the crowd in celebration, but I figured it wasn't befitting of the event.

As we left the stage at the end of the show, Colombia got a goal back to make it close, causing my heart to race for the final few minutes of the match. But by the time it was our turn for a photo op with the Clintons, I was all smiles, celebrating a huge victory for the United States.

~

The US men's team would eventually lose to Brazil on July 4 that year—no shame in that—and looking back upon the whole experience, if I had to make a short list of memorable moments from my big trip to DC, meeting the Clintons, as we did, would come in second behind watching us beat Colombia that day.

Quickly, though, my mind turned back to music. After all that hard work across five years, by July 5, 1994, *Cracked Rear View* sat in record stores all across the Southeast. Thanks to our extensive touring and Tim Sommer's wisdom to concentrate on stocking the shelves in the Carolinas where we had the strongest following, we debuted at #127 on the Billboard 200 album chart. The record hovered between 150 and 200 during the first eight weeks of sales while we toured hard and promoted it, but our single "Hold My Hand" was barely causing a ripple on the Album Rock Tracks charts.

Then, one phone call altered the entire course of our career.

David Letterman wanted us on his show. He'd asked for us personally after hearing the single on the radio in New York, and we were gobsmacked. Most bands would sell their souls for the opportunity, but we had one small conflict: we were scheduled to play a sold-out show in our hometown on the only night Letterman had available. Not wanting to cancel a 3,000-seat, sold-out show, but also knowing we couldn't pass up the chance to play on late night TV, we pulled our first true rock star move and booked a private jet that would deliver us from Letterman to Columbia in time to do both. The plan was to hustle out of the Letterman taping, straight over the George Washington Bridge to Teterboro Airport in New Jersey, and then fly down to Columbia.

For the performance at the Ed Sullivan Theater in New York on September 2, I wore an oversized Carolina Soccer sweatshirt—if this was my only time appearing on national television, I wanted to wear something that meant a lot to me, and give a shout-out to all my Gamecock Soccer guys.

By this point, I'd sat at my drums awaiting the beginning of "Hold My Hand" for five straight years and never once had to put any thought into it (it helps that it's literally one of the easiest drum parts I'd ever written). But now, sitting in the historic, ice-cold Ed Sullivan Theater (Letterman was famous for keeping the studio at around freezing), watching the union crew scrambling to set up around me, and seeing the red lights blinking on the cameras, I was practically frozen with fear. What if I miss a beat? What if I drop a stick? What if, what if, what if?

Then, suddenly, the flashing applause sign lit up and the audience went wild, and I felt a surge of adrenalin. Letterman was off to my left at his desk, and as the stage manager counted down with his fingers "five, four, three, two . . ." and pointed at Dave, the applause faded and a silence came over the theater. In my head, I swear I could hear my mom's voice like we were in our basement and it was 1978: "Come on, Jimmy. Play a little something for us!"

From my drum riser, Letterman's voice was barely audible as he began our introduction, but I thought I heard him say the words, "one of my favorite new bands." I realized that this was the same stage where the Beatles made their television debut thirty years ago, back in the year of my birth, 1964. Paul stood right over there, and John and George, there. And this, right here, was where Ringo had perched on that goofy, circular drum riser as they performed "I Want to Hold Your Hand."

No pressure, Jimmy.

Then Letterman asked if "Hootie" was ready in his usual soft-ly-mocking way, and Darius began strumming the "B add 9" to the "E" chord progression from the song, the same one I'd come up with sitting in my apartment back in 1989, and it ushered a calm all over my body. Seeing a close-up of him in the stage monitor wearing his goofy Miami Dolphins ball cap, and Mark in his same old cutoff shorts, made me realize it was just us, Hootie & the Blowfish, just us playing one of our songs again.

It took just three and a half minutes, but my band, Hootie & the Blowfish, had been launched into the living rooms of millions of people.

It was a game-changer.

It didn't hurt that you could tell Letterman was a true fan of the song. Record sales up to this point had been earned through rigorous touring and our solid regional following, but the opportunity to play a show as important as Letterman was a direct result of the influence that's available at a major label like Atlantic Records. The geographical barriers that had formerly restricted us were gone almost immediately, and the record started to move, too. We were soon booking shows as far afield as Ann Arbor, Michigan, and Toronto, Ontario—in fact, a whole host of new cities that previously didn't know what a Hootie or a Blowfish was. Letterman had tipped the important first tile that made possible a long string of dominoes plunging down onto the next.

thirteen

BIG HEAD

IN 1994, WE were offered a two-week tour as the support act for a band called Big Head Todd and the Monsters, who had a platinum album with Giant Records called *Sister Sweetly*. They were playing in theaters across the Midwest and it was a great opportunity to get in front of bigger crowds out of our market.

At our first tour stop with BHTM in South Bend, Indiana, on October 25, while Dean and I were getting onto our elevator at our hotel, a tall, dark-haired girl was stepping out. She was wearing denim overalls and a black leather coat, and I remember turning to Dean as the elevator doors shut and saying, "Deano, that's why I love the Midwest!" I was referring to her simple, functional fashion, her no-frills beauty, and a purposeful walk that was suggestive of someone who grew up in the blistering cold Midwest.

Just a couple hours later I spotted her again, this time walking through the theater during our sound check. Then, at a nearby restaurant while I was eating dinner, I spotted her a third time. She was sitting with a bunch of people, including a guy who was our radio representative from Atlantic Records. I figured she was somehow connected to the industry, but being pessimistic, I'd already told myself that she must be dating the lead singer of BHTM or something.

Then, as we played our set, in the middle of "Drowning," she came into the hall and got seated about ten rows back. Wanting to get her attention, but limited by my already occupied hands and feet, I went to the next best option, an exaggerated hair-flipping routine. Guitarists and singers have it so easy with their mobility and proximity to the audience, but drummers must be more creative. Unsure of whether I'd caught this girl's attention, in the next song I did what must be done when times are desperate: I went shirtless for the rest of the set.

In the lobby after our set I finally met her.

"Hey, I'm Debbie Mason with Giant Records," she said. "I loved your set!"

"Oh, thanks!" I said. "I'm Jim, but everybody calls me Soni. What do you do for Giant Records?"

"I'm the local radio rep for Giant, and this is one of my markets, along with Milwaukee, Indianapolis, Chicago and some others in the area. Just trying to get some spins at radio."

"Sounds like a fun job. Does that mean you live in one of those cities?"

"I live in Chicago," she said.

This was great news.

"Only my favorite city in the world," I said. "I grew up in Naperville."

And that's how it began.

~

This was about ten months after Alissa's departure from my life, and I still hadn't resolved many of my feelings for her. In fact, I'd only shoved them under the rug, and I wasn't sure what I was looking for in a new relationship.

Debbie and I hit it off immediately, and we spent time together in Milwaukee, Madison, and Minneapolis during the BHTM tour. I was smitten. I loved that she was from Michigan, the state where I was born, and lived in the city of my dreams, Chicago. We both loved discovering new music, and she even loved sports. Once we started dating for real, I made a decision that I wanted this relationship to work. And I promised myself that I would be up-front and honest, and most importantly, faithful.

Time was passing. Two of my brothers, Dave and Mike, were already well down the road to starting families, and I was way behind. I longed to have my own big family and I wanted to start sooner rather than later.

I had just turned thirty years old.

~

And so began our long-distance relationship, based around phone calls and regular trips to Chicago when the band had a few days off. We made each other mixtapes, and mailed letters and postcards from all of the places our careers took us.

After Letterman, sales around the country increased sharply, and we were now officially plugged into that big machine David Crosby warned us about. We were a priority at the label; data the label was looking at suggested our album could be in for a good ride on the charts.

We could never imagine what was actually coming.

~

By December, Atlantic Records had really revved up the promotional machine. We went back to New York, this time to appear on Regis and Kathy Lee, and then we flew to Orlando to pre-tape the Dick Clark New Year's Eve TV show, willingly faking exuberance like it was really a New Year's celebration (it was mid-December). We got to record "Hey, Hey, What Can I Do" for an Atlantic Records/Led Zeppelin tribute album called *Encomium*, and we also shot a video for our second single, "Let Her Cry," in Charlotte, North Carolina.

This all happened in a ten-day period, and by the final day of 1994, the album was up to #56 on the charts.

~

1995 was something else entirely.

We worked and played our asses off during the first five months of that year, beginning with two weeks of club shows and promotion (and hard-drinking) in the UK and Europe. Returning home, we sprinted through fourteen shows in only eighteen days, and a return performance on *Late Night with David Letterman*, singing "Let Her Cry."

We also were blessed to fulfill our dream of touring with Toad the Wet Sprocket. With the exception of maybe R.E.M., I don't think we collectively admired any band more than we did Toad. During our early days in the van, it was one of the few bands you could play on the stereo that no one ever complained about. Whenever we got bored with playing our own Hootie material during afternoon soundchecks, which was often, we always deferred to playing Toad songs. "Come Back Down," "Torn," "Fly From Heaven," "In My Ear," and "Woodburning" were standard, though we didn't always bother ourselves with learning how to play them correctly. On our five-week tour together, without exception, after finishing our set we'd watch their entire show, every night.

A few weeks into the tour, Toad invited Darius up to sing one of our other favorite Toad songs, "Crowing." Upon realizing Darius would be singing with them, I raced out into the audience to watch it from the front of house, crouching down on the front row, blending in relatively unnoticed. As Darius approached the microphone from the shadows, hitting his cue to begin the second verse, the crowd noise swelled in recognition. His baritone voice enriched the song with a velvety layer, as the words he already knew by heart poured out:

> Get over regrets
> While you were sleeping with angels
> He was under the bed
> And the more skin that you shed
> The more that the air in your throat will linger
> When you call him your friend
> And it was never a question
> He was crowing for repair
> You'd give him love and affection
> But you couldn't keep him there

He sounded so strong, yet the constant tugging of his oversized flannel shirt told me he was still a little shy and anxious in the moment. I knew a part of him was living out a meaningful dream.

During the closing moments of the final show of the tour, lead singer Glen Phillips shared a humble thanks and goodnight to the audience, "This has been like, the finest tour, I think, any of us has ever been on." As if his spoken words weren't already sublimely flattering, the musical homage that followed was enough to send the four of us happily to our early graves. With a slight Darius Rucker inflection in his voice and Dean Dinning accompanying him on the organ, Glen strummed the C chord on his guitar and parodied the entire chorus of "Let Her Cry" with lyrics he'd penned himself, singing:

> Letter Y, is a year and yesterday
> Letter C, as in cantaloupe and clay
> Letter O, like an orange on a tree
> But if you wanna spell banana, Letter B,
> ahhhhhh Letter B . . .

The long-running children's TV show *Sesame Street* missed a great opportunity to include Glen's brilliantly educational takeoff of our song for their show, instead redeveloping another song of ours, "Hold My Hand," in a message dedicated to crosswalk safety a few years later.

Out in the real world, "Let Her Cry" rose up the singles chart, and as a result of being locked in our band crush for over a month, the four of us failed to notice the wave of Hootie hysteria that was building day after day across America. *Cracked Rear View* now sat firmly entrenched in the Billboard top ten, and we were content in our little traveling bubble, happily watching Toad the Wet Sprocket perform night after night.

This was the end of an era for Hootie & the Blowfish, though we couldn't see it at the time. It was the end of playing reduced, forty-minute sets as a support act, the end of mingling freely among the fans without needing the help of security, and the end of the innocent spirit you can only feel as you approach to top of the charts for the first time.

~

We were backstage in England during our second trip abroad in late May when we got word that *Cracked Rear View* was about to take over the #1 spot on the charts in America. A year earlier, we would have been happy to be on *any* chart, and now we were going to be sitting at the top of the most important chart of all, Billboard's Top 100.

Shots of Jägermeister were lifted high right before walking on stage. Mark proclaimed, "Here's to #1!" and I remember thinking, *Is this really happening?*

~

Though we loved touring abroad, and were delighted by being a number-one band, back home in South Carolina there was continuing conflict over the Confederate battle flag flying atop our state capitol, and Hootie & the Blowfish would come to be caught up in the controversy.

The subject of the Confederate flag on the state house was so divisive that many simply avoided it altogether. Darius Rucker was not one of those people.

Darius is a proud South Carolinian, with a long heritage that leads all the way back to his own ancestors, who had been held in slavery. So, when the flag topic came up during our interview with *Rolling Stone* magazine, Darius said exactly how he felt.

To his credit, *Rolling Stone* journalist Parke Puterbaugh had done his job researching our music and had picked out some lyrics that confronted the flag issue (from the song "Drowning"). In the interview, Darius called out the entire government of South Carolina as "absolutely asinine" for doing nothing in their power to remove the flag. It was a hurtful symbol to many, which had been hoisted in 1962 in direct opposition to the Civil Rights movement. We agreed with Darius—the flag fostered memories of a controversial, oppressive, and painful time in our state's history, and most folks outside of South Carolina saw it as an indication that we had not progressed socially with the rest of the country.

Since our star had only recently been on the rise, it had been easy to exist without having to declare what we stood for, or what we opposed, if anything. We didn't have to consider how a larger audience would ever view our unplanned "three white guys in an all-Black band" thing.

Too often, though we seamlessly blended together, we still had to face that many others viewed race very differently.

One night, I was sitting at the bar at The Gray Man, in Pawleys Island, South Carolina, in between sets, when some guy behind me said,

"They ain't bad, for having a n***** singer."

One of his friends recognized me and nudged him, saying, "Dude, be cool. The drummer's right there."

I whirled around, and said, "Excuse me?"

I already knew that there is a certain casualness with which the racist, white Southerner speaks in a crowd when they feel comfortable, though the volume always lowers when they realize that someone is listening who might not be so impressed by having the N-word thrown around.

"Oh, I didn't mean anything by it," the douchebag said. "I was just surprised he was, ya know [practically whispering now] . . . *Black*."

Yes, that's how nuts it is. He'd chosen to whisper the word *Black*, while having just spoken the other word out loud.

"Are you talking about our lead singer?" I said, standing up in the guy's face. "His name is Darius. He prefers Darius." The idiot's friends moved to stand between the two of us.

"He's cool," one of them said. "He's just messing around. Really, he didn't mean anything."

With another set to play there was no point starting a fight, so I just walked away muttering, "Fucking moron."

It was much worse for Darius, of course. One time we were approaching a sketchy-looking dive we'd been booked to play in Alabama, and Darius insisted he remove himself from the driver's seat and lay down in the middle of the van where he wouldn't be seen.

"I just don't like how this place feels," he said.

Now, as news of Darius's flag comments started circulating, there were numerous politicians and citizens in South Carolina who were less than thrilled with what he'd said.

The Republican governor at the time, David Beasley, had opposed taking the flag down, and didn't help to improve our view of him when he acted like he'd never heard of the band when asked about us at a press conference. The truth is, two weeks earlier he'd invited our guitarist Mark to come sit with him at a local minor league baseball game, and even complimented Mark on the band's success. We were the biggest band ever to come out of South Carolina, so his attempts to claim he'd never heard of us just made him look silly and craven.

Then, the nasty letters started, and a death threat, which was terrible for Darius, knowing that someone was willing to threaten his life in his own home state simply because of his opinion on a 140-year-old battle flag.

Our racial run-ins weren't confined to the South, either. On the Toad the Wet Sprocket tour, we had an incident in a college town in Michigan. After a gig and some hearty drinking at a club, our crew was suddenly telling me we needed to leave because there were some aggressive racial words being used, and it was gonna be better if it didn't come to blows. We managed to get ourselves out into the snow-covered streets, but it became apparent that our departure from the bar had not quelled the racist fury. As a flying Heineken bottle came crashing to the ground just a few feet from me from across the street, I decided enough was enough. It was time for the gloves to come off. Darius had already come to the same conclusion, and he was exchanging punches with some idiot against the open door of a car in the street. The real problem came when the car started pulling away with Darius and this guy still entangled, half *in* the car and half *out*. I hustled over and threw a few haymakers, which helped Darius get away from the rather frightening situation. I was more than willing to fight for my friend against some bad-mouthing racists, but once the adrenaline wore off, I just felt utterly depressed that there were still people that took such issue with skin color. And though Darius usually shrugged it off and showed a tough exterior, I can't imagine it didn't weigh heavily on him on the inside.

We three white guys could not pretend Darius had the same life experience as we had. We saw the distinct difference between being a person of color in this country, and being white. We couldn't claim to be color-blind, as some do, because if you can't see color and race, then how will you recognize racism? We chose what we thought was the best way forward with the four of us, to always be willing to talk about race, even when it was awkward.

Racism is inane, but listening to comedians like Richard Pryor and Chris Rock, who successfully combined race and humor, gave the four of us a chance to laugh together, and experience a little healing. It helped that Darius also had a talent for finding ways to use race to get a laugh. He was always quick to acknowledge how extra *white* Dean, Mark, and I were when we sang together or tried to dance, and it was absolutely true. If his meal arrived even seconds after the rest of us at a restaurant, he would subtly tap the back of his hand (our signal for implying skin color was an issue) and the four of us would giggle over our inside joke.

But not everyone outside our band and crew understood us. In a band photo shoot, if the photographer placed Darius behind any of us, he would look at the photographer and say, "Oh, I see how it is," and then tap the back of his hand so we could see it. The mortified photographer would be left thinking he'd offended Darius, until the moment he saw the rest of us laughing.

The more we openly discussed race and racism, and called it out when we saw it, the better understanding the four of us would have. But still the flag flew. Though Dean and Mark had been raised in Maryland, and I had spent my formative years in Illinois, all four members of Hootie & the Blowfish ultimately stood together on the race issue and the flag issue—and we were now realizing our voices were louder than ever. It would take twenty more years, the mass murder of nine innocent churchgoers at the hands of a Confederate flag-flaunting racist, and the courage of a strong governor before that particular symbol of hatred would come down.

fourteen

BACK HERE ON THE RISER

WITH OUR RISING profile, it wasn't long before promoters wanted us to fill their bigger venues. Our management, too, convinced us it was time to embark on our first ever headlining tour of outdoor amphitheaters.

This was another pinch-me moment. This was the big time, and it's a place that's difficult to prepare for. We hired a great company from North Carolina, Special Events Services, to put lighting and sound and a large crew together, but we couldn't just go out and *purchase* the experience we needed to entertain crowds of 15,000 to 20,000 fans. We would have to figure that out on our own.

It was difficult for me, back there on my drum riser. Suddenly we were playing on huge stages, and it completely changed the dynamic of the band. I was now separated from my bandmates, and it was like losing sight of my buoys at sea. Suddenly, there were acres of space between Dean and me, and drummers and bass players need to be in sync for a band to be tight. His bass amp, which used to thump thunderously right alongside me in the clubs, was now too far away to feel or hear. But it wasn't just the instruments. Because the rest of the band were at the front of these deep stages it was impossible to have normal communication with them in between songs. For years, we hadn't even used a set list. Basically, Darius would just shout stuff out or briefly turn to discuss it with the three of us between songs. If he got stumped, one of us would throw out a suggestion, and on we'd go.

Darius, who used to be close enough to smell, was now off in the distance looking very small, and all I could see was the growing bald spot he referred to as his "cul-de-sac" on the back of his head when he removed his cap. Mark was off dancing miles away, or working the crowd, and Dean became a speck.

All that said, there was still an extraordinary joy in playing such massive venues, knowing it was our name in big letters on the marquee that had drawn all these people together. The volume level coming at us as we walked out on stage each night was louder than we'd ever experienced and swept over us like a big wave. It scared the hell out of me the first few times I heard 18,000 fans screaming in unison.

It was a wall of sound I grew very fond of hearing.

Romping through one of our favorite closing songs that summer, "Mustang Sally," I looked around at the important friends who had worked hard and were enjoying the ride as much as we were. They were beginning to feel like family. Gary Greene, who we originally hired to sell t-shirts and load gear, now stood on the riser beside me, pounding away on percussion and singing background vocals. Out in the middle of the crowd was our focused front-of-house engineer, Billy Huelin, who'd been with us since the early bar days. Jeff Poland, who had tour-managed us in the club days, was now our security guard, and stood tan and flexing, eyeing the audience like a hawk from behind a stack of speakers. Paul Graham, our college buddy who currently tour-managed us, was in a gleeful conversation with our accountant Lyn Richards between the side stage curtains. Lyn had been with us since we'd barely had enough money to pay taxes. And somewhere out in the distance was our faithful attorney, Gus Gusler. Though for years he'd mostly handled contracts and lawsuits for us, I knew he was now out in the parking lot chasing down bootleggers selling illegal Hootie t-shirts, and loving every minute of it.

We were filling every available gap in the calendar with media and charity opportunities, too. We took part in a moving opening ceremony for the Special Olympics at the Yale Bowl in New Haven, Connecticut, singing "Hold My Hand" to more than 50,000 participants and their supporters. We helped build a Habitat for Humanity house. We played free shows at numerous golf fundraisers (a trend that would continue for years). New videos needed to be filmed, media outlets were begging for interviews, and charities from all over the country were asking for our help. The train called "success" was chugging down the tracks. The only question was: were we the conductors of this thing, or just four passengers?

~

The success of *Cracked Rear View* showed no signs of stopping any time soon. The record sat in the top three of the Billboard charts every week from late May to October of 1995, averaging hundreds of thousands in sales weekly all the way through the summer tour. With each new sales report came the gnawing sensation that we might never reach these heights again. Was there such a thing as too much? Darius was the first to look at the sales projections and share out loud his thoughts.

"You realize we will probably never top this?" he said one day that summer.

Mark said, "Well, Atlantic is an amazing label and they are kicking ass with the record, so, ya never know."

"No," Darius said, "I mean we will NEVER top this again. This record could sell ten million copies [in fact, it sold that before the end of the year]. No rock bands sell ten million records and then follow it up with ten or twelve million more."

Dean said, "Michael Jackson did . . ."

"We're not Michael Jackson," Darius said. "He's the king of pop."

Dean just shrugged and let it drop.

As the numbers mounted, it became clearer and clearer that Darius was probably right—we would never visit these heights again, ever. Though it was tough to accept, we were probably wise to face it sooner rather than later. And that meant facing the need to start moving on and writing new material.

"Should we start working on some new stuff?" Mark said (he loved to write new songs).

"Can we call it Cracked Rear *Two*?" I said, in jest, to a chorus of boos.

~

We weren't downcast, and none of us felt any pressure to top the first record with the second. In fact, we'd faced the task pretty casually, maybe even too casually. We'd decided to follow our hearts instead of our bank books. As artists, we needed to be creative and felt an obligation to get some new music out to our fans, especially the ones who had been supporting us since the early '90s. It simply wasn't in our DNA to put off writing new songs or to purposefully delay a new project just for material gain; plus, we were going to sell millions of copies of the first record, so financially we were about to be in great shape.

Still, we had to deal with Atlantic Records. Initially they'd wanted to optimize their profits by releasing fifth and sixth singles before we released new material, but this wasn't our way. We wanted to deal with the inevitable follow-up issues by simply making a new record, and releasing it. Waiting longer wasn't going to guarantee success for a second album.

Surprisingly, the label didn't push us hard or try to hold us hostage. Instead, they allowed us to start preproduction on the second record, helping us make plans to get us back into the studio with Don Gehman to face this sophomore demon on our own terms.

~

At the end of September 1995, *Cracked Rear View* hit number one for an insane fifth time, and it was showing no signs of slowing down. Since royalty checks were now arriving, we all faced this new thing called *having money*. We had never had any before. We practically had to be begged into investing our first big paychecks by purchasing homes for ourselves. I remember thinking, "Why do we need homes?"

Darius and Dean were still happily living together and, since neither had a significant other, they decided simply to buy a house together. It still makes me chuckle when I think about their big bachelor pad. They made a great couple.

But even then, a manicured lawn, three bedrooms, and a garage with a shiny new car in it weren't of much use to us—the road was still our home.

fifteen

NEIL, JOHN, AND WILLIE

WE WERE HEADING to San Rafael, California, to begin recording Cracked Rear Two, the album title I jokingly tried to push on my bandmates, but on the way we stopped off in Louisville, Kentucky, to perform at the annual Farm Aid concert.

A huge honor for us, the event included the usual hosts John Mellencamp, Willie Nelson, and Neil Young, and several other country/ rock acts. The Dave Matthews Band and Hootie & the Blowfish were newcomers. The week we played Farm Aid, both of our albums sat firmly in the Billboard Top 20.

~

The music of the three hosts—John, Willie, and Neil—spanned most of my life and meant so much to me.

Mellencamp's records always brought to mind memories of long trips back and forth between Illinois and South Carolina in the 1980s, staring out over the endless farmland off Interstate 65 in Indiana, where Mellencamp himself is from. Depending on the particular season of my life, that long stretch of highway brought up a bunch of feelings for me: *excitement*, as I left Illinois for the first time, heading southward to an unknown future in South Carolina as an 18-year-old boy; *letdown*, as I returned eleven months later after failing out of college; and *disillusionment*. I'd taken one of those long drives with my mother, and I was hurt that she and my dad had divorced and I would never have a childhood home to return to. Mellencamp's lyrics of disappointment and rage over the plight of the family farmers were feelings I understood well, and it would take me years to sort through those feelings I kept locked inside.

Willie Nelson, whose music I'd loved all through the years, was an artist I listened to with my dad all the way back in Naperville. It endeared me to my father, and I thought it was so cool that he, who seemed to be just a straight-laced, traditional, sports-loving dad, could hold a longhaired rebel like Willie in such high esteem.

Neil Young made me think of my brother Mike, since he and I really bonded over Neil's music during my first year in South Carolina when we'd repaired our relationship.

Now, the Blowfish were on the same bill as these legends. I had to pinch myself, but still, it hardly felt real.

~

Farm Aid was a first for us, but sharing a stage with Dave Matthews Band was not.

Our careers had been running in parallel all the way back to a Halloween fraternity mixer in Virginia in 1992. It hadn't been my best night, though, for a couple of reasons:

First, I was wandering around the small room where we were going to play, getting my bearings, and I bumped into a guy about my age. I thought maybe he was with the fraternity, but definitely an upperclassman. He was dressed in a snappy knit turtleneck sweater under a sporty tweed jacket. Given that it was Halloween, and thinking he might just be in costume for the party, I said,

"Who are you supposed to be dressed as?"

The guy just said, "What are you talking about?" He was clearly annoyed.

And with that, he stepped up to the microphone for his sound-check, and I realized that it was Dave Matthews.

The night got worse when out of pure laziness I decided to play Carter Beauford's monstrous drum set instead of mine for our set. I didn't feel like lugging my dinky kit from the van, but a couple of songs into our set I realized I was lost amongst the mountains of drums and cymbals Carter had set up, all of which were specifically placed for his reach, not mine. It was really uncomfortable, but too late to fix. I had to completely rethink how to play, and after a couple of blatantly botched drum fills, I was sorry I hadn't taken the extra effort to get my 5-piece out of the van.

Now, though, we were at Farm Aid together, and it proved to be a great opportunity to celebrate our mutual successes with hugs and congratulations. We had carved almost identical paths to get to where we were. We both wrote our own stuff, toured our asses off, and sold our own music along the way without help from a major label. We both put out independent CDs in 1993 that led to recording contracts with major labels. Dave Matthews' RCA debut *Under the Table and Dreaming* came out only months after *Cracked Rear View*, and though rumors had circulated claiming that the two bands didn't like each other, there was no truth to it. Two years earlier, both bands had been grinding out East Coast club tours, and now we were sitting on Willie Nelson's bus together watching him roll fatties while he thanked us for playing his shindig. Now I was too self-conscious (or too high) to bring up to Dave our awkward encounter from the Halloween gig a couple years earlier.

~

I was spending most of my days off with Debbie as she worked and traveled full-time for Giant Records. I was enjoying the feeling of being in love again, and I was benefitting from the music business education she was giving me. It revealed a side of the industry I had no idea existed, apart from what David Crosby had told us and the little I'd seen while dealing with Atlantic Records. I would ride along with her to cities in her market like Fort Wayne, Indianapolis, or Milwaukee, as she worked to convince radio stations to play music by Giant Records artists. I got to see how and why some songs got on the radio while others didn't, and learned quickly that the key factor wasn't necessarily the music; it was *influence*. Lavish dinners punctuated by expensive bottles of wine would be used to help radio programmers make decisions on which singles made it to the airwaves; executives in shiny suits in New York and LA decided which bands would become a priority and get funding for promotion, and which bands would not. While it's a fair business model to prioritize bands from *very important* all the way down to *not very important*, I found it astonishing that the record label continued to tell every band *they* were at the top of the priority list, even when it was clearly not true. Most surprising was realizing how much bartering, deal-making, and politics went into the whole scheme. Believing in the music and the message was nothing but an afterthought by the time the last bottle of champagne had been uncorked.

This was all eye-opening, and it occurred to me that perhaps this was the same process that allowed *our* singles to gain favor at radio stations. I wanted to believe that our success was solely based on the music, and not some dodgy deals happening without our knowledge. I didn't have any inkling that someday in the not-so-distant future we too would fall victim to being deceived, like many other naive or just plain unlucky artists.

sixteen

OL' BLUE EYES

OUR FIRST DAY at The Site in San Rafael, a secluded recording studio north of San Francisco, was a big day in America. Not because Americans were excited to hear we were beginning a new Hootie album, sadly. Instead, it was the day the verdict came down in the O. J. Simpson trial. We still couldn't get over the fact that we'd seen him at the airport on our first day in LA to record our first record, and now here he was again on the first day of our second record, right in front of our eyes on every channel. Both his and our lives had taken dramatic turns during those eighteen months.

We all decided to live at the studio deep in the mountains so we could focus our attention on the new record. After all, we'd had the luxury of writing the first one over a five-year period. We hoped to limit the pressure and distractions so we could give ourselves the best chance possible to concentrate. Our lifestyle in the reclusive mountain studio was a much-needed change from the life of excess we were living out on the road, but as healthy and slow-paced as it was out in the woods, we were never able to stay for long periods before being lured away.

On one occasion, we flew all the way to Hawai'i for a gig and a big pro-am golf tournament. I decided I needed to fly my mom out there to spend some time with her. She had a blast seeing and meeting famous golfers, and she loved the attention of being with the band. "I'm the drummer's mom," she'd tell people.

One night, we decided against going to downtown Lahaina with the group, and instead sat at the hotel bar just chatting. We were in a new place in our relationship. I was no longer little Jimmy on the soccer field, or baseball field, or tennis court; nor was I a college kid struggling with bad grades or trying to keep a steady girlfriend. I was her grown son in the middle of a successful career, bringing her to Hawai'i. I'm sure I'd been a frustrating kid for the past thirty years, but this trip felt like a tiny offering of thanks for all the love and attention she'd given me.

The next day we played tennis—it was always something we loved to do together. I'm sure the time change and humidity and Jäger shots the previous night didn't help our physical state, but this was the first time I remember noticing her being overly short of breath. I was taken aback and couldn't figure out that while she looked exactly the same, something on the inside seemed to be drastically different. She was active, but she had also been a lifelong smoker. Never had I given it serious thought that her cigarettes might finally be catching up to her, but now I was wondering if there could really be something wrong. Mom just deflected the obvious physical suffering with humor, saying, "I just need a cigarette and I'll feel better."

∼

The band made a bunch of other trips, too, during the making of the new record—to Las Vegas for a VH1 celebrity golf tournament; to New York to speak at a law school as a favor to some friends in the industry and to play a charity show for Boomer Esiason and the Cystic Fibrosis Foundation. But nothing quite compared to the trip we took to LA to play at a tribute concert for Frank Sinatra's eightieth birthday.

Rubbing shoulders with celebrities was a big deal to us, and the Sinatra gig was another example of this surreal life we'd fallen into. We'd be performing "The Lady is a Tramp," a song Darius played whenever he was the DJ in our van or at whichever Columbia bar we found ourselves. I thought we knocked it out of the park, mostly thanks to Darius's vocal performance and the Big Band that was supporting us. And there we all were, in suits nonetheless. I even wore a big ol' fedora as I swung along with the band.

As big a thrill as it was to perform right in front of Frank Sinatra, there was the added excitement of being in the presence of all the stars he had gathered around him. We got to brush shoulders with Tony Bennett, Ray Charles, Danny Aiello, Don Rickles, Bruce Springsteen, and Patti LaBelle, among others. It was an amazing night.

~

With the Sinatra gig done, I also managed to make several trips to Chicago and Detroit to see Debbie and her family. I loved that we had a similar background. She came from a middle-class suburb of Detroit and, like me, had a lot of family scattered all around Michigan. Our relationship was getting more serious even though it was never easy finding time to be together, with both of us working in different places and now on different coasts. I felt I was in a good place though, staying committed and enjoying our development into a serious relationship.

While I was still cranking up my partying on our trips away, I was able to string together multiple days of sobriety in San Rafael as we recorded. I took advantage of the treadmill in the living room, logging mile after mile every afternoon. We played two-on-two basketball daily on the hoop outside the front door of the studio. But the process of making what would become *Fairweather Johnson* (our pet name for fair-weather sports fans) was not an easy one compared to *Cracked Rear View*. We disagreed on what to do with a handful of older songs that had been well-received by our pre-*CRV* live audience but hadn't made the cut for *CRV*. As a result, catchy tunes like "If You're Going My Way" and "Sorry's Not Enough" (from *Kootchypop*) were ditched, never to resurface. A song previously titled "Kiss Me" mutated into "Silly Little Pop Song" by altering the lyrics and the instrumentation slightly, but the changes that were meant to satisfy all of us ended up satisfying none of us. The song "Old Man and Me" suffered in a similar way—in an effort to revamp it, it lost its luster for half of us—yet it still showed enough promise to become our first single off the album.

With all of the busy-ness and business crowding our lives, a dozen nearly finished songs sat frozen in time, awaiting lyrics. When some of my more poppy lyrics were ditched for lyrics that were more personal and introspective to Darius, I took it personally. I was too sensitive for my own good. Writing songs as a group requires sacrifice and patience, and I was struggling with both of these. At length, our team debated the value of each song, and sometimes it was just Don, Tim, and me deep in discussion well after our daily recording sessions were finished. I couldn't tell if we were overthinking things or underthinking them.

For all of these new frustrations we experienced, the four of us were still just Hootie & the Blowfish—four guys that celebrated living, loving, and laughing together. We still kept weird inside jokes and reminisced about the simplicity of our college days. Just for fun, Darius declared Dean to be the official name-giver of all the new songs—something we'd never done before. So, as we plodded through a dozen songs, they all received odd names because Dean, well, Dean can be odd at times. "A Day at the Zoo," "Lace Satin," "Sloth," "Revenge of JCP" . . . All of these unrelated titles became just another chance to giggle.

We experimented with a big hookah pipe we found at the studio one day, too, thinking some very powerful northern California weed might expand our minds and help us reach some higher level of understanding or musicianship. Everything seemed fine until Mark, without explanation, put down his guitar and walked out of the studio during the middle of recording the track, "When I'm Lonely." We all attempted to hide our laughter, continuing to play along without him. In the end it was Hookah pipe, 1 – Mark Bryan, 0.

By the end of the sessions, we somehow narrowed the diverse heap of songs down to twelve. There were disappointments and differences of opinion. But we got it done.

Our mellow life at the studio had given me a chance to clear my head and gain some perspective. It took slowing my life down for a minute to realize how much I really missed my family back in Columbia. This crazy ride I'd been on with the band didn't appear to have a jumping-off point, not one that I could see anyway. Conversations about booking another tour and more overseas opportunities, while exciting, left me wondering if I'd ever see my people any time soon.

seventeen

FAIRWEATHER "FRIENDS," AND *FRIENDS*

THE INSANE TRAJECTORY Hootie & the Blowfish experienced in 1995 spilled right over into 1996. Our fourth single, "Time," was racing up the charts, following in the footsteps of "Only Wanna Be With You," which, with the help of our goofy, sports-centered music video, assured our fans that we didn't take ourselves too seriously.

Our careers and lives were melding into pop culture in ways we had never imagined possible. Sitting in the family room at The Site one evening, our phones began blowing up with calls from friends back on the East Coast to tell us a Hootie & the Blowfish concert was the plot of an episode of *Friends*. (I had no idea of the significance of this, because I didn't have time to watch prime time television anymore.) On another day, we received a fax from Henry Winkler's wife requesting our presence at his surprise fiftieth-birthday bash.

So the Fonz liked us, but others didn't. We had become an easy target for music critics as we continued selling millions of records (critics hate it when you do that), but it was much more hurtful to hear our musical peers slagging us, too. The band Journey had come by to inquire about using the same studio in northern California where we had recorded *Fairweather Johnson,* and they couldn't stop telling the studio team how lame and insignificant they thought we were. I was crushed to learn that a band I'd grown up admiring was talking trash about us. Is it not enough to be successful in your own career without having to take shots at another band for their success? I still have no idea why they'd do that.

Green Day's lead singer Billie Joe Armstrong was another one who jabbed at us. When asked by an interviewer in late 1995 if the next Green Day album would be a "laid-back, acoustic affair," he said, "Yeah, we're going to sound like Hootie & the Blowfish. I've taken up golf lately, too." He quickly assured the interviewer that he was joking.

It hurt because, like Journey, Green Day was a band I deeply admired, and like us, Green Day had worked hard writing and play-ing their original music regionally until they got a break and signed a record deal. Though it's easy to see how our bands differed in our musical DNA, there were also similarities: both bands wrote anthe-mic choruses and gave great live shows. Maybe Armstrong was just one of those "in the closet" Hootie fans, outwardly mocking our acoustic guitars and our mid-tempo songs, but secretly was locked in his bedroom belting out "Let Her Cry" when no one was watching. I get it. Not everyone who enjoyed our poppy choruses was willing to boldly don a Hootie t-shirt and tell the world about it. Armstrong had the kind of tough-guy, rebel thing to uphold anyway, though it was notable that eighteen months after he'd made those snide comments, he'd released his biggest hit, an acoustic guitar-laden, mid-tempo song, "Time of Your Life."

I wonder where that inspiration came from. . . . You're welcome, Billie Joe.

Bands on our own Warner, Electra, Atlantic label family weren't holding back, either. For some of them, we just could never be cool enough. I gasped when I heard the band Everything But The Girl promising they were going to "save the world from Hootie & the Blowfish." I wasn't aware we were harming the world, frankly.

And then there was alt-rock darling Trent Reznor, who declared "Death to Hootie" when he decided we were too safe for how *he* defined rock and roll. I don't know Trent Reznor, but I know *he* didn't invent rock 'n' roll, nor does *he* get to define it for the rest of us out here making our own version of it. I didn't join Hootie & the Blowfish to be an anarchist or to be dangerous, and we weren't claiming to be something we weren't in any case. We were comfortable in our own skins and 100% authentic

~

It wasn't all bad news. Some of our musical heroes treated us as their musical peers. Neil Young offered us a slot on his stage again, this time for the Bridge School Benefit, along with Bruce Springsteen, The Pretenders, Emmylou Harris, Steven Tyler, Beck, and Daniel Lanois.

And then there were the award shows. In September 1995, we'd won MTV's "Best New Artist in a Video," and in the following months we pulled down awards at the Billboard Music Awards, the American Music Awards, and the Grammys. The most surreal moment of these shows was accepting one of our two Grammys from KISS and the other from Tupac Shakur. KISS were my childhood heroes, bigger than life for me. I'd collected their posters and albums and trading cards, and one of my first concerts had been seeing them in Chicago in the late 1970s. They hadn't appeared in public with the original lineup in years. Though my self-doubt wouldn't allow me to think we might actually win a Grammy, I suddenly found myself on stage, face-to-face with 6'2" KISS bassist Gene Simmons, probably 6'8" in his costume heels. He leaned in toward me with his dark brown eyes and demon-painted face, now inches away, and said with his smooth, baritone voice, "You look good" in the most serious tone imaginable.

I froze; I was sure he was just meaning it as a congratulatory compliment, but to me it was if I was caught in his spell, like he was about to take my virginity, like he was about to *take* me. I popped out of it and back to earth, holding a Grammy for Best Pop Performance by a Duo or Group, for our song, "Let Her Cry."

At the same award show, I escaped the lengthy program to take a quick bathroom break. While standing at the wall urinal I notice a small figure step up, two urinals down—Bob frickin' Dylan. This guy . . . an icon to most, perhaps, but not to me. My band and I had just lost a painful copyright dispute with Mr. Dylan. He, or his people, had allowed us to use lyrics from an old tune of his called "Idiot Wind" for our 1993 recording of "Only Wanna Be With You" on the *Kootchypop* CD. Perhaps we were the real idiots though. When we rerecorded the song only a year later, in March of 1994, we assumed we were still in the clear to use the lyrics again, in the exact same manner, which we proceeded to do. All was well until "Only Wanna Be With You" became a smash hit across America in the summer of 1995. In the music business, no one fights about copping lyrics until there is something substantial to fight about; namely, money. When Dylan's attorneys came a-knockin' we had to face the music, or in this case, the lyrics. In an attempt to save a shitload of *money* on lawyers and a shitload of our *time* on a courtroom battle, we just agreed to write him a big, fat check and be done with it—but it didn't make it hurt any less. Now, standing alone next to the aging legend, my first thought was revenge. What would feel better than to just shuffle over a few steps and piss right down the side of him? Dude probably wouldn't know what hit him until it was too late. I'd say, "Here's to your bastard lawyers and your fucking 'Idiot Wind'!" As I turned my head back to Dylan to make a final assessment before what would undoubtedly be the stupidest career move ever, I noticed his gigantic bodyguard filling most of the doorway, staring right back at me. It's as if he knew exactly what I was thinking. Without words, his stare told me, "Don't do it, you moron." I owe it to that guy; he saved me that night. As I passed through the men's room exit, though, I don't know what I regretted more, the massive amount of money we dished out, or not pissing on Dylan when I had the chance.

~

Perhaps the most gratifying moment, though, was when Garth Brooks called us out at the American Music Awards. After receiving the Artist of the Year Award, he actually refused to take it, saying, "For all the people who should be honored with this award, I'm gonna leave it right here," which was an incredible gesture to the other nominees, but he made his real thoughts clear in the press interviews after the ceremony.

"It wasn't fair for me to walk away with that award," Brooks said. "Maybe a year or two ago, when we had a really good year. But I've been around talking to retailers . . . and every one of them credits Hootie for keeping them alive in 1995 and I couldn't agree more. So I thought that's who should've won."

~

On our third trip to the United Kingdom and Europe in the spring of 1996 we brought along another Atlantic Records artist named Francis Dunnery to support us.

Debbie had given me a couple of his CDs, and I had instantly fallen in love with the authenticity and beauty of his music. Francis had been hugely popular in the United Kingdom a few years earlier as the lead singer/guitarist of his prog rock band, It Bites. Francis fit right in with our band and crew, regularly sharing colorful stories of his tough British upbringing and his spiritual views, as well as his previous alcoholic behavior and his newfound sobriety. He became a kind of guru/therapist to us. We were all half-lit most of the time, but it didn't seem to faze him, and he was one of the few people I'd met, besides Don Gehman and David Crosby, who had told me they'd once used and abused drugs and alcohol and later had to quit altogether.

This was an insane concept to me. What could make someone quit? As I'd done when hanging around Don Gehman in the studio, I asked Francis one or two questions about his journey into cleaner living. The thing is, back then I didn't think I'd ever have to face taking that journey myself. Both he and Don planted some seeds in me that showed me there was a happy, contented life to be lived that did not include alcohol binges and trips on mind-altering substances.

As we cruised around Europe, the parallel universes of The Dave Matthews Band and Hootie & the Blowfish crisscrossed once again. Both of our latest records had been released within a week of one another in late April, and now, as we found ourselves doing a concert together in Germany, our *Fairweather Johnson* sat at #1, and their *Crash* sat at #2 on the Billboard Top 200 list.

Their show was amazing, and I continued to admire them, though mostly I just stared all night in awe of Carter Beauford's amazing drumming. Afterward, the two bands sat together in the backstage area congratulating one another by passing around bottles of liquor and big-ass blunts. It's always nice to be on top of the world—or in our case the musical world—but it's even better to be able to do so with friends.

Being a significant part of the '90s pop/rock music scene was surreal. We relished opportunities to interact with some of rock 'n' roll's biggest celebrities, witnessing firsthand the different results of life as a touring musician.

On tour in the Ireland, I wandered through the lobby of the Clarence Hotel on Wellington Quay in Dublin, Ireland, and noticed world-famous lead singer of U2, Bono. He was comfortably concealed in the corner behind a big newspaper he held up with his hands, enjoying a morning hot beverage. I recognized him as the paper dipped down momentarily and revealed his eccentric eyeglasses. This was rock 'n' roll royalty for me. We'd heard he was one of the investors in the hotel, so to some degree I wasn't surprised to see him in his own hotel lobby. Yet there he sat silently, not drawing attention to himself. I wondered, "How does he carry himself in such a composed manner, the world at his feet, a massive rock star, just sitting here so calm, cool, and collected?" I envied how he appeared to have it together, even after so many years of touring and stardom. Though I'd hoped for an interaction with him, my shyness got the best of me. The fanboy inside me shrunk in fear and I decided to leave him uninterrupted, to continue in his peaceful moment.

Meeting Aerosmith's lead singer Steven Tyler for the first time, I was also starstruck, but since we were being introduced at a music event, it was more suitable to engage in a conversation. With his raspy New England accent, he greeted us first, "So how are we doing, Blowfish?" He was smiling the whole time, congenial, and dressed as if he were about to walk onstage.

"We're great, man! Really nice to finally meet you. We're huge fans," Mark and I replied, talking over one another excitedly.

Though he was probably just shy of forty years old, the creases on his face told me he'd lived some hard years. His bouts with drug abuse and rehab were public knowledge, and as we spoke about music-making and Aerosmith's recent renaissance I wondered if he was chemically altered or clean and serene.

Regardless, it was obvious by our fluid chat that he was a social butterfly.

Before we parted ways, Steven granted Mark's request to jump on his cell phone to give a shout out to Laura, Mark's significant other, who was back in South Carolina. With the glee of a child, he grabbed Mark's flip-phone, "Hey Laura! This is Steven Tyler!"

At Rock im Park, a giant music festival in Germany, we shared an outdoor backstage space with the other bands on the bill. To my surprise, exiting the trailer directly across from ours were Eddie and

Alex Van Halen. *Are you kidding me? Van fricking Halen!* This band was my gateway into hard rock and were the top of the list on the soundtrack to my high school years with my partying friends.

As Eddie made his way down a few stairs from their trailer to the patio, I could see he was relying heavily on the railing for assistance. As he got to the bottom, he brandished a walking cane from his other hand and used it to gingerly move forward. He was gaunt and pasty.

Right behind him, Alex appeared in the doorway. He surveyed his surroundings by turning his entire body to the left to see in that direction, and then stiffly swinging it all the way back around to the right, to see that way. As I looked for the cause for Alex's rather bizarre bodily movement, I noticed he was wearing a full-sized neck brace.

My image of what two high-flying metal warriors should look like was quickly quashed. This scene looked more like a hospital ward than backstage at a rock festival. Here were two of my hard-rock heroes, broken and bandaged, limping around as if they'd just returned from battle, and seeing their ailing bodies put a cold shiver of fear in me.

But I couldn't miss this moment for a quick hello, partly so I could tell my old friends how I had met Eddie and Alex(!), so I briskly walked over to them for a handshake.

A smile broke through sweet Eddie's lips as I confessed my adoration of his band.

Back in our trailer, I was chatting with Gary Greene, who had lucked into a much longer conversation with the Van Halens.

"Man, those guys were super-nice, especially considering their sad physical state! Alex told me he's got three ruptured vertebrae! Can you believe that?" Gary said, shaking his head, "And Eddie may be looking at having to replace his hip!"

"Man, I thought I liked to have a good time," I said. "Makes me wonder what those dudes were doing to get those sorts of injuries? Holy shit!"

"Don't know if I could do it, playing with injuries like that," Gary said.

"Let's hope we never have to find out," I replied.

Brushes with these stars suggested the different paths available for sustaining a career in rock 'n' roll. I witnessed a graceful picture of Bono, Steven Tyler during a tranquil moment of an otherwise roller-coaster ride of a career, and the Van Halens experiencing cause and effect, coupled with some bad luck. (Eddie's bad hip turned out to be avascular necrosis). I tried to keep an inventory of these helpful lessons and warnings.

I couldn't help but wonder: *How will I deal with our career going forward, or possibly downward? What bruises and scars will I pick up along the way? And most importantly, will I successfully balance the circus life of touring with some sort of normal family life at home?*

I certainly wished for both.

~

In June 1996, Mark became the first of our merry gang to tie the knot. He married Laura Brunty at a big Southern wedding in Myrtle Beach.

Debbie and I also got married three months later in suburban Detroit, Michigan, on September 28. Though often spending long stretches apart from one another, our relationship had been smooth, and I was anxious to start a family. The wedding came off without a hitch—we'd invited about 130 close friends—and its success was notable given that we'd planned it while also doing a fifty-city summer tour. We'd also appeared again on Letterman, on Conan, on Rosie O'Donnell, and *Showtime at The Apollo*. And as if we had all the time in the world, we'd also decided to shoot the music video for "Sad Caper" in late August, outdoors, dressed in wool marching band outfits, in Las Vegas. My only memory of shooting that video, after staying up all night drinking the night before, was stopping briefly to watch Darius dry heave all over the 100-degree pavement.

I don't ever remember seeing that video on TV. That was a first for one of our music videos, and it should have concerned us. But we were too busy to notice.

~

Hootie & the Blowfish were not good at sitting still for long. As my honeymoon ended, we got to host Farm Aid in Columbia. Six months before I would officially join the Blowfish, they'd passed the hat to help me after the fire in my apartment, and now, it remained meaningful to us to leverage the band's popularity for good. Our modest local fundraising golf event, Monday After the Masters, was only a year or two old now, so bringing together 35,000 people for Farm Aid was a proud moment for us. It was also one of those blank spots in my memory of an insanely busy few years that makes me glad someone took a few pictures I can remember it by. As the last empty beer cup was tossed into the trash and the final folding chair was hoisted onto its rack, our buses were warming up their engines to head back out across North America. We managed to stuff another forty-five shows between my honeymoon and the end of the year, including covering a long string of hockey arenas in Canada and another three-week trip back to Europe.

That jaunt across Canada was brutally cold. I woke one morning to find frost growing on the inside of my bunk wall. If there was frost on the inside of the bus, I wondered what in the world it could be like on the outside. I stared out at the huge piles of snow, the icy wind whipping hard, knowing I would eventually have to race through it all to get to the backstage door. If I was lucky enough to make it inside without busting my ass on the ice or dying of frostbite, the feeling of relief was always squelched by the realization that our dressing room was once again the visiting team's locker room.

The smell is enough to knock you dead.

eighteen
CAN'T STAY PUT

AS WE TRUDGED through Canada and the Midwest in 1996, I felt a little glum for the first time in my career. I caught myself looking at the empty seats in the venues and it made me wonder if things were slowing down a bit. *Fairweather* had a strong run on the charts. After spending three weeks in the #1 spot, it remained in the Top Ten into July and the Top Forty until the middle of September. Any other band out there would be pleased to sell as many records as we were selling. But as much as we had already conceded that we would never again achieve *Cracked Rear View* levels, there's a big difference between talking about it and seeing it happen.

By the time we'd played Farm Aid on October 12, *Fairweather* was already sitting down at #75. I was content to ignore the charts, but every magazine or radio interviewer opened with the same questions: "To what do you attribute the weak sales of *Fairweather Johnson?*" or, "How does it feel to sell ten million records on your debut and far fewer on your follow-up?"

~

As Debbie Mason became Debbie Sonefeld, I booted out my old roommates Jeff and Ford (also band employees) and moved my foosball table from the center of the living room to someplace more inconspicuous. With fewer band commitments in 1997—a purposeful choice by us—I was free to stay home with Debbie and pretend like my life was normal, but there is nothing normal about being a celebrity in a place like South Carolina. Not a conversation could go by without some mention of Hootie & the Blowfish. I was extremely grateful for our success and all the gifts it brought, but the chance to unwind and detach from the band was pretty much impossible. Part of me loved the attention, but I didn't like the inability to control it, to turn it off when I didn't want it.

There were plenty of upsides, of course: It's great to get free tickets from concert promoters and get out of tickets from the police. It was nice when people wanted to buy me drinks, and I did my best never to turn one down, but the price was always Hootie, Hootie, Hootie.

~

Not everyone was nice to me.

I found myself part of a mini tennis tournament in Atlanta, featuring some retired big-name stars like Stefan Edberg, John McEnroe, and one of my childhood heroes, Jimmy Connors. As part of the event, McEnroe and a local Atlanta TV personality were to do a brief celebrity doubles hit-around with Jimmy Connors and me.

I loved tennis and still played a little, so to be able to do a celebrity event was a real thrill. The scheduled celebrity hit-around would be followed by McEnroe's rock band (The Johnny Smyth Band) closing the night with a concert. I was a solid tennis player, but my nerves were getting the best of me as the event ran later and later and I stood in the wings at the old Omni Coliseum. Finally, my part of the night arrived . . . right as McEnroe's legendary pouty attitude showed up, too.

After I tried unsuccessfully serving several balls into his court, he announced to the crowd that he should serve a few to "Big Mr. Blowfish." And so he did, at top speed. I barely even saw the first one, and just about got my racket on the second. The third was the quickest of all, hard and right at me, and I jumped out of the way in time to stop from being hit. Then he threw in some sarcastic remark about Hootie & the Blowfish. Honestly, I was crushed. When we finished after just a few minutes, I walked off the court dumfounded by what had just happened.

Was this guy just impatient and eager to get to the concert part of the evening with his band? Was he sick of tennis, or celebrity hit-arounds? Did he hate Hootie & the Blowfish?

Was he just a dick?

The last I saw of McEnroe was in the bar afterward, loudly berating the promoter for something or other; security even had to pull him off the guy. I didn't have the balls to tell him what I thought of him. I was too busy drowning my sorrows with a bunch of Jack Daniels. I got so drunk, in fact, that Debbie ended up having to drive us all the way back to where we were staying, while I vomited out the window down the side of the car onto Highway 400.

nineteen

THE ASS OF ALEXI LALAS

BEFORE WE KNEW it we were preparing songs for a third Atlantic Records release in 1998, *Musical Chairs*. We were still touring on the back of the success of *Cracked Rear View*, and to a lesser extent *Fairweather Johnson*, but new trends and new artists and fickle radio programmers force you either to keep your gas pedal mashed down or to move over to one of the slower lanes.

For the new record, we had attempted writing sessions in Jackson Hole, Wyoming, and Desert Mountain, Arizona, but neither proved to be musically fruitful. We were happy to hang out, golf a little, eat pot brownies, laugh our asses off, and share musical ideas, but I was underwhelmed by the quantity and quality of songs we were coming up with. Still, it didn't stop us from booking studio time with Don Gehman back in Los Angeles since we knew we wanted to release the record before the end of the year.

We moved into our new California digs in the late spring of 1998 for the recording. We were convinced the proper place for us to live was an enormous, rented mansion on Sunset Boulevard—a far cry from our unpretentious two-bedroom apartment four years earlier. We had our own swimming pool. We rented nice cars and drove separately over Laurel Canyon each day to Royaltone Studios in the Valley. Being in LA now was different than four years ago. Back then, we were like fish out of water, newbies hoping to make our mark. Now we were established recording artists residing among the movers, shakers, and stars. The thought of that gave me a high as I drove around in the Southern California sunshine, hair blowing in the wind.

We worked hard in the studio. Darius's vocals were strong and crisp. He and Don had a reliable process for recording vocals by now, and most importantly, a trust, after two albums together. Darius could be boisterous watching sports or in a backstage party, but in the obscurity of the vocal isolation booth attempting final tracks, I saw a different side of him: studious and undistracted, he was seemingly at peace, with only a microphone, a cup of warm tea, and that voice.

I would stretch out on the control room couch and listen as the two of them worked. Darius was out of Don's view, yet the connection was intimate. Don would suggest doing a few takes to warm up his voice, to which Darius often said, "I'm good. I don't need a warm-up. Just hit record." We still recorded on two-inch tape back then, so there wasn't infinite digital space to record take after take after take. Darius rarely needed it anyway. He nailed a lot of the keeper vocals "live" while we were tracking bass, guitar, and drums. Then, trying to improve on those tracks, Don would turn the volume low on the smashing cymbals and distorted guitars, revealing the thick, textured tone of Darius's voice. What a powerful gift it was. When Don would catch an exceptional moment of singing, he would swivel his chair around to me and say, "Darius makes my job very easy. That's just magic. I could listen to him all day."

Mark put in extra hours perfecting guitar parts and honing his sound, and the rest of would always clear out of the studio for that arduous task. Dean's bass was really beginning to stand out, as was his songwriting, with "Michelle Post" and "Answer Man." My confidence as a drummer was beginning to grow in the studio setting, too. The problem was, we hadn't shown up with a wealth of material. We'd only brought fourteen ideas, of which thirteen would need to comprise the album. It was a diverse group of styles, mixing country, rock, blues, ballads, even a little soul, but we had not been diligent enough with our writing. To get a dozen *great* songs you should write at least twice that many, and then pick the best ones.

We absolutely did not do that.

Looking into the control room from my drum kit, I watched Don and Tim Sommer leaning into each other, deep in conversation about song arrangement, instrumentation, and performance, all of which they tactfully participated in for each song. Tim was a huge asset to the band musically, personally, and professionally. Though he officially worked for Atlantic Records, he was such a champion of the band that a discussion developed around whose interest he was really serving, the label or the artist? It was a fair question. For us, his value was immeasurable, and that was undeniable.

I was spending a decent amount of my free time chasing soccer games around the West Coast as the United States men's national team prepared for another World Cup; I even got Darius to sing the National Anthem for the official, final match/send-off at RFK Stadium in Washington, DC, before the team (and Debbie and I) headed off to France.

Having already seen one World Cup in person, I didn't want to miss 1998. Our France trip did not disappoint, even though the United States suffered a quick departure from the tournament. Debbie loved the spectacle of sports, in general, and we'd spent lots of time attending NFL, MLB, and NBA games together. I loved that she was always up for a sports adventure, and, of course, the opportunity to meet a famous sports figure. Her years in the music business gave her plenty of valuable experience interacting with notable performers and she was always smooth in those situations, whether she was meeting Dan Marino or Garth Brooks. I never had to worry about Deb's answer when suggesting a trip to Wrigley Field, or hopping in a car for a road trip to see whatever sports team I was chasing. Now, in France, we stood in awe of the hordes of colorful, jubilant fans from South America, Asia, Africa, the Middle East, Europe, North and Central America, and the Caribbean. The stunning visual tapestry of the darkest Africans dressed in their gold and green and red, set against groups of pale/sunburnt Scots in their plaid blue and green kilts, all dancing and chanting together, was incredible. I laughed as stoic Norwegians with painted faces ogled a loud parade of barely dressed Brazilian dancers and drummers, while a family of South Koreans stared as though they were watching an alien movie. I was so happy to be part of this peaceful international extravaganza.

~

Back in the United States, Hootie's Monday After the Masters charity golf tournament was now in its fifth year, becoming one of the most impactful single-day charity events in the state of South Carolina. Big names from golf and the sporting and entertainment world convened in Columbia every spring to support the pro-am golf fundraiser. On the one hand, I was glad we never shied away from our love of sports because it was authentic for us, but I had also begun to wonder if the whole music/sports marriage—especially when it came to golf—wasn't having some negative effects. Was it possible we relied too heavily on the sporting connection for publicity? Was the slew of athletic affiliations distracting from the real reason we were in the spotlight, namely, the music? Mark always agreed with me on this topic. "Doesn't anybody want to talk about the music?" he would say.

We certainly were receiving a lot of attention through the many sports-related events we found ourselves doing, like playing Super

Bowl parties, attending charity basketball events, singing National Anthems, and throwing out first pitches. Even the record label that represented us in Europe, Warner, thought it fitting to have a professional soccer team, Hammarby, in Sweden, feature our name down the sleeve of their green and white jerseys. (We sponsored them.)

Ultimately, Atlantic Records supported any kind of promotions we could conjure, even if they were predominantly sports-related, because they drew attention to the band and usually cost them nothing.

Musical Chairs managed to hit the Billboard charts at #4 during its first week in September 1998. But the title of the first single, "I Will Wait," seemed to foretell the unwanted truth about our current charting power, that we would indeed have to wait for some other day to score a hit single. It was hard to interpret whether the label was impressed or disappointed by the result, because our main thread of communication had been severed before the album even came out. Tim Sommer had been let go from Atlantic. Our main strategist, lobbyist, and influencer to the bigwigs at the label was gone. His absence left us weakened. With no inside connection, we would have no voice. No voice meant no influence. And influence? *Influence* in this business was *everything*.

We thought we'd done every type of promotion possible for radio, and there had been lots of hype and talk, but it hadn't resulted in much airplay. The label seemed willing to tell our management whatever they thought they wanted to hear, while not bothering to come through with those promises. (From what I'd learned from Debbie, and seen firsthand about the business, this was not a stretch to believe.) Maybe we hadn't given them much to work with on *Musical Chairs*. Maybe nothing on this record was up to the standard of the first four or five singles that had been so successful for us. Maybe we lacked one important, yet elusive ingredient necessary for chart success: good timing?

We asked why all of the radio stations we'd been doing appearances and free shows for were not reciprocating by playing our new song, but we were unable to get straight answers from Atlantic. I used every bit of my energy trying to get answers—even personally scouring radio station playlists and statistical charts. We had been a golden goose for Atlantic Records, and they were still swimming in the insane profits of *Cracked Rear View*—could they really be letting us drift away?

All evidence pointed to one conclusion: Atlantic Records was done using their influence to push a Hootie & the Blowfish single up the charts, and with no one on the inside to represent us, there wasn't much we could do. The new album quickly sailed off the charts, and I think I was the only one who wasn't surprised.

$\sim$

Our willingness to find a positive outlet, even in those times of doubt, led us abroad again. The United Kingdom and continental Europe were still growing for us. We barely broke even financially with all the expenses for flights, shipping gear, hotels, and taxation, but it was worth it to us. Although we had already been to Southeast Asia, Australia, and New Zealand, we were eager to see more of the world.

I used my influence within Hootie to bring along a guy who had ties to the soccer world, Alexi Lalas. Alexi was the most recognizable face in US soccer, with his fiery red mop of hair and his goatee, but in stalking him as a soccer hero I realized we had more in common than our love of the sport. Lalas was both a Michigander and a singer-songwriter. His power-guitar-pop album *Ginger* had been released on the same day as *Musical Chairs*. I was a big fan of the record and thought it would be a lot of fun to hang out in Europe together and make some noise.

With Alexi attached, our tour was about as American as apple pie, and everyone in both bands enjoyed the camaraderie of being

American music exports in a foreign land. Alexi and his band tried hard to keep up with our partying pace and often childish behavior, but we were not an easy group to keep up with.

We weren't afraid to use peer pressure, either, especially when it came to drinking, and if you attempted to take a night off you always heard about it. One late night out in Hamburg, Germany, our band and crew were wandering about in drunken oblivion when we spotted Lalas passing us on the opposite side of the street, happily carrying a pizza box and presumably hoping we didn't notice him. We weren't going to let him off that easy, and began hurling a series of names and taunts at him. To Alexi's credit, he stayed in character, never once acknowledging the screams directed at him.

On stage, Lalas's music went over very well, even to the curiosity-seekers who wanted to see if this soccer player could really play and sing. Turns out, he could.

On the final night of the tour, when it came time to do some traditional pranking onstage as a gesture of friendship and respect, Alexi and his band pulled off, literally and figuratively, one of the best pranks we'd ever seen. As we got about halfway through "Only Wanna Be With You," out Alexi and his band walked, doing a synchronized striptease dance right down to their underwear. They took their positions in between Dean, Darius, and Mark, and then as the last chorus arrived, all four turned, pulled down their boxers, bent toward the now-howling audience, and revealed the words ONLY——WANNA——BE WITH——YOU, written very large and legibly on their asses.

I was relieved to be in the back behind my drums so I didn't have to get a close-up view of that. It takes a close bond between friends to handwrite lyrics on one another's butts.

It takes an even closer bond to scrub them off.

~

Encouraged and inspired by a one-off trip to Bosnia to perform for our troops back in 1996, we dedicated the second leg of the 1998 tour to USO concerts in the Middle East. That meant using some military transport planes and helicopters and wearing protective gear while traveling into places that were not considered completely safe from enemy fire. By this point in my career, I was accustomed to the comforts of spacious first-class flights, free drinks, and warm towels to wipe away the day's worry. Now, we were being fitted for flak vests.

For reasons I didn't care to ask about, our flight into Prince Sultan's Air Base had to take place during nighttime. But it was worth it when we were greeted by several thousand smiling faces in tan and brown camouflage as we took the stage in a refitted hangar. As far as my eyes could see beyond the servicemen and -women, there was sand—thousands and thousands of miles of it.

That show wasn't the only thrill; I got to help land a spy plane. Because of the limited visibility and the fact that pilots are landing on two side-by-side skinny wheels under the center of the plane, they need assistance coming to earth. We got to be in the chaser car—a speedy Ford Mustang—to help guide the pilot on the runway. Wearing what seemed to be just Air Force-issued football helmets for protection, we held our breath as the plane came in over our shoulders, and the driver hit the gas and sped up to about 130–140 mph in order to get as close to the tail of the plane as possible. Then, via radio, he told the pilot approximately how close to earth the plane wheels were, until it gently touched down.

~

At a stop in Jebel Ali, United Arab Emirates, we played for a standing crowd right next to the *USS Enterprise*, our country's first nuclear-powered aircraft carrier. We stood right behind former president George H. W. Bush as he pumped up the crowd. . . . Yes, that means that former President Bush was Hootie's warm-up act.

I always took time to meet as many soldiers as possible—over a beer or a game of ping-pong. I wanted to find out about their lives and families, and to thank them for their service. A few of them mentioned that they were on high alert, and I couldn't imagine living with that sort of underlying anxiousness. Only five days after we finished this USO tour, America unleashed a major four-day bombing campaign called Operation Desert Fox on military and security targets in Iraq. Most of the planes used on this mission flew from the very decks of the *USS Enterprise* on which we had recently stood. It was a sobering reminder of what the military faces every day.

twenty

CAMERON SHAY

WE ARRIVED BACK home for Christmas after the long flights from South Africa, where we had closed out the final leg of the tour.

I began the final twelve months of the twentieth century waiting for some new chapter of my life to unfold. I was desperate to become a father and desperate for the band to get back on the charts. But, for now, having a drink in my hand seemed to suffice.

Being the shirtless, long-haired drummer for Hootie & the Blowfish was beginning to feel rather empty. I was growing tired of the redundant conversations in my Hootie-centric life, but who would I be if I woke up one day and wasn't "that Blowfish guy"? From the outside, it looked like a life not many would turn down; on the inside, I was tangled up.

My bandmates were changing their lives all around me.

Darius moved away from Columbia back to Charleston and bought a beautiful house near the beach. Dean had found love with a Columbia girl named Laurie Hutchinson, and they too headed for the South Carolina coast (marrying in early 1999). Then Mark and

Laura bolted from Columbia, too, to a cute little neighborhood near Darius—they were pregnant with a second child, too.

Meanwhile, Deb and I decided to stay put in Columbia. Two of my brothers, my mom, and Grandma Hornberger lived there. Mom had been diagnosed with idiopathic pulmonary fibrosis by this point and I couldn't imagine moving further away from her. Plus, we still had our Hootie offices and our beloved Gamecocks to follow. Being in Columbia also allowed us easy access to the Blue Ridge Mountains, so Debbie and I purchased a second home there, a little cabin with a million-dollar view.

I told myself all of this movement by and separation from the band was perfectly fine, but in truth I was a bit resentful. My twisted pride told me I was somehow more loyal than they were for holding out and staying in the city where Hootie had started. This thought was complete bullshit, of course. I was no better than them just because I'd decided to remain in Columbia.

On the professional front, Hootie's schedule began looking a bit random. Management was doing its best to bring us reputable gigs, as well as gigs that paid well, but when you don't have the leverage of being the *current* top-selling band, you have to scrape together whatever the market bears to make touring work. We were still doing some events I was proud of—Austin City Limits; the David Letterman show again; a traditional music festival called "Merle Fest"; and more USO-sponsored shows for our troops abroad—but, whereas in previous years we could string together whole tours of amphitheater-sized venues, we were now filling in a growing number of holes with corporate shows, casinos, festivals, and even state fairs.

And the growing number of empty seats each night was catching my eye.

~

My partying had begun to ratchet up, too. I realized I was using every opportunity to gather our band and crew together to celebrate with a drink and raise a toast to life.

I had a special gift for using the hair of the dog as a cure for a hangover, but it was also a curse, of course. I was the only person in our pack who bounced back from a big night with another big night. In fact, I wore it like a badge of honor. If there were no volunteers to partake in my consistent drinking I would prod them with phrases like, "*Every* day is a drinking day!" If I was being questioned as to *why* I was drinking hard again, I would proclaim with all the sincerity I could muster, "I drink to make people more interesting." If someone's tone ever became too serious, I would claim that I got sick if I didn't drink. Evidence showed this to be true, especially as my drinking stretches started lasting longer and longer. My tolerance to alcohol was building up, and I would develop what felt like a flu or a harsh cold every time I made a conscious effort to quit, even for a few days. I had no idea I was suffering from alcohol withdrawal syndrome, a serious medical condition. My body was detoxing, and I had no conception that heavy drinking over long periods, interrupted by quitting cold turkey, could not only be dangerous, but in some cases potentially life-threatening.

I was lucky I was still in great shape. I randomly entered 10k road races and would post great times, usually 5.5- to 6-minute miles. But coming home off the road wasn't enough to buck the drinking trend, however fit I felt. Since Debbie loved to socialize, we were either out to dinner nightly with friends or hosting gatherings at our house. Both allowed me to camouflage my drinking by being in a crowd.

~

The new century opened with the amazing news that Debbie was finally pregnant. This brought me great joy, although I was a bit paranoid that all my years of drinking and drugging might have a direct and negative effect on the health of our child. An amniocentesis test eventually showed the fetus to be healthy.

The only band project we were working on was an album of cover tunes, but as many of the tracks were already finished B-sides from other recording sessions, the project didn't take as long as a normal Hootie record. We played a Super Bowl XXXIV pregame party in Atlanta, attended out-of-town music festivals in North Carolina and New Orleans, and I attended a smattering of celebrity golf tournaments, charity events, and corporate gigs.

Otherwise, Debbie and I headed off to the mountain cabin. I wondered if I should moderate my drinking, given that we were having a baby, but having a temporary designated driver everywhere I went wasn't exactly motivation for me to drink less. As the months rolled by and Debbie's belly grew, I continued my steady drinking. I liked to drink, and if I could do it without big episodes or drunken outbursts, then I felt it wasn't a problem. I didn't need to drink during the day, nor was I sneaking swigs of cheap vodka when she wasn't looking, but I made every excuse in the world to justify making drinks *every* night. The meek voice inside me suggesting I make more appropriate choices didn't stand a chance against the bully within demanding that first drink by happy hour. The meek voice sometimes said, "Take the night off, because Debbie will be so happy you decided not to drink tonight," but the bully scoffed at that, too.

If my bandmates noted that they weren't drinking as hard as me off the road, I'd say things like, "It's important to stay in drinking shape while at home because if I show up on the road out of shape, that shit will hit me hard." That one always got a laugh, though the laughs grew shorter and fewer over time.

~

One night, in mid-July 2000, with Debbie only weeks from her due date, we found ourselves (unsurprisingly) at a bar called the Elbow

Room. There was almost nothing that could come between the two of us and our desire to see a great rock show, even if it meant hobbling heavily through a crowded college bar that reeked of stale beer and cigarette smoke. As I remember it, though my memories of this period are clouded by my heavy drinking, we were there to watch our favorite New Orleans rock band, Cowboy Mouth, perform. Debbie did not last long in this environment, though, and decided she needed to go home, get off her feet, and take a nice bath. How she got home is another detail somehow lost in this important yet hazy period of my life. For my part, valor and chivalry stood no chance against my thirst for a few more drinks and some rock 'n' roll camaraderie. So, just like a self-centered alcoholic, I stayed on to listen to more music.

And then I got the urgent call telling me to come home asap. Her water had broken. There was no godly voice to intercede; no repentance; no idea that I should quit my excessive partying to focus on a childbirth and becoming the best father I could be. If there was an inner voice speaking to me, it was drowned out by the thumping bass drum and distorted electric guitars. I stood there like a deer in headlights, then chugged what was left of my bourbon and headed for the door.

At 1:37 a.m. on July 18, with the liquor still on my breath, we became the proud parents of a baby girl, Cameron Shay Sonefeld.

~

A new baby wasn't the only change in my life. After six years in Columbia, the band decided to move the Monday After the Masters charity event to Kiawah Island, located near Charleston, South Carolina. We had been so lucky to have raised almost 1.5 million dollars for state charities, but we envisioned something even bigger and better in a more suitable location.

About a month later, the band and our long-time manager Rusty Harmon parted ways. It was a difficult business decision to move forward separately, since the five of us were friends as well as business partners. We had been through a lot together. Our relationship with Rusty spanned eleven years, from rags to riches to our current state, which was basically just trying to stay relevant. We were suddenly free agents.

All this reordering in my life served to unnerve me. Hootie & the Blowfish seemed to lack definition now. What had for years seemed like a career marked by endless growth and record label support, now seemed arbitrary and unpromising. Our 2000 release of covers, *Scattered, Smothered, and Covered*, hadn't set the world on fire, and it felt like we were just pacifying Atlantic Records as we chipped away at the long record contract we had signed. There was no single; no video, either. Having no A&R person fighting for us at the label didn't help us.

Corporate and private events still paid handsomely and were sustaining us, but our regular ticket-buying fans would sometimes ask us what we'd been up to lately. Hearing this is never a good sign for a band's career. Along the way, Darius was spending more and more time working on his first solo project, an R & B record, and I wondered if he would perhaps leave the band for greener pastures if presented with the right offer.

~

The bright spot in my life was my growing baby girl, Cameron Shay. Holding her in my arms and caressing those warm, soft cheeks on her face, hearing her laughter—it was all magical. And yet the joys of fatherhood were being undermined by my denial about the drinking. I kept telling myself I was getting more out of life through my drinking and drugs, even when it clearly wasn't true. Yes, there was that initial buzz, but it was followed by an unyielding craving for more, one I could never seem to fully satisfy. I kept chasing a good time, but night after night I would end up alone with my final drink.

It's not as though I'd never been warned about the perils of drinking. The Catholic nuns of my youth had attempted to drill line after line into us from the Old Testament book of Proverbs. "Who hath woe? Who hath sorrow? Who hath contentions? Who hath babbling? Who hath wounds without cause? Who hath redness of eyes? They that tarry long at the wine . . . at the last it biteth like a serpent and stingeth like an adder." Those archaic phrases rarely made it through my thick skull, especially with the confusing language in the King James version of the Bible we were using. Now though, the warning about excessive drinking made complete sense to me.

The price I often paid was missing the first moments of Cameron's day, clutching her warm body from the crib as she first woke, or a father/daughter bonding over a morning feeding. I'd spend my mornings groggy, or grumpy, and by the afternoon I'd find myself obsessing about when I could get my first drink. My attempts to recruit others to this game continued, too, but I wasn't above going it alone.

Actually, sometimes it was easier that way.

~

Debbie and I had built a wonderful, two-story detached studio/apartment behind our house where I could work on music. I would head out there, saying "I'm going back to work on a new song. I won't be too late." But even as the words were rolling off my lips, they were leaving a bitter taste. I knew in my heart I didn't have any idea how late it would be, and Deb would likely be asleep when I returned. I justified my deceptiveness toward her by telling myself that *my* songs were what had built this back house, *my* work had bought both of our homes. What I didn't see was the lie. I knew I would never consider staying up late to write music if no alcohol was involved. It wasn't a mere coincidence there was a fully stocked bar and easy places to hide a little weed or blow.

And no one had to know; or so I thought.

twenty-one

ALL THOSE MISSED CALLS

WHEN WE WERE trying to write new material in the early 2000s, the band would gather at Mark and Laura's second home on the Intracoastal Waterway in Awendaw, northeast of Charleston. The first time Mark told me about the place, he simply said, "You've just gotta see it to believe it. Words don't do it justice. It's a little slice of heaven."

He was right. It was pure heaven out there in nature, with views of Bulls Bay and the Atlantic Ocean. Mark had outfitted much of the second story of the house with instruments and recording equipment and a crusty, classic beer can collection from the '70s. It was the perfect place to make noise, and no one ever bothered us out there. If we were doing multiple days of writing, I found it easier just to sleep there, since I lived two hours away.

The Intracoastal Waterway in Awendaw is dotted with elevated homes and long docks extending hundreds of feet out through the marsh to the deep water. You are more likely to see an alligator than a neighbor. Making it even more peaceful was the limited access to TV and internet. I had my cell phone, but since I used it only for phone calls, I was not yet obsessed with having it on me at all times, even though I had a wife and 1-year old baby at home.

One night in September 2001 after finishing rehearsing, all the Charlestonians headed back to their homes for the night, leaving me by myself until our next scheduled rehearsal the following afternoon. I was thrilled; I'd get to be alone and untethered. I'd rarely experienced that, growing up in the middle of a large family of seven, so being alone as an adult made me feel sort of kingly. A voice whispered in my head, "You can do whatever you like. No one is here. No one is looking."

That night in Awendaw, I took advantage by mixing up several stiff drinks, taking a few sniffs of the white, powdery stuff, and playing a little guitar. (I was "working"). Time flies when there's cocaine around, and suddenly it was four in the morning. There never seems to be enough time when the demons of addiction are calling you to have just one more.

Before the darkness of Monday night could turn into the light of Tuesday morning, I smoked a little weed to try to wind down after realizing the song I'd been working on wasn't going anywhere. I decided to take in the low country ambience by walking out to the end of the long dock to smell the fresh salt air and listen to the water.

It was soothing out there, but in my head I couldn't avoid the ugly truth. I was no functioning songwriter or responsible father; I was just a completely addicted asshole staying up late chasing a good feeling. I did some math in my head—also a symptom of being in the grips of cocaine—to measure how much sleep I could get before folks started to show up around lunchtime. Somewhere around 5:00 a.m., in one of the guest bedrooms, I finally fell sleep.

At around noon I woke up, hardly able to make sense of where I was, what day it was. All I knew was that I needed to put something in my body to make me feel human. I struggled up the staircase to the kitchen on the third floor. There was threatening weather outside, which I was grateful for, given how I felt. The last thing I needed was a bright, shiny day to make made me feel even more like a vampire.

Suddenly, the front door on the second floor flew open and slammed shut and I could hear fast footsteps coming up the stairs. It was Mark.

"We've been trying to call you!" he said. "Debbie has been trying to call you! Why aren't you picking up your phone? The twin towers in New York have been knocked down by planes! Our country is being attacked! What have you been doing out here?"

Nothing he was saying made any sense.

"Dude, just settle down and take a deep breath," I said. "What are you talking about?"

"You need to drive back to Columbia right now to be with your family," Mark said. "And, in the future, you should try and check your phone more often."

As quickly as I could get my bag and head together, I hit Highway 17. I headed out of town during what I was sure was the darkest, most deafening thunderstorm to ever engulf Charleston. Coupled with the radio broadcasts I was hearing, I thought the world might be coming to an end. As I drove, I remembered that just five nights earlier we'd played a club gig ten short blocks from the Towers at our favorite New York City haunt, The Wetlands Preserve.

It was almost 3:00 p.m. on September 11th when I finally arrived home and saw my first glimpses of the horrid scenes unfolding in New York, DC, and Pennsylvania. For many people, that day would prompt conversations about where you were when it happened. This would never be my story. Where had I been as these cataclysmic horrors unfolded? It would take me another few years to discover the real answer. But if this was an opportunity to take stock of my life, consider its worth, and make some adjustments, then I missed the opportunity completely.

twenty-two

THE TRUCKEE BENCH

IN THE FALL of 2001, Debbie and I celebrated our fifth wedding anniversary, and with Cameron now almost fifteen months old, I found myself hoping for another baby or two. Mark and Laura had already had their second child, Kenny, in September 1999; and Darius and Beth had become parents, too, with the birth of Daniella Rose in May 2001 (she was Darius's second child). Dean and Laurie had Gracie in 2001, and had already announced they were pregnant again.

There was no sign of a second baby for us, though, even though I deeply yearned for more children. I loved kids—I found hanging out with them to be more invigorating than being with most adults. The short attention span of a child suited me, and it was better than being stuck in small talk with a big person. Playing animated games and making up ridiculous voices with the kids got my lifeblood flowing and felt like being in a circus with acrobats and jugglers. It was a brilliant relief from the world of adults I lived with on the road.

Maybe I was just afraid of growing up.

~

As a kid, I loved to skateboard, and now I was deeply into its icy sibling, snowboarding. My first snowboard run down the mountain had given me that same wonderful feeling as skateboarding, with even more speed, and once my hips and knees started loosening up, I like to think that I looked natural. A bunch of my friends and I began meeting regularly for springtime boarding and bonding out West. It was no coincidence that these guys enjoyed a good time as much as I did, so our gatherings always included drinking.

In 2002, we converged on the California side of Lake Tahoe to do some boarding at the Northstar Resort. As was typical with us, to celebrate an incredible day on the powder-filled slopes we headed to the nearest bar at the bottom of the mountain. Though my internal gauge for my own drunkenness wasn't the worst in the world, increasingly I was discovering my gauge to be faulty. On this particular night, I completely failed to adjust my drinking to the high altitude and the fact that we'd played and sweated hard all day. I had a few beers to rehydrate in the first bar, but then I went straight into the hard liquor. Trash was talked and shots were shot. Eventually hunger and logic—neither belonged to me—set in, and the gang of us ended up in the nearby, old-timey town of Truckee with plans to sit down for dinner. By the time we were seated at a table, I was shit-faced and moving on to red wine. I vaguely remember leaning heavily on one of my friends. Luckily, we were squished so tightly into our booth that I was able to stay upright by the sheer pressure of the surrounding bodies. I was accused of passing out, which was probably true. Dinner finally arrived, and the boys were relieved to see my drunk ass was going to get some solid food in him.

It didn't end well. I stumbled out of our booth sideways, barely finding the bathroom in time. Unfortunately I didn't find the toilet, and proceeded to lose my guts right in the sink. With that, I looked into the mirror at the three of me, said "goodnight" out loud, and walked directly out of the restaurant to the nearest bench, where I laid down to sleep in the 27-degree air.

Time flies when you're passed out. I was floating in that heavenly realm between two ugly worlds—the out-of-control woozy one I'd just left, and the painfully hungover one that had yet to arrive. But my passed-out paradise in the refreshing mountain air would prove to be short-lived.

"Hey, wake up. Yo, get up. There's no sleeping on these benches. Gotta move along." When my eyes finally focused, I realized who owned the voice I thought I'd been dreaming: a Truckee police officer.

Thank God my boys came to my rescue. Being the ever-responsible pals they are, they told the officer they'd take care of me. (And by taking care of me they meant gently pouring me into the back of the covered pickup truck we were using to get around. My limp body blended in with the snowboarding gear, old newspapers, a shovel, and a frozen garden hose.)

~

In the mid-to-late 1990s I might have cooled my jets for a few days after an incident like that, but not anymore. There was no such thing as a night off from drinking. Since I refused to admit that alcohol was controlling me, I always had to get right back up on my horse after a fall to prove it.

Worse was to come.

One day before a show, I was in the Hootie dressing room, which was basically a trailer separated into two halves by a curtain. No one heard me come in. But from the other side of the curtain I could hear two of our road crew talking.

"I'm not sure what is up with him." one of them said. "Is he having some problems at home or something?"

The other person said, "I don't know, but his behavior is so erratic. I'm not sure if I'm even comfortable approaching him to talk about it, but I'm worried something bad is gonna happen if he keeps it up."

This is juicy, I thought. *I wonder who they're talking about?*

"In the ten years I've known him, he's always loved to party, but now there's sort of a dark edge to it. I'm scared there's something going on with him that he needs to address. A couple of other crew guys have mentioned it as well and they're wondering if someone should say something?"

My thought was, should I offer to help out the poor soul they were talking about? If it was an employee of the band, then I needed to know about it.

"Well, he's a good guy, but you're right. Something's got to give with his partying. It's out of control."

"I love *Soni*," the second voice said, "but I hate to see him throwing his life away like this."

Time slowed, and my heart stopped. I was mortified, realizing they were discussing *me*. I felt like a failure. I wasn't sorry that I'd worried those working around me, just dejected for losing the approval of my friends. Instead of accepting that I had a legitimate problem with drinking and drugs, my only takeaway was thinking I needed to do a better job at hiding it.

And so I made a commitment to conceal my alcohol and chemical intake more effectively. I was being ruled by something more powerful than me, and I had no idea.

～

"He who goes forth with a fifth on the fourth, may not be around on the fifth to go forth" was the kind of thing my mother said to us growing up, all in order to help us see the dangers of underage drinking. Now, in my late thirties, she was still warning me about the dangers of liquor.

I wasn't looking for advice on the subject, but she wanted to tell me the truth as she saw it, while she still had the chance to. She had made it into her sixties, at least, and though she had a youthful spirit, her body was not well. She had idiopathic pulmonary fibrosis, a disease that leaves you shorter and shorter of breath as the lungs scar over and fail. That, in turn, raises your blood pressure, which often leads to heart failure. Doctors estimate three to five years' life expectancy for sufferers once the illness is diagnosed. She'd made it to the outer limits of that span, but I think she knew she was living on borrowed time and therefore began to speak her mind more openly about everything. For a start, my mother sure as hell wasn't about to let her son drink himself to death, so she began speaking out about it, because she loved me.

~

Since Mom was not doing well, we thought a trip might lift her spirits. We decided to bring her to visit my oldest brother Dave and his wife Deanna and their three kids in Austin, Texas. We didn't know how many trips like this she might have left in her.

After a long day of airports and loading and unloading, we arrived safely at the house. That first night we had a few drinks over a competitive game of Scrabble with Dave and Mom, an old family tradition; the next night we took in some live music on Sixth Street; by the third night everyone was taking it a bit easier after a couple of nights of drinking. As for me, well, I was forced to rummage deep into a cupboard above the refrigerator for something to drink, so I wouldn't have to go to the liquor store all by myself.

As I stood with one foot on a kitchen chair, my long arm stretched out and digging into this obscure cabinet, Mom chimed in without even looking up from her *Better Homes and Garden* magazine.

"Jim, what are you looking for?" she asked.

She knew exactly what I was looking for in the cabinet, of course. As I stepped down off the chair clutching an unopened bottle of Jack Daniels she said, "You're drinking again? Is there a night you take *off* from drinking?"

My sister-in-law Deanna took this as her opportunity to join in.

"Do you drink when you're at home after being gone touring? Isn't it hard to get up in the morning?"

"Y'all obviously have me confused with someone who gives a shit," I said.

"Well, that's not a very nice thing to say," Deanna said, not unreasonably.

"I know, but y'all are ganging up on me."

"Don't be a pill. I was just noticing this is your third straight night drinking," Mom said.

"Well, do you know what tomorrow will be?" I said. "My fourth straight night drinking."

"Very funny, Jim" Mom said. "What does Debbie think about you drinking at home every night? Is she concerned?"

"Well," I said, "Deb knows there are really only two times that I like to drink."

"Oh really? What are those?"

"*Day* time" I said, "and *night* time."

twenty-three
WAS NOT WAS

ON THE ROAD there was minimal resistance to a lifestyle that included nightly drinking and shenanigans. One day it was nearly noon when the four of us dragged ourselves off the bus, which sat idling at the curb in front of our hotel on a day off from touring. We plodded into the lobby like a parade of half-dead zombies, marching toward our new tour manager Mike Kelly, who stood holding a stack of room keys. He addressed us plainly, trying to keep a straight face, "Artesian Wells, room is ready. Jefferson Johnson, ready." He handed Mark the third packet, "Percival Sweetwater, here you go."

With a bit of false bravado, he looked at me and announced, "And last but not least, Senator Bucket. Senator George T. Bucket. What does the 'T' stand for again?"

"Thunder," I responded. "Thunder Bucket."

"That's right! And, how is the Senator feeling this morning? You still seemed to be going strong when I bailed out of the party around 2:00 a.m."

"There were no victims, your honor. All ready for a new day," I said, confirming that the late night of partying had left no negative impact on me.

We'd been using pseudonyms at our hotels for years to avoid being discovered by intrusive fans or overly curious press, and a part of me enjoyed the figurative mask I slipped on each time the alias was used. These fake titles were a concoction of middle names, old street names, and inside jokes. For a period, Mark and I, who had both lived on Burney Drive, were George and William Burney. Darius and Dean, who had lived together on Edisto Avenue were The Edisto Brothers, Carlos and Everett. Darius eventually turned into Virgil Runnels—the real name of the famous wrestler Dusty Rhodes. Dean morphed into Brew End Holland, words taken from the label of a Heineken beer bottle. Mark simplified to Mr. Mel Low, and me, to the almost funny pun, Alan Rentsch.

Something sinister inside me brewed with excitement knowing no one could find me unless they knew my secret name. On some level, temporarily assuming a moniker allowed me to compartmentalize my life inside that hotel suite from the reality outside of it. More and more, I hoped the derelict behavior behind the closed doors would not be connected with the persona I wanted those around me to see. Perhaps my bandmates didn't think this way? Maybe they just thought of the name changes as some goofy prank.

I convinced myself that my excessive partying, though increasingly done in isolation, was feeding my inner artistry and creativity. Surely there was value to an edgy life, free from others' judgment, straddling the line where sanity and insanity diverged. There, I could delve deeper and thereby write better songs. Maybe I'd become one of those Jim Morrison-type characters who used extreme drug and alcohol binges to reach some artistic climax? (Minus the whole dying of an overdose in a tub part, of course.)

I knew I couldn't live like a recluse, alone in some hotel room forever, because we all lived together on our bus while touring. With my escalating drunken forays and my increasing desire to seek out cocaine, I would often end up in some random house or apartment in which I shouldn't have been. Maybe I just needed more people around me who would approve of my silliness, hijinks, and excessive behavior.

Enter: Don Was.

~

Hootie's new manager was the legendary Doc McGhee (he'd handled KISS, Bon Jovi, and Mötley Crüe, to name but a few), and in concert with his entertainment company we began looking for someone to produce our next studio album.

We were contractually obligated to make several more records for Atlantic, even though they didn't seem too concerned with promoting us anymore. With that in mind, we thought a new producer—in this case Don Was—would help get the label's attention once again.

Was is a Grammy Award-winning producer and musician. The hugely successful albums he'd made with Bonnie Raitt in the late '80s and early '90s were played incessantly by Darius in our van days, so we were all familiar with his production skills.

Don is a cool motherfucker. Somehow, he's both smooth and trustworthy, two traits not always found together; he's also whip-smart and sincere. His darkly tinted glasses distract from the fact that there is always a little grin breaking out on his face. He wears a wide-brimmed hat that isn't country or Western or Southern or anything, but it still makes you feel it has a purpose. His dark, messy hair is desperately trying to get out from underneath the hat, and though it's in disarray, he somehow makes it look thought-out.

In March 2002, we loaded into Beacon Street Studios, in Venice, California, to make our fifth, and what would turn out to be our final, studio album for Atlantic Records. Doc McGhee had been savvy enough to get our Atlantic Records agreement greatly reduced. The studio was much smaller and less expensive than any other one we'd used since Atlantic started funding our recordings, too, but since our long-time studio keyboardist John Nau ran the place, we felt confident we could make a high-quality record there.

As we started sorting through songs with Don and Ed Cherney, who would assist on the record, they wanted to discover what environment would make the band comfortable so they could get the best performances as possible out of us. On the first Monday, after finding the remnants of our party weekend strewn about the studio, Don pulled a couple of us aside for a little private conference.

"So, it seems like you guys like to party a bit. What are you guys into? Because it would make sense to me if we all got on the same page for this thing."

For a brief moment I was afraid, as though he was one of my parents and he had busted us for drinking and now he wanted to know what other substances we were using. But pretty quicky I realized this was not an intervention, more like an open forum to discuss exactly *how* we liked to party.

"Well, I have been known to enjoy a few bourbon drinks," I said, the king of understatement. In fact, I was holding a glass of bourbon in my hand as I said it.

Don was unimpressed.

"No, I mean what is it you guys like to do that *you're not already telling me about?*" Before I could respond again he made himself even clearer.

"'Cause it just makes sense that if, for instance, the drummer and the bass player are going to trip on mushrooms, then the rest of us should, too. Or, if several people are doing blow they should not have to conceal it. Ya know what I'm saying?"

With the door now kicked wide open, I spoke up.

"Well," I said, "some of us like to smoke a little weed. We all like to drink, some of us more than others. And, if there were some blow around, be assured you won't have to do it all by yourself."

With that, Was then went down a checklist of other drugs to see if we were holding back or, perhaps, to find out if we were offended by their mere presence.

"So, you guys don't do ludes or X or acid or hash or uppers or downers?"

It was time for Darius to chime in.

"Listen man, we've seen all this stuff and done some of it ourselves, so knock yourself out. We're not here to judge, or to be judged."

That was all Don Was needed to hear. For me, this was the green light to finally make every day a drinking day (even though every day already was a drinking day—now I just didn't have to hide it). Unaware of how an addictive mind works, or in my case, how it *doesn't* work, I looked at this new way of recording a record as a great opportunity to have a more open and honest forum about drugs and alcohol and creating a tolerant atmosphere for those of us who wanted to alter our minds a bit more.

But for someone like me, who was losing his ability to recognize when enough was enough, this was also extremely dangerous territory.

Within a couple of weeks of tracking tunes, Don pulled out another suggestion.

"What would you guys think about trying to capture the 'live' energy in a setting you've grown so accustomed to, by inviting some friends here to the studio while we record? You know, sort of performing *for* them, while recording the music? It could add a real buzz to this room, like a club scene. You guys seem so sociable and have plenty of acquaintances around here, it would be easy to do." Again, he didn't need to convince us. He was suggesting something we already believed: more people = more fun.

~

You might imagine that recording an album in sunny, beachy Southern California would inspire me to write some upbeat, positive new songs for the album, but it was not the case. The material I contributed sounded as though it were written by someone who'd been stuck in Alaska all winter and had run out of vodka halfway through. There was the morose "Tears Fall Down," which Don and I stayed up all night working on, deep in an abyss of loops, effects, and cocaine while trying to produce the perfect drum track. There was the despondent "When She's Gone," written as a foreshadowing to my own mother's death, and how broken up her children would be.

They were good songs, but it was also true that it had been several years since I last wrote any tunes that could be considered cheery. From our *Fairweather Johnson* album came the song "Tootie," an account of my best friend's final moments with his dying father in a hospital room. On *Musical Chairs*, I contributed "Only Lonely," which hardly required a shrink to conclude that its author might need some therapy. Life had dealt me only a minimal amount of personal pain and suffering. I still had all of my siblings and both of my parents were alive. I had money and friends. Even an outside assessment of my marriage would have deemed it healthy *enough*. But if you read the lyrics to my songs, you could see there were a whole lot of unresolved feelings I had yet to come to terms with.

The unintended consequence of having the green light to combine partying and recording created a battle in me to push back the temptations of the first drink as far along in the day as possible. The longer I could push back making the *first* one, the longer I could avoid getting trapped in a cycle where the only good answer was *another* one, and another, and another. I obsessed over wanting the thrill ride to begin while at the same time fearing what the ride might bring.

Pacing is everything if you are an alcoholic trying to function in a work setting. I'd walk by the booze and mixers saying to myself, *Not yet; this doesn't have to start already. Get a couple hours of recording done first and then you won't look so out of place. Did I have a full meal yet today? Is there enough blow to keep me focused? Should I sneak a drink or push others to drink with me openly? Am I crazy? Why can't I stop thinking about this?*

On and on it went, consuming my thoughts. Unfortunately, the side effects of my substance abuse were becoming difficult to conceal. My continuing excuse for incessant nasal sniffing and dripping was that I was suffering from allergies. Not everyone was convinced that it was my allergies, though, even when I began to jokingly call it my "California Cold."

All the coke had a negative effect on my singing voice, too; consistent snorting causes the chemical to drip down to the back of your throat with a bitter, unnatural taste and numbing sensation. Over time, you just feel like there's something stuck in your throat or that you have an ongoing scratchiness. I was constantly making excuses when I couldn't hit the high notes, or any good notes at all.

I also had a hard time with eating. Eating becomes difficult when you're combining a depressive liquid drug—alcohol—with loads of sugary mixers and a powdered stimulant that gives you energy while arresting your hunger. For an inactive person, a low-calorie diet like this might be fine, but I was *not* an inactive person. I loved running and rollerblading and snowboarding, and even in my sickness and chemical addiction I somehow maintained a high level of cardio workouts.

My love of a good sweat had never been just a hobby—it was a need. Whatever inner peace I had through the years was a direct result of my ability to work out regularly. Even after my organized soccer career unofficially ended in 1987, I still worked out all the time. I used to have the ability to work out in the morning, but now with my nights getting later and later, and with my consumption rising, it became impossible. Severely altered sleeping hours coupled with my inability to eat left my mind wondering which was more important: the peace I gained feeding my chemical dependency, or the peace I gained through my physical fitness routine.

~

For the first time ever during a major recording session, the four band members were living separately from one another. Dean, Darius, and I had individual condos at a complex in Santa Monica; Mark decided to get his own place on Venice Beach. With this set-up, I found myself missing our usual uncomplicated approach to recording, those days when we would record for eight or nine hours and then drink together until we got tired or passed out.

One night after all the bars had closed, I convinced one of our crew to hang out a little longer for a drink and a line at my condo. We kept convincing ourselves we would do only one more line to take the edge off, and then we'd laugh at ourselves, because we knew you can't take the edge off of cocaine with cocaine. The hours rolled on, and the night became day. I closed the curtains, trying to keep the sunlight out and the paranoia from setting in. I aimlessly sat staring at my TV, hoping to find something conducive to the situation. I came upon an episode of "Winnie the Pooh," and my mood quickly darkened. I was wasted and wasting away, and two thousand miles away Cameron was probably sitting in front of our television watching the same show. A wave of guilt rolled over me. I knew this was horrible use of my time, my money, and my life. I knew if the phone rang at that moment and it was Deb and Cameron, I'd probably not pick it up, fearing that they would discover who I really was. I wondered, not for the first time, why I was living—if you called it living—in this drug-induced prison.

How the fuck did I get here?

twenty-four

BACK TO NAPERVILLE

IN EARLY 2003, the self-titled *Hootie & the Blowfish* album we'd made with Don Was slithered unnoticed onto the shelves of the few remaining record stores left in America. Even though I was not at my strongest during the making of this record, there was a lot I was proud of in the end. A cover of the Continental Drifters song, "The Rain Song," is still one of my favorites. Mark's "Deeper Side" was so much fun to produce and play, as well. And I think "Little Darlin'" is one of our most creative inventions. But the song that definitely stood out above all others, and showed Dean's continued songwriting prowess, was "Innocence." We were rehearsing and writing at Awendaw during the period after 9/11, seeing peril in our country and around the globe, and feeling the distress and downturn we'd been through together as a band. We reminisced about the simpler times. This was our fight song for better days, but no matter how hard we tried to get this single on the charts, it just wouldn't move up. Radio programmers seemed content spinning our hits from the mid-'90s. Atlantic Records didn't have any answers. The stars again were not aligning for us.

But there was better news on the horizon, at least personally. Deb was pregnant with our second child, due in October.

That summer, the band went on tour, hitting some smaller cities like Modesto, Kelseyville, Temecula, Oneida, Beloit, Interlochen, and Livermore. Though in terms of pure numbers our audience was still shrinking, we could at least look out and see mostly full houses. Looking out to see 3,500 people dotting an 8,000-seat venue, as had been the case for a while, can suck the life right out of you, but seeing the exact same 3,500 fans packed into a 3,500-seat venue can make you feel great.

The most fun I had that summer was a hometown show in Naperville. By now, the bean fields and cornfields of my youth had been gobbled up by suburban developers, who'd laid down McMansions and shopping malls. Our concert happened to line up with the twentieth anniversary of my graduation from Naperville Central High School. Staring at my old school behind the crowd of 30,000 screaming fans (it was free admission), I found myself getting lost in memories of the place. The teachers who'd done their best to prepare us for the world were mostly gone; only a few remained. I wondered if any of them were at this concert and what they might think of me now, or if they had thought anything of me back then.

As I moved from behind the drums to make a cameo playing guitar, I wondered how a kid like me who could barely get the attention of one cute girl in high school was now shaking his ass in front of all these people from my hometown. I wondered how it was that, twenty-five years earlier, my deviant high school buddies and I were being chased around by a cop named George Pradel, a man who was now the esteemed mayor of Naperville and heading onto the stage to thank me and the band for coming to town.

To me, this was proof the world was not governed by some wrathful God I'd learned about as a kid, because if He were a vengeful God, I certainly wouldn't be on this stage having the time of my life. I was told kids like me weren't supposed to thrive under a judgmental God's rule. I was either the luckiest little Catholic around, or God wasn't watching very closely.

~

Something else, much darker, was also coming into focus.

Looked at from the outside, being the drummer in a hugely popular band should signify you're either happy or rich, or both. I only had the money. As Darius once said in an interview when asked if fame and fortune had provided him with happiness, "Money can't buy you happiness, but it sure makes being miserable a helluva lot easier." That tour was the first time that I started to struggle onstage. My mind drifted. One minute I'd be flipping my hair wildly, and the next I'd catch myself staring off into the distance, going through the motions. Or I'd suddenly want to be up front with Mark, Dean, and Darius, where all the dancing and up-close interaction was; then the next moment I'd decide I cared nothing about what was going on at the front of the stage.

Offstage, I displayed a similar Jekyll-and-Hyde personality. Sometimes, I'd be delighted to see the friends, family, and business associates who gathered after our shows to greet us and party; sometimes, I'd hate it. My temper would flare up when accommodations were clunky or transportation was slow. If I were feeling unwanted or unimportant, I would make a stand on some meaningless point until I felt like I was being listened to and respected.

A lot of my mood swings would boil down to whether or not I had enough white powder. I was becoming a handful, and though I wasn't proud of my behavior, it was clear to the circle of people around me on the road that I had a disturbance somewhere in my life.

At the end of the third month of that summer tour of 2003, and the night before heading back for a few days off in Columbia, things got really ugly.

We were playing another second-tier gig outside of St. Louis in a place that seemed to be a combination of a farm and a flood zone, with a small carnival attached. There were no showers on site, the place had no real dressing room, and it was a van ride to the nearest hotel. The real kicker was having to leave shortly after the show to drive the nearly six hours up to Chicago's O'Hare Airport to catch early flights back home.

Travel plans like that are a bitch for a drunk. If I had had some coke left, I would have simply stayed up all night chatting to the bus driver, then rolled up to the airport wide awake—smelling like a still, of course, but at least I would have felt okay. On this night, there was nothing but booze and regret for me.

The aftershow had been fine. Some friends from my college soccer days and their families had come backstage and we'd gotten to hang out for a bit. I was psyched that they brought their kids along, and I wrestled and played with them, frolicking in the grass and taking pictures together. I had a solid buzz going, but it didn't feel sloppy or reckless. Then our tour manager Mike warily approached me and pulled me aside.

"So, uh Soni, looks like we're gonna need to start heading to O'Hare if we're gonna make our 6:45 a.m. flights home, buddy. Can you tell your friends it's time to go bye-bye?"

The devil had already snuck up on me. Staring through Mike as if I hadn't heard a word he said, I declared, "I need to make a drink. Yeah, I definitely need to make a drink." Something in me had snapped.

And with that, I just turned back to my friends, basically ignoring him. The fact was, I would do anything to avoid the inevitable departure. Mike's job was to get ten people on a tour bus and stay on schedule, and I was making his job more difficult than it needed to be. Ten minutes later, Mike approached again, this time a little less gracefully.

"Dude, we really gotta go. We got 342 miles in front of us."

"Dude, fucking chill!" I barked. "I'm saying goodnight to my friends. Can you give me a second?"

My St. Louis friends could see something was up and immediately began saying their goodbyes. I then made my way to the bus, but I was steaming. I'd lost my ability to step back, take a deep breath, and look critically at my own actions and their effects.

There was a conflict in my soul, an emotional disturbance for which I was blaming others, but the real disturbance was me.

I wanted to party, *and* I wanted a full night of sleep. I wanted control, but I'd *lost* control.

I wanted my life to be simple, but it continued to become more confusing. I had to hide the alcohol I was drinking from certain people, and I had to hide the cocaine I was snorting from certain *other* people, all the while greatly downplaying the increasing use of both to everyone. I had to lie—about little trips to drug dealers, taking shots of liquor while picking up pizzas for the family, and unexplained bank withdrawals. I had to deceive—slyly handing-off blow in public, or hiding it, omitting parts of stories from my separate life on the road. The hardest part was juggling all of these stories and trying not to get caught in my own web. It was just too much.

Walking onto the bus and slamming the door, logic left me. I clenched my right hand, gritted my teeth, and threw a committed punch to the closed bathroom door. My fist hit with a loud thud and the only thing that crumbled were my knuckles against the wooden door. Now I was even more pissed—there's nothing worse than punching a door that won't break. A second punch crashed through the door; and while pulling out my hand after a third and last punch, a stream of blood spewed out like a hose from my knuckle. Suddenly, several people were on me. There was panic as they tried to figure out just what the fuck had happened and why there was blood everywhere.

What happened was that I was a drunken mess, and my mess was spilling literally and figuratively onto those around me. The air in the small tour bus was filled with a sense of disappointment and pity, and it was all aimed at me.

~

For a guy who makes his living using his hands, I sure wasn't treating them with much respect. My job, not to mention the jobs of several dozen others around me, depended on my having two healthy hands with which to beat a drumkit.

The next time the band met up, the questions started.

"Hey, is everything okay with you?" Mark asked. "It seems like you're drinking an awful lot and we're kind of, ya know, worried about you."

"Well, it's probably just nerves about the new baby getting ready to arrive," I lied. "I appreciate it, but I'm all right."

"You know you can talk to us about this sort of thing. We love you, man. Just want to make sure you're good."

"Well, I appreciate you looking out for me. I'm planning on getting this thing worked out. You guys don't have to worry."

Dean pulled me aside for a similar conversation. To paraphrase his words: We love you. You seem to be struggling. You are kind of acting like an asshole. Do you need to consider rehab?

Though Darius chose fewer words to voice his concerns about my lifestyle, I completely understood him when he uttered, "Hey man, you good?"

"Yeah, man. I'm good."

"*We* good?"

"Yeah. We're good. Just going through some shit."

I was thankful for their concern, and I was resentful. Though I understood their message, and even considered their intervention to be thoughtful, I didn't think I needed to suppress my partying for the greater good. I just needed to tone down some of my more explosive behavior. If I could just practice more self-control, then my family and friends wouldn't be burdened with all this anxiety, and I wouldn't have to engage in any self-sacrifice.

I found myself in a cycle:

1. Obsession to get the first drink
2. Inability to stop once I started drinking
3. Emotional explosion or blunder
4. Spiral of shame, guilt, and regret
5. Start over from #1

I guess normal people, after experiencing consistent remorse from their actions, would either choose different actions or humbly ask for help. I chose to medicate myself. Unwilling to adjust my drinking to make my life more bearable, I tried to manage the world around me and continue with the same drinking pattern, but none of it worked.

～

After recent interventions, Soni the party machine may have been down, but I wasn't counting myself out. I flew with the band to New Hampshire for a commitment to an annual charity concert and golf tournament. We regularly shared this bill with our friends from Florida, Sister Hazel, who'd hit it big with their catchy singalongs "All For You" (1997) and "Change Your Mind" (2000), and fellow South Carolinian Edwin McCain, whose hits "I'll Be" (1998) and "I Could Not Ask For More" (1999) solidified his national status as a songwriter/performer. These were our closest musical friends from the road, and we all had a heart for philanthropy, as well as a big desire to celebrate our collective successes. And, like many bands, each was made up of individuals whose drinking and partying ranged from social to excessive.

Based on the previous year's late-night exploits, the bar had been set pretty low when it came to acceptable behavior. The first year we played the event, I partied too late, completely missing a scheduled visit to speak to students at a local school. When I finally arrived at the golf tournament, a hungover Edwin told me, "I'm not sure getting in front of those kids was such a fantastic idea. One of them looked up at me and stated, 'You smell like grandpa!'"

Another year, I was reprimanded by the local fire department when the bonfire I had taken charge of on the beach became a concern for locals who were out on their early morning walks. It was 6:00 a.m., and I was still up drinking. It didn't help that I was using furniture from the host's home as firewood to stoke the blaze.

Still, my hope for the next day and a half was to fly under the radar without unneeded attention.

I rarely drank alcohol before a show. It takes too much focus to play music and sing for two hours, so I could never afford to arrive buzzed. Once the show officially started though, it was a different story. My routine was to do a shot of Jäger or some liquor with the band right before walking on stage, and then bring a stiff mixed drink to my drum riser and place it in my cup holder. I would drink that during the course of the show, perhaps starting a second one toward the end of the set if I could get the attention of our percussionist Gary or the guitar tech to make me one.

That night at the show, the crowd was pressed up against the metal barricades, and the shallow casino stage meant I was up close and personal with them, just the way I like it. I probably drank one healthy-sized liquor drink (the equivalent of three normal drinks) as we rocked through our ninety-minute set. I was invigorated as we walked off stage, and as several of us stood in the dressing room hoisting our drinks high to toast another successful show, I spotted Edwin ducking out of the side exit, making an escape from the merriment. Normally at the center of the party, Edwin was now in a period of drying out, attempting to get people worried about his excessive partying off his back.

I thought maybe it would be an uneventful night until I saw a baggie full of cocaine being passed around. My heart raced with anticipation as I reached my hand out. One snort led to another. An hour later, I decided to eat a few mushroom caps. Before I knew it, it was 3:00 a.m., and then 5:00 a.m. Should I ride it out? Riding it out was our term for *not sleeping at all*, pushing right through usually with the help of amphetamines and/or peer pressure. It can be exciting, and a little dangerous, but it has no real benefits that I can think of.

Accordingly, I made it without any troubles (that I can recall) late into the following afternoon, but after a travel day, a full show, a party night, a charity golf tournament, and no sleep, my time of reckoning arrived.

After being up for almost thirty-six hours, the last twenty-one on an alcoholic bender, my thoughts were tangled. First, my entitlement to party as I damn well pleased was suddenly challenged by the guilt of remembering I had a very pregnant wife at home taking care of our three-year-old daughter. Next, my shriveled, screaming stomach, which hadn't been fed recently, was not cooperating. As a result, my temper was becoming short. The party, long into overtime by this point, was coming to an end, and I couldn't face it.

I stood in my little second-floor room in the hotel, the bus idling on the curb below, scheduled to leave in thirty minutes. It looked like a small tornado had just blown through the room. My shit was everywhere, and it irritated me to see my belongings carelessly scattered about. There was no way I could begin to put them back together in any orderly way. Confusion was setting in. A brief phone conversation with Debbie—which was interrupted twice by calls from Mike Kelly to remind me we were leaving soon—ended in a shouting match and me angrily slamming things around my room.

My stack finally blew, and rearing back like a major league pitcher, I attempted to throw my entire medical kit across the room and out into the street below. Most of the kit and its contents came apart as it sailed through the open sliding glass door, my deodorant, mini-shampoo, and Q-tips taking flight in the late September air. A container of baby powder didn't make it out though, exploding as it hit the door frame, causing a giant white cloud to slowly envelop the room.

Drew, one of our friends from Sister Hazel, whose room was next to mine, heard the commotion and came to see what was up. With the knock on the door I quickly changed from tantrum man to mild-mannered musician feigning sobriety.

"Hey man," Drew said when I opened the door, "how ya doing? Everything okay with you?"

"It's all good here," I said, attempting to mask my madness. "Just trying to get my shit together so we can head out on our long bus ride. As you can see, I had a little accident with my baby powder."

"Okay, I thought I heard some loud noises or something. Is anything wrong?" He tilted his head, acknowledging the big, white cloud behind me.

"Yeah," I said, "I was on a rather heated phone call. I got it sorted, though."

With Drew placated, I knew I had to eat something solid, preferably salty and fried, before getting on the bus, so I rammed what was left of my stuff into a couple of bags and headed down to the restaurant/bar. I'd scarfed only a handful of fries when I saw Mike Kelly heading toward me from across the bar. I was late, and I was guessing he was dreading the moment he had to tell me that the bus was about to leave.

"Dude, this really is the last call," Mike said. "The bus driver's been waiting out there for a while now."

"I'm eating," I said.

"Dude, come on. I'm trying to be nice about this."

"Okay, just gonna finish my dinner," I said, and proceeded to eat one French fry at a time while staring directly into the middle distance.

Our personalities shine during a promotional photo shoot in Miami, 2000. (Photo by Lorenzo Agius)

The influential Francis Dunnery, with Mark and me backstage in a German rock club in 1996.

Playing on *MTV's Unplugged*, Columbia, South Carolina. April 1996. (Photo by Jeff Amberg)

(Above left) Looking sharp for Frank Sinatra's 80th birthday show. Los Angeles, California, October 1995. (Above right) Soccer star Alexi Lalas offered great musical support and friendship on European tour. 1998.

Hootie and the Blowfish with former president Bill Clinton in July 1994, Washington, DC.

Goofing off with former president George Bush in the Persian Gulf before a show for the sailors on the USS Enterprise. December 1998. (Photo by Chester Simpson)

Dad, Baby Mason Sonefeld, and Mom share a moment of joy shortly before her death. Columbia, South Carolina, 2004.

(Above) Somebody needs a nap! I'm with newborn Cameron Shay Sonefeld in July 2000. (Right) Grateful, sober daddy with Cameron on the first day of school.

The blended Bryan/Sonefeld crew showing their love and their teeth! December 2011.

Everyone all grown, on the Group Therapy Tour in New York City. 2019.

Highflying Mark in front of our hometown crowd closing out the 2019 Group Therapy Tour. (Photo by Todd and Chris Owyoung)

The three of us singing at the front of the stage is one of my favorite moments of our set. (Photo by Andy Lavalley)

Happy drummer at our favorite Glasgow venue, The Barrowland Ballroom in Scotland. 2019. (Photo by Carney James Turner)

After back-to-back sold out shows in Madison Square Garden, with our indispensable musician/friends Peter Holsapple, Garry Murray, and Gary Greene. 2019. (Photo by Todd and Chris Owyoung)

Singing for hope, love, and recovery. 2019. (Photo by Katie Smith)

twenty-five

MASON JAMES AND MOM

OUR SON WAS born on October 26, 2003. We named him Mason James Sonefeld.

We were back to the grind of diaper changing, bottle feeding, and everything else that goes with a newborn. Plus, we had an exuberant three-year-old to watch, but it didn't do much to curtail my drinking. I had come to know every creak in the wooden hallway floor between our kitchen and the front room, where our liquor cabinet stood. It was a victory if I could simultaneously sprint while tippy-toeing through the maze of toys strewn about the house to mix a drink while Deb was using the bathroom or changing a load of laundry. Could I silently get the cubes of ice into an empty glass, lift and pour a heavy, half-gallon bourbon bottle, all without knocking it against the edges of the cabinet? I tried like hell to unscrew the lid from a plastic ginger ale container without its loud hissing sound echoing through the house, the noise that announced, "Daddy is making another drink."

Unfortunately, most drunks are not as subtle as they think they are.

We were blessed to have the presence of Debbie's mom Doris to help us. Her mothering skills and patience were key to our keeping the ship running smoothly, especially when I wasn't firing on all cylinders. Debbie's dad Colin Mason was a fun-loving and mischievous Brit who came to America via boat at the ripe young age of seventeen with about forty bucks in his pocket. He was also a big help, too, since he was an amazing handyman and loved his grandkids dearly. He was always busy building, fixing, or cleaning something for us.

He was also my drinking buddy.

To have Colin be the one to pour my first one meant that I didn't have to look like I needed a drink; I was just playing along. And there's nothing that an active alcoholic needs more than to mask the truth of his own disturbing drinking patterns. Deb wasn't happy about the amount of drinking I was doing, but I knew she wasn't going to say much about it. As long as I didn't do something completely stupid, she was more likely to let my drinking slide than to chastise me for it. Who knows if she really knew the extent of my drinking? She certainly had her hands full with other things.

~

I was in my mom's doctor's office with my brother Mike when the doctor dropped the bomb.

"Well, I'll cut right to the point. Though last week the oncologist diagnosed you with Stage Four lung cancer and signs of emphysema— and thereby gave an estimate of roughly six months to live—I am not so optimistic, based on your previously diagnosed pulmonary fibrosis and your generally poor health. I think realistically you're looking at half of that time: three months. I'm sorry."

Mom, the queen of using humor to diffuse an otherwise painful situation, used her well-worn line, "I need a cigarette."

This time, I don't think she wasn't trying to be funny.

"Go ahead," the doctor said. "It's okay, Mary Lou. Really, it's up to you. I'm not sure how much a few more cigarettes are going to matter at this point."

Mom and Dad had raised us kids to have compassion, but, sitting there, I simply couldn't come up with anything comforting. I was in shock. For the moment, all I knew to do was to hold my mom's hand. I wished through osmosis I could transmit a meaningful sentiment to her that said, "Hold on to me tight, Mom, because I'm not going to let go." But the real voice inside my head was that of a scared little boy.

The days ahead were filled with family and old friends coming through town trying not to appear as though they were *only* here to say goodbye, though for many of them it was indeed the case. I imagine it was hardest for Mom—Mary Lou—stuck at home as the throngs of visitors came and went. Mike, for his part, did an amazing job of caretaking, listening, and keeping my mother's spirit up. When he was younger, he was a real thorn in her side, always in trouble at school or with the authorities, but having risen through the ranks of firefighting, his glorious, authentic servant's heart burst to the surface. I admired him greatly for that. He was always her rock, through her pulmonary fibrosis diagnosis, her hip replacement, her transition into full-time oxygen tanks, the steroids, and the other setbacks that she'd had to face. He knew all about the MRIs, the PET scans, the CT scans, the bone scans, the blood work, the bronchoscopies. He knew the cardiologist, the internist, the oncologist, the pulmonologist, and many of her nurses. He knew about the Wound Center, the pain management clinic, and radiation treatment. He was the angel she needed.

Since my brother Steve and I were local, we also chipped in to help out when we could, though my constant traveling made it difficult to be a caretaker for Mom. Dave and Katie lived out of state, but they, too, did everything in their power to love and support her, often traveling back and forth long distances.

I'd been able to buy her a car and make her condo payments, but the thing I wished I would have given her more of was my time, and I failed horribly in that way. My decision not to immediately cancel concert dates to make room for what might be our final days together was one I would regret for many years to come.

And so, I plowed on. I wondered if the timetable was truly accurate. Was there a chance that she might experience one of those miracles where six months is suddenly five years? But this was just my denial masquerading as hope. The more I believed that fairy tale, the better I could cling to the feeling that everything was still normal. I could keep drinking and telling myself I was happy. But really, like all of us, I was powerless.

~

Eventually (though not every day), I just started saying fuck it and drank overtly, all the while developing techniques to attempt to diminish or absorb any backlash I incurred. One of those involved my taking a demented pride in my abilities to drink at an Olympian level. Another was delighting in the creativity with which I defended my outlandish habit. I would sometimes announce with pride when the drinking day had begun and then try to recruit others. I enjoyed the game in which I'd throw out a comment and hope that someone would take the bait and drink with me—or the opposite: challenge me to not drink. "Who thinks Tuesday should become an official weekend day, so we don't have to wait till Friday comes? Can someone call the governor and get that arranged?" Or how about, "This tequila is going out-of-date soon and I'll never be able to finish it myself. Who's going to be a gentleman and help me drink it before it goes to waste?"

One particular afternoon, the band and wives, and their growing legion of little kids and babies, together with various friends of ours, all gathered around Darius's pool. We had a day off between a series of shows at a nearby beach club, The Windjammer. At one point, drink in hand, I announced, "All right, who wants get their day heading in the right direction with some classy Caribbean lubricant? I have a healthy liquid treat full of vitamin C and other natural ingredients waiting for a willing participant."

Corey, our massively muscular ex-NFL football-playing friend, was standing over the grill sweating, engulfed in smoke. "Whatcha got there, Soni?" Corey said. "Let me try a little sippy-sip of your concoction." With that, he grabbed my cup, took a gulp, looked sideways at me, and said, "Damn, Soni! Is there really any juice in that thing?"

"Well, I would say it's the proper ratio of liquor to juice, given my size, weight, and professionalism. 70% liquor to 30% juice, roughly."

Darius's wife Beth, irked by my nonchalance, said, "Soni, are you already drinking liquor?"

This was what I wanted—a chance to put my smart-ass personality to work. Her question allowed me to start some banter on the virtues, or perhaps pitfalls, of my drinking.

"Well, since it is *still* today, and I *do* have a drink in my hand, then technically I am *already drinking liquor today*. But, since you can't really drink yesterday, and there are no guarantees about tomorrow, then to me this is the wisest of my options, to drink today. I mean, what other day can I count on?"

I know my point didn't make much sense, but it was okay because it would either wind her up or shut her down, and I was so gone to the drinking that both options seemed fine by me.

"Plus, this is my day off," I said, "so it's not as if I'm going to get in trouble for showing up to work under the influence."

An older member of Beth's family who was listening to the conversation—and whom I'd never seen drinking alcohol—said quietly, "Looks like we've got a live one here." His inference, I suppose, was that I was an untreated alcoholic who needed help.

I took no offense. It was a statement I couldn't even begin to defend.

I was an active alcoholic.

twenty-six

LEAN ON ME

AT MOM'S CONDO, various stacks made up of bills, photos, newspaper articles, and unsent greeting cards covered the entire dining room table and shelf space behind her on the hutch. Some of the stacks were only an inch or so high. Others wobbled near collapse. Hunched down in a chair in front it all, oxygen tubes hissing, eyeglasses balancing off the tip of her nose, sat Mom in her nightgown.

"Seriously mom," I said, "do you want me to buy you a couple of little file cabinets or something so you can put this stuff in order?"

Without looking up, she drew from the most abundant heap of them all, one that I hadn't even noticed on the floor next to her. It began on the carpet next to her chair and reached all the way up to where she could comfortably grab from the top of the pile.

"I have a *system*, you know," Mom said. "I know where everything is, so just shut up." She emphasized the word *system* as if she thought I'd never heard her say it before, but she'd been using that word for most of her life regarding her unique way with paperwork.

"Yeah, mom. I know about your system. You're the only one who knows where everything is, even if every *thing* is every *where*."

"And anyway," she said, "I've got to get this done now, so you kids don't have to do it yourself."

If she lasted only as long as the doctor predicted, which was maybe another month or two, it was likely that all of us kids, or at least Mike, would be left to sort through her massive system, and it was unlikely that we'd be able to make any sense of it.

I backed off to go take a peek in the cabinet I spent the most time looking through in her condo: the liquor cabinet. If my memory serves me, I thought, there should be at least a third of a bottle of Jim Beam in there. The cabinet was a hilarious hodgepodge of booze that covered a span of probably twenty years, even though she'd only lived in this condo for less than a decade. There was a bottle of Absolut vodka dating back to a quaint New Year's I spent visiting Mom when she lived in Atlanta a few years after the divorce. Further back was some museum-quality stuff—a crusty bottle of crème de menthe from the '70s that had adhered to the shelf; and furthest in the back was a big bottle of Jose Cuervo tequila, still half-full. That one was a classic. I could tell it dated all the way back to Napervillle by the perfectly legible *Alton Drugs & Liquors* logo on it, but when I touched it there was a scummy, sticky residue. The faded price tag read $3.99.

"Mom, you planning a party or something, or can I toss out some of this old booze?"

"Don't be smart with me. And don't drink any of it!"

I grabbed the Jim Beam and scooted to the kitchen for a glass.

Back at the table, I found her hand. I really wanted to ask her a serious question about how she was feeling mentally and emotionally, but I was filled with trepidation.

"Mom, how are you doing?" I said. "How are you *really* doing? Is there anything I can do for you right now?"

This was the same woman who for the eighteen years I lived at home had expressed every human emotion possible, yet now she just couldn't.

"Yes, you can make me a glass of water."

"Mom! That's not what I'm talking about. I want to know how you are *feeling*, not if you are thirsty!"

Eventually she said, "I just don't want to miss out on all those grandkids, them growing up, and graduating and playing soccer, and tennis, and living life."

She stopped. We cried.

"I'm just sad," she said, "I just don't want to miss it."

~

That spring, Hootie had played twenty shows by the time we arrived in Chicago in late June to perform at a celebrity roast for our friend, ESPN's Dan Patrick. I checked in regularly with Mike, but there weren't really any big changes to report about Mom.

The Dan Patrick roast was an escape for me and helped me to forget, for a little while at least, my mother's looming death. I was unable to score any coke to help steady my ship during the course of the evening, and by the time I got to a blues bar after the event, I was already drunk. As the Jäger shots were proudly held high, I could hardly get them to my mouth. I knew if I drank another ounce I'd be vomiting. I pulled a runner, heading for the exit without telling a soul. I vaguely remember the driver asking me if I was okay as I clumsily got into the back of his cab. I hated that feeling. I liked being in control, and I was clearly out of control physically and mentally.

Back in my hotel room, I found myself standing in front of the bathroom mirror wiping vomit off my hands and mouth. I was slipping and stumbling and angry, mad at myself for being blind drunk and pathetic. As I was slurring the words, "You're an asshole," into the mirror—which, given that I was so drunk, appeared to be a moving target—I swung my fist. I hated the man I was looking at. My right hand connected with the wall and the mirror, causing the mirror to shatter all over the sink and the floor. My hand was bleeding.

"You're a fucking idiot, loser."

I continued to slur, slipping again down to one knee. I tried to focus my eyes on the faucet as I let the running water flow over my hand. I found a towel, then I got back to my feet.

Eventually, I passed out.

And that was Dan Patrick's roast.

~

I took the kids to see Mom in early July. She smiled at a cute and talkative Cameron, just a few weeks short of four years old, who had raced into the living room for a hug. Mason was eight months old and huge for his size, but not yet walking. Mom had trouble fully holding him with the combination of his squirminess and her weakened state. She didn't get frustrated though. Did she realize that she might not have many more chances to hold him? He became obsessed with the tubing that ran between her oxygen tank and her nose, gnawing on it. I took photos. Though my kids would likely have no memory of their wonderful Grandma Lou, at least they'd have these pictures.

"How have the shows been going?" Mom asked.

"Not bad. I had a little *too* much fun at John Daly's charity event in Arkansas. I ended up buying a guided fishing trip at the auction, and as you know, I don't really fish."

"Oh, Lord. Is John still a mess? You weren't out drinking with *him* were you?"

"No, Mom. I don't need John Daly to help get me get drunk. I do a perfectly good job on my own."

By then, Mom's arms were pockmarked with a combination of collapsed veins, lacerations, and needle marks. With all the medications she'd been on, her skin had become paper-thin and easily bruised, or it bled with even the slightest contact. I saw her hands shaking and a twinge of guilt hit me for talking about all this traveling and seeing friends on the road.

Mom turned serious on me.

"And you, how have *you* been doing?" she asked.

I didn't know where to begin. As a kid, I was never good at sharing my real feelings. I would often end up alone in my room, upset or disappointed or sad, and Mom would come find me and try to get me to talk, but I would just shake my head from side to side as if to say, "I can't, Mom." I *had* feelings, of course, but I just couldn't put them into words. And here I was now, at age 39, once again unwilling to share my deepest state, so I gave her a lame answer that didn't begin to scratch the surface of my real thoughts.

"Well, I guess I'm just trying to keep everything in my life balanced; my road life, my home life, my partying. Trying not to do too much of this, or too much of that." On top of my traditional unwillingness to share my troubles, I also didn't want to burden Mom with a bunch of my problems at this delicate time of her journey. I tried to offer something hopeful.

"I think Deb is enjoying everything at home with the kids, so that's good news."

I wasn't sure if she was convinced by my words.

"Well, I just want you to be careful," she said, looking concerned. "I worry about you, and all the traveling, and whether you are taking care of yourself. And you look tired."

"Thanks, Mom."

When she left the room, dragging her endless oxygen tube looping over the table, I picked up her monthly planner that sat open to July. As I turned the page back to a few months ago, I noticed that her once-impeccable cursive had deteriorated since the start of the year. Letters and lines that used to flow now seemed messy, as though she'd been filling out her calendar in the back of a pickup truck riding down a bumpy dirt road.

By July, her entries had become disjointed, and some even illegible, as if she had to stop in the middle of a word, and then restart. Though some of this was undoubtedly a result of her fragile body and motor skills wearing down, I also took it as a sign of her hidden emotional and mental condition. Her handwriting style had always been an extension of her state of mind and her personality. Now, the once buoyant and hopeful person was at the end of the line, and this grim reality came through in the way she wrote.

Flipping forward to August, my spirit was crushed anew: she had only two entries—the birthdays of a grandson and her only brother, Phil. No doctor's appointments. No salon appointments. No visitors listed. September was empty. So was October, and onward. The only ink on these pages were a few illegible scribbles that appeared as though she had either fallen asleep while writing, or maybe that she no longer believed that she would be here at all.

~

I darted in and out of town: Pittsburgh. St. Louis. Toledo. Before each little run of concerts, I wondered if I'd need to have the *I may never see you again* conversation with Mom. Now, in the middle of July and facing a two-week run of shows on the West Coast, I realized the time had come. I drove across town to see her.

Her condo continued to be a busy place, but it also had the eerie feel of a coastal town awaiting the arrival of a hurricane, a distant blip on the radar swirling ever closer. You can try to keep calm because there's still time to plan, but something terrible awaits you and your family.

That said, the mood that day was genuinely upbeat, considering the circumstances. Mom would have it no other way. She and I beat around the bush talking about how her car was running, her back screen door that needed fixing—all to put off the real conversation, at least from my side.

Eventually, I sat down at the table with her. Grasping her hand I said, "Mom. You know I love you, and I'm scared, and I'm sad about all of this, but I have this trip I have to go on."

Mom interrupted me without making eye contact. "Yeah, me too," she said.

It's funny, and not funny.

"I don't know if I'm going to see you again, and that really sucks."

Our attempts to be strong ended as we started to cry.

"I just want you to know I love you, Mom."

She could barely look at me. Perhaps it was her way of dealing with this indigestible truth. Who *really* wants to stare into their child's eyes to say goodbye forever?

"I know you do. I know. And I love you, too."

As I stood and gave her a gentle kiss on her sweaty forehead, she squeezed my hand in hers.

~

In the middle of a long bike ride from our gig on Shelter Island to Embarcadero Park on the waterfront in downtown San Diego, I realized my phone was ringing. I immediately thought of Mike back home with Mom and the last words he and I had shared before I left for the road. He had pulled me aside to tell me he wouldn't be surprised if the bad news came sooner rather than later—as soon as a week or maybe ten days. I stopped my bike and pulled my phone out to see that it was indeed my brother. Seeing his number, a feeling of doom came over me. I'd only been gone for forty-eight hours.

"I think it's happening," Mike said. "Just wanted to let you know."

I dismounted my bike and it dropped onto the road. I didn't care.

"Fuck. Really? What's going on?"

"Well, she's started saying some kind of crazy shit and has been pacing around the condo all morning. Way more than usual. Some of it isn't making any sense at all. She seemed pretty normal last night, and now she's a weird combination of confused and agitated. It's probably a sign that she's not getting proper oxygen to her brain and that things are, well, shutting down."

I didn't know what to say.

"It sucks," Mike said. "I'm sorry you have to be out there. I called Steve to let him know, and he's coming over, so we'll both be here for whatever happens."

"I'm really glad you guys will both be there," I said.

That night, I put on my best fake rock 'n' roll face for the crowd, and I drank, of course. Afterward, I knew I couldn't face a whole bunch of drunk, excited people crowded into the small bar, so I stayed back with some friends around the backstage area and near the tour buses, where it was fairly quiet. Eventually I made it back to my room, and then my phone rang once more.

It was Mike.

"She's gone. She fought it a little, but in the end she went peacefully."

Silence fell over the phone line. We were two brothers on opposite coasts of a huge continent, both silently trying to comprehend the death of their mother. Two people who loved each other deeply but had no ability to pull the words up out of our broken hearts and say them aloud.

It's strange that, growing up together, our emotional and spiritual paths had almost never intersected, even when we lived in the same small house, ate at the same dinner table, and brushed our teeth in front of the same mirror. But at that moment, though we were thousands of miles apart, I don't think I ever felt closer to him.

~

I was pleased that my dad made it to Columbia for the funeral gathering. I witnessed his interactions with Mary Lou's side of the family, many of whom he hadn't seen since his and Mom's divorce seventeen years ago. I admired his composure, but I also sensed his discomfort. Through the years, he'd privately shared with me his thoughts on their breakup and the aftermath, and I'd felt growing compassion toward him. It took years to understand his deep suffering, not only for the split but from watching Mary Lou move away to Georgia with his only daughter Katie, who'd been a teenager at the time. Pain and suffering were feelings I never associated with Dad because, like his own dad, he rarely showed them.

At the time of their breakup, I was too wrapped up with college eight hundred miles away to understand what it must have felt like for him. Coming home for Christmas break for the first time after the divorce, I was angry at Mom, as the divorce appeared to be initiated by her. But it was hard to stay mad at my own mom. Luckily, on that same visit, someone shared a phrase with me, or maybe I read it, that said, "Forgiveness is the greatest revenge." It struck me as profoundly useful, and never since have I looked back at her in anger.

Now, I watched my dad easing through the crowd with a gentle and reverent posture, no matter who he had to face. Arriving to the open casket, he whispered his final words over the body of the inherently sweet and loving woman who had borne him five children and then broke his heart twenty-six years later.

∼

Standing in the foyer of the funeral home for mom's visitation, I noticed Mark and Laura Bryan enter. They were having a heated discussion about something. And though the sight of them feuding was hardly new—they had often seemed to fight—as they got closer I realized that *my name* was at the center of their discussion. Mark was whispering, "*Why* don't you want to talk to him? His mom just passed away and you need to say *something* to him!"

"I don't need to say *anything* to him," Laura said. "I think he's an asshole. And a drunk."

Mark put his body between us as if to block Laura's words from reaching me.

"You can't just come here and ignore him."

"Yes, I can," Laura said. "Watch me! There are plenty of other Sonefelds in attendance I actually like: Katie, Mike, Steve, Dave, Otto. If you need me I'll be talking to one of *them*."

Laura departed, and Mark came over.

"Dude, how are you feeling?"

Perhaps he thought I hadn't heard their conversation, but in any case, in my haze of grief and jet lag, I had neither the energy to bring it up to him, nor the self-esteem to care that Laura was pissed at something I'd done or said.

"I'm all right, all things considered. Glad you guys could make it here. It must be crazy with three kids now," I said.

"You can't even imagine," he replied, shaking his head.

∼

The funeral for Mom took place on a hot, humid day in mid-July. We had wanted to play "Lean On Me," the one song she'd requested for her final departure, but because of some ridiculous rule, the Catholic Church wouldn't allow it to be played inside the church walls. Accordingly, we were forced to celebrate her life via that song while standing in the brutal heat outside. Sweating through our suits, my band and I and a small host of others sang and cried, as I added another resentment against the Catholic Church to my already long list.

twenty-seven
TIGER'S WEDDING

"DO YOU SEE a man who is wise in his own eyes? There is more hope for a fool than for him." The words of King Solomon pretty much defined me by the fall of 2004.

I had dug in deep, way down into the trench of denial, even as Deb and others around me tried to intervene. This was the script in my head: "I have a college degree, a successful band, three cars, two homes, and money in the bank. I have Grammys on a shelf and a bullet-proof spirit. I am a strong, affluent man. Don't tell me who I am or what I can or cannot deal with."

Meanwhile, in the background, alcohol just laughed at me. As many times as I said, "I got this," I clearly didn't. My life was imploding.

~

In early October 2004, and seventy-five days after my Mom's death—which was equal to seventy-five drunk days and nights—the band and our spouses found ourselves on the island of Barbados for Tiger Woods's wedding.

Deb and I had just said goodnight to Charles Barkley and Michael Jordan when we became embroiled in an argument in the elevator on the way back to our room. As the doors reopened, Mark Bryan was standing outside, waiting to get in. We continued, ignoring his presence.

"I wasn't ready to leave yet; that's why I wanted to stay," I was saying, displaying all the logic for which alcoholics are famous.

"Everyone was drunk, including you, and everyone was leaving anyway," Deb said.

This was hardly the first time we'd found ourselves in this situation.

"You guys done for the night?" Mark said.

"We are now," I said.

"Jim didn't want to leave his man-crush, Michael Jordan," Deb said.

"Wait, I wasn't the one trying to get his room key!"

"That was a joke, if you couldn't tell. I wasn't ever going to his room!" Deb said.

"Well, you sure could've fooled me!"

This was what we'd come to. Mark tried to change the subject.

"Well, our friggin' door key won't work and I've got to go all the way back to the lobby a mile away to get a new one."

Mark finally hopped in as we got off on our floor. Suddenly, Laura Bryan appeared.

"You!" she said, pointing at Debbie. "Go to your room and do whatever you like, because I have something to say to him in private." She was pointing at me.

Deb looked at me for reassurance, and I nodded at her; she headed to our room, located right in front of the elevators, and Laura and I sat down on a couple of chairs, also right next to the elevator.

Laura cut to the chase, as she was known to do.

"Listen. This whole celebrity thing is gross, and embarrassing." She had clearly heard a bit of our argument. "All this partying, all of this excess. I'm just done with it. Don't *you* ever get sick of it and wonder if there is something different, something better for you?"

I had no answer, so I just shrugged.

"Have you ever asked yourself *why* you continue living like this? Why you keep drinking like this?"

No one had ever bothered asking me the deeper question of *why* I kept drinking and acting like I did. They just continued to tell me that the *results* of my drinking were horrible, without digging into the causes.

"You know, we only get one chance at this life on earth. How do you want to live it? Don't you want to feel better about yourself? Don't you think you are worth more than the way you've been treating yourself, and treating your body, and treating your family?"

I was silent. She was on a roll, now.

"You need to figure out if you even value yourself, because based on what I've seen lately, I'm not sure you do. Do you know that you are valuable?"

Tears began streaming down my face.

"I suggest you figure out just how valuable you are," Laura said. "We've all made mistakes; I have plenty of regrets myself. But don't you want the best for your life, and for your family?"

"I do. I really do."

"We all have crap that blocks us from a higher level of peace, and I think alcohol is one of those things for me. In fact, I am done with drinking."

This was Laura Bryan. I'd known her for years, and I'd never had to read between the lines with her, but was she really admitting she had a problem with alcohol?

This was certainly not any normal intervention. No one who'd ever tried to help me had admitted they had a problem, too. Somehow this was reassuring.

"Wow, I can't believe I just told you all that." Laura said. "Take some time to think about what's important in your life. And if you come up with a list of things that are valuable in your life, maybe you'll consider putting yourself on that list as well."

~

On October 20, 2004, I turned 40. In the days since Laura's confession at Tiger's wedding, I'd continued to try to find relief by drinking every night, but had reached only dead ends.

Deb put together a big group of friends to go out to a restaurant to mark the occasion of my birthday. It looked like a celebration: gag gifts, alcohol, a cake. But I couldn't escape the nagging feeling I was careening out of control. Mason would turn one in just a week, and I got to wondering how many more of his birthdays I'd get to celebrate with him. I was suffocating under the stress and chaos of life, and the alcohol and drugs had long since stopped working as a remedy. Continuing at this rate was like attempting suicide by the installment plan—one bottle of liquor at a time—though fortunately I hadn't yet reached the point of looking for a quicker way out. I flashed back to my time working at the State Mental Hospital and wondered if any of those folks had found themselves in this state of mind. The smell of cigarette smoke and floor cleaner came to me. I pictured myself wearing one of the patient-issued robes. Was that my next stop?

~

Twenty-six days later, Cameron woke me up on the couch in the back house and uttered to me a simple question, one whose impact I could barely imagine at the time. "Dad, what are you doing?"

As I took that walk of shame, plodding through our small yard littered with bikes, balls, and toys, I knew something must be done today. I couldn't tell whether it was desperation or divine intervention that was dragging me through that backyard. Rather than face my family directly, I headed to the bathroom to brush my teeth and try to cover my reeking breath. I walked into my closet and saw a messy, scribbled note on the shelf. It read, GET HELP TODAY, and strangely I recognized it as my own handwriting. What sense does it make that at 1:00 a.m. the night before, unable to stop myself from heading to the back house, I still had the ability to write myself a drunken note?

Elsewhere in the closet, I found the number of a friend (Laura's brother) named John, whom I hadn't seen out at the bars in forever, and I needed to find him, today. This guy had never tried to pressure me into cleaning up my act, never tried to convince me how much he thought I was screwing up my life, but he had given me his number one day and suggested I call him when I was ready.

So, right there and then, I dialed the number, and made a call that would change the course of my life.

"Dude," I said, "can you please take me to wherever it is you've been going lately. I need to get some help."

"Yeah man, sure," John said. "Whatever you want to do. I can make it happen. Are you okay?"

"Well, I'm not feeling so great at the moment, but I gotta figure this thing out. I need to find out what the fuck is up."

"I'm glad you called me. But I have to warn you that the only meeting I know of is later tonight, sponsored by gays and lesbians at 7:00 p.m. Are you cool with that?"

"I don't care if it's a room full of three-legged donkeys riding unicycles, as long as they can tell me something about my fucking drinking. I think it's about to kill me."

I hung up and took a big breath and let it out. I was relieved to have made the call, but then it hit me that I'd just committed myself to going to my first 12-Step meeting. *What the fuck am I getting into?* As I pondered this, Deb yelled from the hallway that she was taking the kids out for a while. She didn't sound happy and didn't wait for a reply.

~

It wasn't even lunchtime, and I had hours until meeting up with John. *What if I find out at this meeting that I'm truly an alcoholic, and I need to stop drinking?* That would mean that last night was the end of it.

I was unsettled by this, so I headed to the garage like a zombie, walking a slow, determined line directly to the freezer. I pulled out a bottle of frosted-over Jägermeister and took a large swig. It burned going down my throat, then warmed me. I truly had lost the power of choice about drinking. I had zero willpower. And as for logic . . . well, this was as ridiculous as my mom wanting to smoke a cigarette in the doctor's office after being told she had terminal lung cancer.

I spent the next several hours trying to occupy myself, sweeping the sidewalks, straightening the garage, and drinking Jäger, making sure to get into the house to brush my teeth before the family returned. When Deb got back, I finally told her that I was meeting with a friend and going to a 12-Step meeting.

"Good," she said, and that one-word answer was all I deserved. For several years, Debbie and I had been cautiously walking the thin line that ran between acknowledging my drinking and ignoring it. Neither of us enjoyed direct verbal confrontation, but I think we both knew that my drinking was a major flaw and an impediment to our relationship, and there were few things I would do if they *didn't* involve drinking. I'd deceived her to hide my addictions, and allowed them to take me to places I wasn't proud of. My bingeing had cheated us out of time together as the isolation had increased. We'd have a blowout argument every once in a while, too, but we both found it unpleasant, and since neither of us was willing to be completely vulnerable, we had ended up sweeping our discomfort under the rug, where it slowly piled up, unresolved.

I knew that Deb hoped one night I would pass up the glass of wine at dinner, or not go straight to our bar to make a big liquor drink before the dishes were even washed. It was fair to assume she'd be happier if I went to bed at the same time as she did instead of always staying up to consume another drink or two. But the more she suppressed her feelings, the more I told myself my behavior was acceptable, and the emotional void grew between us.

~

There's one more party to have; always one more party.

I was determined to squeeze in a few more drinks and a few lines of coke before meeting with John. I headed out to see two friends, Dan and Reggie, who were hanging out at Dan's bachelor pad.

As a child, I had suffered from the Sunday Blues, that depressing feeling as the weekend is coming to a close. Even through college and working a day job, and during my music career, Sunday afternoons left me feeling melancholy. Over time, I had learned that drinking alleviated that down feeling, and a good Sunday buzz represented a middle-fingered salute to those who had quit partying on Saturday night and those expecting me to be at work first thing Monday morning

That Sunday, I figured I was going to go out in a little blaze of glory. I think I needed to believe I was still bucking the system.

When I arrived, Dan and Reggie were watching football.

"So, Soni, what has you out and about on a Sunday afternoon?" Dan asked. "How'd you get a hall pass?"

"Well, you'll never believe this, but I'm on my way to my very first AA meeting," I said. They both stared at me.

"Damn, dude," Reggie said.

"You're going WHERE?" asked Dan, laughing. "Give that man another drink!"

Taking a long slug of my bourbon and ginger ale, I said, "Yeah, I'm going to meet our old buddy John after I leave here. He's taking me. I've got to figure something out with my drinking. Not sure what I'm going to hear there, but I'm going in. It's time."

Dan replied, "Be careful with that. I heard it's like some kind of a cult. They might kidnap you!"

Reggie was more compassionate. "Well, dude, good luck. I'm interested to hear what they have to tell ya. Lemme know how it goes."

We clinked our glasses together and toasted the moment, though I wasn't exactly sure what it was we were celebrating.

twenty-eight
TAKING STOCK

HEARING A COUPLE dozen recovering addicts frankly discussing their alcoholism, along with the solution they used for liberation from their living hell, was a major eye-opener for me. In just sixty minutes, I caught not only a glimpse of what my problem likely was, but what the solution could be. For the first time since my drinking had developed from social into the near-solitary state I was currently in, I knew I would never again have to feel alone.

Back at home later that night, it was apparent to Debbie that something profound had occurred to me.

"Well, how was it? Are you okay?" she said.

I was staring off into the distance.

"Can you tell me how it went?"

I could barely put the enormity of what I'd just been through in words, but after a pause and a deep breath I tried.

"I think I'm an alcoholic and I don't think I can ever drink again."

The words even surprised me as they came out of my mouth. Tears streamed down my face. Deb looked stunned.

"What does that mean, exactly?"

This was a fair question to ask, but I had had only sixty more minutes of education on the topic than she had. I couldn't imagine the impact of realizing for the very first time that you're married to an alcoholic. She certainly had been wanting me to get control of my partying, but I can't fathom that she was thinking it would come to this. I rambled on, mentioning a few important highlights from the meeting. I don't know how much sense I was making, or if any of it made her feel any better, but at least it felt good to say the words "I am an alcoholic" out loud.

We briefly discussed the life that presumably lay ahead of us. No more bottles of red wine over dinner or champagne together on New Year's Eve. No more doing shots with the band before every show, hanging out drinking in my brother's garage; no more Skins/ Cowboys Monday Night Football party. I realized that *everything* in the life I had built included alcohol. Every person I hung out with, every place we gathered, every plan I made, every event I committed to—everything—was connected to alcohol. I wondered how I would go on being the *funny guy* without that incendiary device called alcohol. This was a real fear for me. And did I have the ability to write a song without the elixir that I believed made my artistic thoughts flow? Even the idea of performing completely sober in front of thousands of fans seemed implausible.

I now confronted a life-changing question: would I make an honest attempt at abstinence from alcohol? Sure, I had quit a few times before, but I could never stay clean for long. I could *get* sober, I just could never *stay* sober. It wasn't insane that when I drank to excess I would end up acting crazy or stupid, because even a *non*-alcoholic can have that reaction. The insanity for me—a man who knew alcohol was affecting him negatively, if not killing him—was that when I was completely, physically sober-minded, I would pick up the first drink to begin *another* binge. *That* was my insanity, choosing to consume a drug that I knew was killing me.

By now, whatever buzz I'd gotten from the drinks with Dan and Reggie had fully worn off, and I was amazed to find I had no desire to sneak off to make a drink. This was a miracle in itself.

The people at the meeting told me I needed at least one trait if I had any chance at succeeding going forward: *willingness*. Willingness to go back to a second meeting, and a third meeting, to hear what they had to say. I sincerely hoped I could keep it up.

I cried myself to sleep that night; I had no idea what was to come.

~

It was 7:15 a.m. on a Monday morning in August 2005, and five-year-old Cameron Shay Sonefeld looked all grown up with her perfectly-brushed long brown hair and super-cute outfit. On her shoulders, she wore a bright-colored backpack full of new school supplies. On her face was a nervous smile. As we approached a big set of double doors, she shook my hand from hers, and it was hard to tell which of us was sweating more. Seconds later, we walked through the doors of Rosewood Elementary for her first day of kindergarten.

We were both nervous, but the apprehension I had leaving my firstborn behind on her first day of public school was dwarfed by the gratitude I had for another day of waking up clean and sober. It was hard to believe I'd put together six consecutive months of sobriety, one day at a time. I managed seventy-four consecutive clean days at the beginning, but I had relapsed and been counting days ever since. My body was adjusting to its new diet, which no longer included a massive daily intake of liquor and cocaine. I was eating regularly and had reached 170 pounds for the first time in several years—still a bit skinny for my 6'2" frame, but I'd take it. My sleep habits were better too, as I was going to bed earlier and finding peace in the quiet morning hours I used to despise.

Though the urge to use was still with me, the gray fog of an addicted life was lifting, and I was able to see and feel more clearly.

I had been granted some new space in my head that was previously cluttered with planning for the first drink or meeting up with a drug dealer. I met regularly with other addicts and alcoholics to discuss how to keep recovering. As a result, I gained a growing awareness of how important it was for me to be more involved with Cameron and Mason as they rapidly grew and changed before my eyes.

I continued traveling and performing with the band, and part of me missed all the late-night brotherly fun and mischief. The wheels of chaos on the road seemed to be spinning at their normal pace even though I'd jumped off the ride. I caught myself trying vicariously to enjoy some of the pleasures, and I imagine the people around me were slyly scanning me, too, either in pity—or in sadness? Maybe this was just all in my head. Each night, I was torn between jumping back into the ring or running like hell.

Circled up with the band as we prepared to walk on stage, I took a big whiff from the non-alcoholic shot that had been devised for me before I drank it: Gatorade, or Red Bull, or a mixture of the two. "Woahhhhhh, I'm so dangerous! Look at me mixing Mango Extremo and an energy drink!" I still struggled with feeling like a quitter, a pariah who couldn't control the amount of booze he consumed, so he couldn't have any more. Some nights, I fell into a state of self-pity, or even anger, and I'd think, *This is just fucking lame.* I saw the others on stage drinking and carrying on with the crowd, and a little pang of jealousy shadowed across my heart. They seemed to be having a much better time than I was. Why couldn't I just drink a little? Then I'd flash back to the final few years of my drinking. They were hardly successful. Despite repeated attempts to get back to the glory days—when my drinking was just a brief detachment from the worries of life, filled with carefree camaraderie—I just couldn't get them back. I pleaded for my drinking to produce joy and joviality, but things always turned dark and demented.

That said, I fully accepted that abstinence from alcohol was the only way forward for me.

I had suffered, and had caused great suffering to those around me. Thankfully, no one had to be burdened with finding my lifeless body in a hotel room or discovering me in pieces all over the side of a road after getting behind the wheel of my car under the influence. Short of becoming a father twice, the early 2000s had been miserable as I became increasingly enslaved to the chemicals and the unhealthy relationships that accompanied them.

For now, I was satisfied just to get to my bed each night without drinking. Laying my face onto a cool, cotton pillowcase sober was heavenly. I never thought I'd be so grateful for such a simple thing, but there I was.

At times, I felt I'd gotten the monkey off my back, but it was noted by my sober confidante Jamie that I was *still in the circus*. Yes, I'd quit drinking, but if I didn't get to the root of my *thinking* problems and straighten them out, I was likely to reach back to the bottle for relief. Jamie suggested I write out an honest and thorough personal inventory of my life, to squarely find and face the truth of my past actions.

I wasn't thrilled by the thought of doing this wholesale inventory at the age of forty; there was just so much crap in there I would rather have kept buried. But the idea of a spiritual house-cleaning did make sense. I wanted to move forward in a healthier manner, and if that meant discovering and letting go of the deficient behavior that had caused my emotional entanglement, then I was all in.

While scouring the pages of a recovery Bible a friend had given me when I first got sober, it became clear that I was now willingly living by some of the same biblical tenets I had first rejected as a child. I'd never heeded the words in the book of James, which suggests "we confess our sins to one another and pray for each other so that we may be healed," but this was exactly what I was doing with Jamie in the present. In my extensive rejection of the Bible throughout my twenties and thirties, it now appeared as though I'd thrown out the baby with the bath water.

I trusted Jamie. He didn't ask me to do any spiritual lifting he hadn't already done in his own life. He was patient with me, but as we spent considerable time talking, he did not hold back in telling me the truth as he saw it. He said, "It takes someone that has *been* full of shit, to recognize someone who *is* full of shit." Unlike my Church teachers as a child, he didn't demand that I believe a certain theology, or threaten that a maleficent god was coming for me if I didn't do it. He merely told me the steps he'd taken to arrest his drinking. I hungered for the type of peace I saw in him, so I followed his lead.

As I did so, I was confronted with a plot twist I never saw coming. It appeared alcohol was *not* to blame for most of my poor decision-making. When I heard that, I thought, "What? Alcohol *is* the problem, and if I stay away from it, my problems will go away!" But this was just the thinking of an unschooled rookie.

~

My drinking, I came to learn, was merely a symptom of my disease of alcohol*ism*— a two-fold illness of the body and of the mind. I couldn't stop the obsession in my mind that told me I could drink successfully, even when there was evidence to the contrary. And when I put alcohol in my system, it produced an actual physical craving which made it impossible to stop drinking. If I couldn't drink because of my body, and I couldn't stay sober because of my mind, I was basically powerless over alcohol. THIS was my problem. So, I acknowledged my powerlessness and decided to take the suggestions of other recoverers who'd been able to stay sober—not because anyone told me I had to, but because I saw the evidence that *it works*.

Writing out my inventory, I found some serious failings. I uncovered where I'd wrongly blamed others and had been self-pitying. I saw I had an excess of self-centered pride and fear, and a general lack of acceptance for the disappointment and heartache I encountered in life. I found I'd sought the approval of others to a point that was unhealthy. I had an over-inflated ego and a strong need to be right. I was lustful and greedy. I began to see more clearly how some of my natural desires had been warped over time. While I was pretty sure everyone struggled with their own shortcomings and failures—it's part of being human—I seemed not to have developed the proper tools to deal with my own limitations, so I'd used alcohol to relieve the frustration.

~

There were things from my past I had written out in my inventory that I simply couldn't imagine sharing face-to-face with Jamie, yet keeping them inside only stood to clog my spiritual development. So, I timidly let them out. What could be more valuable than *exposing the things that are likely to trip you up in life?*

There was another category, a list of things I couldn't officially call *memories*, because they were too vague or too blurry. Thoughts of girls I'd drunkenly hooked up with, but whose names I couldn't recall. Flashbacks to periods of extreme intoxication, but I only *sort of* remembered the places, and I only *kind of* recalled how things had ended. The stories were incomplete, and they indicated the depth to which an alcoholic life can sink. I wasn't typically a blackout drinker, someone who remains upright and awake, sometimes for hours on end, but has no memory of what took place during the period of drunkenness. But, I can't say I *never* blacked out. Who *remembers* a blackout, anyway? That's what friends are for, to fill in the blank spaces we can't seem to recall.

My new life as a sober person was daunting, though. There was my first Monday After the Masters weekend. Getting through it without a drink felt more like being put through the wringer than a victory. I white-knuckled it with sweat on my brow, restless and discontent, often hitting my knees to pray. I couldn't help but notice the people around me drinking, slurring, talking loudly, and repeating themselves, and my patience wore thin. I found myself judging them, forgetting I had been doing the same thing for years. I've never been so glad to finally get away from a party.

Then there was the making of our fifth studio album, which we would name *Looking for Lucky*. While I was truly thankful for each sober day during the production of that record, I was unprepared to take part in such an important creative process while my head was transitioning into life without alcohol. It was nice to be in a friendly town like Nashville, where we chose to reunite with producer Don Gehman after seven years apart; it was free of any demons lurking from my past, and I had a strong recovery community surrounding me. But when we started collaborating with Nashville's finest song-writers, at the request of our management and label, I was suddenly lacking confidence. This was new territory, and I just felt unqualified working in that setting—three hours to start and finish a song with a writing partner you'd never met before. Faith in my own skills plummeted when my songwriting sessions failed to yield anything the band liked. My ego took a shot and I fell back to my old tactic of sulking and shutting down when I couldn't face the disappointment.

In the studio, my drumming was tentative, too. Working with a click track as a guide for the first time in my career didn't suit me well. I felt rigid and mechanical, trying to follow the unforgiving pattern. I never got comfortable sitting in the one place that always had felt like home to me: behind my drum kit. No longer able to use alcohol to numb the pain, I was forced to *feel*.

I was lucky in two major ways, though. My band, sensing my fragility, and perhaps worrying about my general welfare, were abso-lutely brilliant with me. They never once pressured me to drink, or smoke, or go partying at the bars. They made me feel like I was welcome to join them, of course, but there was none of the peer pressure or the guilt-tripping that often resulted when any of the four of us bailed on partying. We had always been inseparable when it came to carousing, but now they recognized my vulnerability.

I was also lucky that even though I struggled creatively with my songwriting, my band rose to the occasion and came up with a lot of really good material. It's one of our strongest records, to my ears anyway. Mark again generated the most of anyone, bringing in rockers like "Another Year's Gone By" and "State Your Peace," and collaborated on some others: "Hey Sister Pretty" (with Nick Brophy), "One Love" (with Philip Lamens), and "A Smile"(with Walter Salas-Humara). Dean had two killer cowrites: "Can I See You?" (with Derek George), and "Waltz Into Me" (with Hank Futch). A song Darius wrote with Matraca Berg called "The Killing Stone" fully captured my attention, too. The biblical lyrics, *You without sin / Pick up that stone*, fit my situation perfectly. I was a man who had harmed others, but I was praying that God and those around me would not judge me harshly, and instead offer me some grace.

I made the choice to skip a few events I really loved, fearful of falling back into drinking or discovering that I couldn't find a way to enjoy myself without alcohol. I stayed home from the snowboarding trip out West; I steered clear of several Gamecock and NFL football games and their attendant tailgating; I made early exits from a lot of our aftershow meet-and-greets. I found the small talk no longer meaningful, and the adoration of fans felt uninspiring. But from Birmingham to the Bahamas, Honolulu to Houston, Saginaw to Sunset Boulevard, I managed to stay connected with other people in recovery, and this ongoing connection started to ease me from the grips of the addiction.

As I discovered the exact nature of past failures and current flaws, hitting my knees and crying out to a higher power, or God, or Jesus, seemed to diffuse the suffering. I can't explain how it worked, only that it *did* work. I can't tell you that there is some specific master-god in the cloudy heavens who moves and controls things, because I just don't know that. But I do know one thing for sure: I gained relief and peace in those moments by submitting. I felt calm when I was able to put my body in a passive, yielding position and speak out loud to the universe. I experienced the anxiety dissipating, if only momentarily, until I could sort out what the *next right thing* to do would look like.

Don't misunderstand me. I didn't suddenly claim to fully understand God, or Christianity, but the critical evaluation of self, and sharing it out loud with another person, was invaluable. As I voiced my inventory to Jamie, admitting only *my* faults in each disturbing story, a huge weight lifted from me. I was liberated from the main source of much of my discontent: my own secrets.

From that day forward I would rethink the old adage that society preached: that men need to lead, to achieve, and to triumph, and that strength, stoicism, and success define who you are. When it came to my recovery, I found out that the opposite would be true: my Grammy Awards and gold records weren't gonna fix me; owning homes and cars wouldn't heal my spirit. Keeping my feelings stuffed away was dangerous. Fame was not who I was, though I'd never seen it that way before.

twenty-nine

THE DUFFLE BAG

I WAS LEARNING to face and resolve challenges rather than push them under the rug or drink them away, but a friend warned me that life was not guaranteed to improve just because I began practicing a spiritual program and sobriety.

"*Life* may not get better, but *you* will!" my friend said.

It turned out to be true.

~

We released our fifth studio album, *Looking for Lucky*, and once again it was met with a tepid response, dying a swift death on the charts. But instead of obsessing about its failure or claiming there was a conspiracy against us, I chose to let it go.

Then, while out West during a swing of shows, I received a dreadful and panicked call: Deb's father, Colin, had suddenly died. Instead of numbing my mind and body over it, though, I chose to do the right thing and headed home as soon as possible to console Debbie and help with the kids. (Gary, our percussionist, stepped up and skillfully filled in for me for the gig I missed.)

~

There was an unforeseen change in my relationship with Deb after I got sober. Debbie was able to enjoy spending time out with her friends without having to babysit her drunk husband, and I was content to stay home with the kids. Honestly, I was neither comfortable nor even really interested in going out anymore. But this only served to widen the gap between us.

All the work I'd been doing on myself to stay sober, peeling back layers of lies to expose the truth, had revealed something I could no longer ignore: my marriage was broken—the connection we once had was too far gone to fix.

There is never a good time to start a conversation about ending a marriage, especially when there are kids involved, but finally I had to bring it up to Deb. When I did, my words were clunky. I struggled to be direct. I kept my eyes averted from hers. Perhaps I had an under-developed understanding of what love truly is? I thought of the time I was touring in Australia and Deb arrived at my hotel room door an entire day earlier than we'd planned, to surprise me. Even though we'd only been married a year or two, my reaction was admittedly under-whelming when she yelled, "Surprise!" After a brief hug and kiss I could only muster, "Hey—I'm about to go down to the gym, would you like to join me?" Was this a bad sign? Perhaps I was immature or too hasty in my decision-making to get married in the first place, too eager to find someone who would start a family with me?

None of these theories made our reality any less heartbreaking. It certainly didn't help that this all appeared to be coming out of nowhere to Deb, but the truth was that it had been brewing in me for some time, and it was my failure not to have brought it up in conversation sooner.

We tried some marriage counseling sessions, but my heart was not in it. I took steps toward separating in early 2007, at first spending nights sleeping in the back house, then a week later moving to a friend of a friend's house. I took just one duffle bag full of clothes with me.

Sadly, we were not the only Hootie couple to be struggling. Mark and Laura had separated at the beginning of 2006 and appeared to be headed toward divorce. And Dean and Laurie had already divorced back in 2003.

There was no turning back for me. We spent the next weeks and months hiding our separation, fearing the reaction we might get from the kids. (They were six and three years old at the time.) We were only trying to protect the kids from our mess at the time, but it was also an act of cowardice, putting off the inevitable.

$$\sim$$

As my marriage was dissolving, I embarked on my first solo music project. I had an array of musical and lyrical ideas built up and no place to go with them. There was nothing new on the horizon for the band. No conversations about another studio record; just a smattering of shows dotting the calendar. I was hoping this project could fill a creative void as I searched for my authenticity.

Ironically, the guy I convinced to produce the album was the talented Francis Dunnery, the Brit who'd toured with Hootie back in the '90s and who had also sung at our wedding. He seemed to be specializing in producing records with artists/songwriters who were not traditional lead vocalists. (I was the perfect fit for this category.) I loved the results he was getting with his other artists, like Squeeze's Chris Difford and a relative unknown, Stephen Harris.

Francis was ridiculously talented, and I had always loved his demented sense of humor. The incredible thing was, he didn't need alcohol or drugs to activate any of his bizarre thinking. I relished the chance to take in more of his eccentric personality. In March 2007, I flew to New York City to spend a couple of days with him. I brought only my acoustic guitar and a notebook full of lyrics to sing to him.

I was nervous because even though we were friends, I had no idea about his music-making process. He was a genius-level musician and singer; I was a drummer and a songwriter who lacked confidence and who had no experience whatsoever as a musical leader.

At some point during our first meeting, Francis promised, "We will make a record you will never forget, and you'll forever look back on it with love and appreciation. It will be fun, and ultimately represent this exact chapter in your life." *This* exact chapter of my life certainly had its contradictions. After sharing my inventory with Jamie, I had spent months making amends to many of the people I'd hurt in my life—and I was trying hard to practice principles such as patience, honesty, tolerance, kindness, and unconditional love as part of my recovery. But I was a work in progress. Anger, codependency, and stubbornness still had their grips on me. For every two steps I took forward in the spiritual process, there was often a step backward.

Still, I was sold by Francis's proposition of capturing this moment of my life—and he convinced me that writing and singing about my battles would be therapeutic.

After recording all the basic tracks in New York City in just four days with two fabulously talented musicians we'd brought in from England—Nathan King and Trevor Smith—Francis and I met at my mountain house in North Carolina to start doing my vocals and overdubs for the record. Then he told me he had something important to convey.

"Sonic (his nickname for me), before you go forward on this monumental spiritual and musical journey, there's something we need to do."

I was immediately nervous, wondering what insane idea he had on his mind.

As I held my breath he continued. "We're gonna shave that fucking head of yours."

He stared at me encouragingly, nodding his head up and down, perhaps wondering why I wasn't more excited.

Shocked, I said, "You wanna shave ALL of it off?"

Francis could barely contain his glee. He had chopped his long hair off twelve years earlier during his own journey, one that had also included a new-found sobriety as well as a fresh musical direction. I, on the other hand, was vainly hanging on to my long blond mop after twenty years. The thought of losing *the look* that I thought defined me was terrifying. But some intuition told me to trust Francis on this. Maybe I did need to let go of my past to walk liberated into the future.

The next thing I knew, I was sitting in the Main Street barbershop in nearby Jefferson, North Carolina. Francis was with me and eagerly told the barber, "Just leave him a little fuzz so he doesn't get cold, heeheehee!"

As big clumps of my hair hit the floor and I looked up to see a fresh version of me I'd never seen before, I thought, *I can be something different. I can be something new. I can be something better.*

Shorn, I felt the afternoon sun on my head as I walked out into the Blue Ridge Mountains, the warmth of those rays promising a kind of reawakening. I felt a little hopeful. Then I thought, *What the fuck are my kids gonna think?*

~

Francis helped me find harmony in my soul via the music, and a new way to see myself via the barbershop, but he was persuading me to do some pretty heavy spiritual lifting, too. He had studied psychology, Taoism, and Eckhart Tolle, and he had some ideas that were critical of Christianity and the Bible.

Though I'd spent twenty-five years away from the Bible, I had hesitantly begun reading it again a few months after I stopped drinking. We had some long discussions in Dunnery's studio that challenged some of my thinking, as I was still trying to find my way through some biblical mazes. Francis didn't want to take away my desire to follow Jesus, but he also wasn't afraid to share the long list of problems he found in the hierarchal church system. Some of the stuff he said sailed well over my head, and some of it clashed with beliefs I held deeply, even beliefs I held about myself. His most useful proclamation was, "Sonic, don't believe everything that comes out of your mouth."

He was right, too, because I was still struggling to be fully honest with myself. In the end, Francis would always allow me to take only what I needed or wanted from his offbeat lectures. Even when he staunchly believed in something, he would end his speech with, "I'm telling you, Sonic, you can believe it, *or not*. I'm not going to shove any dogma up your arse. That's the Catholic Church's job!" This image seemed to make him laugh—and just left me shaking my head while he giggled.

~

After a productive period of music-making and soul-searching, it was back to the unfolding drama at home. Driving up to the house, my new look was met with a variety of reactions. First there were Cameron's tears; then there was Mason, who at four years old still had the gift of 100% honesty.

He said, "Who's that?"

Deb's face seemed to ask the same question.

The principles I was trying to live by—like patience, tolerance, and acceptance—were being tested weekly by a lawyer who it seemed would love to have made our divorce stretch out a few years, racking up hundreds of thousands of dollars for himself in exorbitant hourly fees. The nasty tactics of slowing the process with unnecessary paperwork, while creating an environment of fear and distrust where they otherwise didn't exist, drove me mad.

Thankfully, Jamie talked me off several cliffs when I was refusing to see anything positive about the situation. He reminded me that blame is a useless tactic, and justifiable anger was not something I could afford to hang onto. The only way to solve my problems was to look inside myself and work out the parts I was responsible for.

Jamie was a godsend. I had started working closely with him after my brief relapse at the beginning of 2005. He showed me how spiritual principles worked in his life, but he never left out the messy truth that he, too, was human. He still had shortcomings which would cause him to use poor judgment at times and to struggle with certain relationships. By being humble enough to let me see that he, too, was flawed, I could never put him on a pedestal, and this was crucial to our relationship.

Jamie gave me hope as I transitioned from long-haired drummer to crew-cutted lead singer, from married man to single man, from someone who was afraid to be honest to someone seeking to be more open. But it wasn't easy.

Even though at times it all felt so hard, Jamie constantly reminded me that just because I couldn't see what was ahead for me (and the unknown scared me), this didn't necessarily mean that the future was going to be a worse place; in fact, there might just be a *better* life ahead for me. At least it would be free of the chaos.

When I had frustrations about lawyers or my band life, or fear of becoming a single dad, he let me vent—and he was always man enough to admit when he didn't have the answers. He never promised that everything would be perfect—just that if I continued to grow spiritually, there would surely be some important revelations along the way.

And that was all I needed to hear.

thirty

I CAN ONLY IMAGINE

TIRED OF LIVING out of a duffle bag and sleeping in a twin bed, I decided to buy a house. Flying under the radar to do this was next to impossible, but I was lucky to find a sweet, older couple who promised to keep the sale on the down-low. The secrecy didn't last long; a gossipy parent broke the news before I could, and Cameron came home from school during the first few weeks of second grade and said, "Dad, did you buy a new house on Monroe Street?"

It was finally time for Deb and me to have that serious talk with the kids we'd been putting off.

~

Deb and I decided we needed to sell the mountaintop getaway, and I was set to fill my new place with a lot of its stuff. I planned my final trip up there around a forthcoming concert in Charlotte by a contemporary Christian artist named Chris Tomlin.

Laura Bryan had given me a couple of CDs of contemporary Christian artists Casting Crowns and Jeremy Camp back when she realized that I was beginning a spiritual journey. She was already on that path, feeling pulled to live into a better version of herself and seeking nourishment through Christian literature, music, and church. At first I found the mixture of electric guitars and evangelizing on the albums to be kind of offensive, even cringeworthy. On top of that, praising God through singing brought up feelings I'd had from long ago when I'd been forced into singing at church. I was shy and unsure of my faith and my singing voice as a child, and I certainly hadn't wanted to have to sing in front of my own brothers or classmates. I hated the memory, and I think it tainted my feelings toward Christian music.

I'd been with Mark, Laura, and a few others in a car back in 2005, a few months after I'd gotten sober. The Christian radio station was playing a song called "I Can Only Imagine" by the band MercyMe. I'd happily mocked it out loud; Laura had defended it, and insisted that the volume be turned up.

"What is he even singing about?" I'd said while rolling my eyes. "And what is it he is imagining over and over and over?"

"It's God he's talking about," Laura said, "and he's imagining meeting God face-to-face."

"What is he doing standing in the sun?"

"It's the son, S-O-N, as in the Son of God, as in Jesus."

"Well, I think it's weird," I said, "I just don't get it."

"You wouldn't," Laura said. (With Laura, you never had to wonder what she was thinking.)

But times had changed, and Chris Tomlin was one of the artists I now looked to for spiritual inspiration and direction. My growing collection of CDs included the David Crowder Band, Matthew West, Matt Redman, Martin Chalk, and even MercyMe, whose song I had derided just a couple years earlier. Along with becoming a regular attendee at a local contemporary Methodist service, these songs were beginning to influence me to seek a better understanding of the teaching of a loving Jesus, one I could trust. I was discovering an idea of God that was different from the wrathful, finger-pointing one I'd remembered from childhood. I still pushed back against the needless, male-centric, legalistic precepts from the Bible, and I detested anything that smelled of that sort of control, but I was able to begin celebrating a new faith in my heart.

That night at the concert in Charlotte, I was overwhelmed. Here were 10,000 people peaceably gathered to sing and worship. As I looked around, I couldn't believe there was so much unbridled joy (and they weren't even selling alcohol at the concessions!). I began to cry like a baby—in fact, I think I was in some ways a spiritual baby that night, fresh and full of wonder. The powerful message melding with the music, combined with whatever spirit was working on me, was strong—one I could barely describe, let alone begin to understand.

It was surrender. And hope. And liberation. And victory.

It was love.

~

It was time to make other changes, too.

After roughly two and a half years of touring on and off with the band since I had found sobriety, my patience for being the only guy not partying at a never-ending party was wearing thin. So, too, was my enthusiasm for the constant packing and unpacking of suitcases. Worse yet, Cameron and Mason were now old enough to ask me where I was going and when I'd be getting back, and it was getting harder and harder to constantly leave them behind. I was missing too much of their childhoods. A key question they were beginning to ask was did I *really* have to go to work?

One of my favorite tasks was picking up Cameron after school. I would pull four-year-old Mason in a two-wheeled bike trailer behind me, and we'd discuss everything we saw around us, from bright red northern cardinals to mud-covered yellow bulldozers. On the way home, Cameron would hop up on my seat to "ride double," holding onto my shirt for balance. How many moments like this was I missing because I couldn't control the number of days I traveled? One day, Cameron asked, "Daddy, whyyyyy do you have to go to rock and roll again?" To the kids, rock and roll was a place, not a thing you do. This was a hard one to answer. Was I just so used to this "come and go" lifestyle that I had never considered there could be an alternative.

I'd been keeping a running total of how many days I was on the road versus how many days I was in Columbia with the kids, and I didn't like what the numbers showed. With an impending divorce and the likelihood of Debbie and me splitting time with the kids, it would only get worse. The intuition to make a change became stronger. But how could I create more time to make sure I could be an important part of my kids' lives?

~

The end of our marriage officially came in January 2008. We were already having the kids spend time with me at my house on a limited basis when I wasn't performing with the band or finishing up my record with Francis. Finally, after months of obsessing over the quandary of creating more time for my children in my life, I came to a conclusion and scheduled a meeting with the band. It was time to make a bold request to the three friends I'd worked hard with and played even harder with for more than eighteen years.

I really didn't have a full plan together by the time we were sitting face-to-face on that March afternoon, but I knew in my heart that now was the right time to have this conversation. I didn't want to be stuck with regrets down the road.

Band meetings were never a thing I looked forward to. They usually signified big business discussions, or sorting out some personal conflict. But now, even though I was nervous, I was also confident. This was time for my truth. I owed it to myself and my bandmates to put it out there.

We'd had an insane stretch of performing and partying, but when I got sober, it left me on an island separated from my fellow band members. I wasn't hanging out with them after shows; I didn't head to the bar with them; I was no longer the ringleader for day-drinking and late-night parties. And, truth be told, the band vibe had never quite been the same after I quit drinking.

"I've been doing a lot of thinking lately," I said, "about my divorce and our child custody situation, and about our touring. And, I've decided I just don't want to keep going this way, at this pace, in this format. Packing. Unpacking. Saying goodbye to the kids. All these corporate gigs and casinos.

"I don't want to miss watching my kids grow up. I don't want to wake up one day and have them look at me and say, 'Who the fuck are you?' I feel the best way for me to protect that is by being home. So I guess what I'm saying is I need to stop touring."

Before anyone could react I wanted to make myself perfectly clear.

"I am definitely not quitting the band, or saying you guys need to stop touring, by any means," I said. "If you need to hire another drummer to take over the touring, or move Gary into that position, I would not be offended or upset. And Darius, I know you're hoping to dedicate some time to your country project; this certainly would give you more freedom to do that."

I knew if the timing was ever right for Darius to want to slow down the Hootie touring machine, it was now. He had already dedicated a ton of time to writing and recording the new project and was about to release his first single, so there was a good chance he might see taking time off from Hootie & the Blowfish as a good idea.

The guys let me have my say.

"Feel free to disagree with me, but maybe we could all use some time to take a closer look at where we are in our lives and what is important to us? With three of the four of us divorced now, maybe we could all benefit by taking stock of what's meaningful to us as we move forward?"

It wasn't easy for me to air all this. The mood in the room reminded me of when we'd first realized our dubious record deal with JRS had failed back in the early '90s.

Dean spoke next.

"Well, there's a lot to think about here, most obviously the financial impact of making a big decision like this. We'd have to talk to management and our accountant and money people to figure out if we've saved enough money to get by in the present, and more importantly how far down the road it might support us."

"We also have to see what the health insurance landscape looks like," Mark said.

I looked specifically at Darius, "What do you think, man?"

Darius, perhaps not willing to show all of his cards, lifted his ballcap and scratched his head with the same hand (typically a sign of his discomfort).

"Yeah, man," he said. "Whatever you need to do. I mean, I'm more than happy to have the extra time to work my record, but there's some shit we'll have to figure out, too."

These were fair points, but I'd at least spoken my mind, and there had been no major explosion or kickback.

The math for figuring out how much money we needed to stay afloat, to keep health insurance for our families, and whether we could still draw any sort of partial paycheck, was monumental. We met with our accountant, our lawyer, our financial advisor, and all levels of management, all in order to try to understand what the overall picture looked like. Had we saved well? Would royalties from record sales sustain us? And perhaps the most difficult piece of the puzzle to solve: *who* in our staff, which included many long-term employees we considered family, would be let go as a result of our downsizing? I tried my best to lead the charge into investigating all of these details;

after all, it was my push to make this transition. I'm not a numbers guy, though, and was frankly amazed at how complicated the math ended up being.

It would be no easy task to make such a big change. As the summer tour began, though, the four of us agreed that we'd enter a period of dormancy immediately following the end of the tour. No touring. No recording. Indefinitely. It was a mutual decision, but with no official date stamped on the end of it, a daunting one. We decided against making an official announcement—though we did not all agree on this point. For a start, what if no one cared we were going dormant? What if fans thought we were already gone? My suggestion was to just slide out of the scene without drawing any attention to it. It typified the sort of goodbyes to which I'd become accustomed: no grand hoopla, just more of a disappearing act.

The thing that was most meaningful to us—raising money for South Carolina charities via Monday After the Masters, Hootie at Bulls Bay, and the Homegrown Back to School Roundup—would continue. This was good news, and something we all firmly agreed on.

thirty-one

LAURA

DIVORCE CAN FEEL like you're living inside a tornado. The hardest part is navigating feelings of guilt and shame, and worrying about the negative effects the split may have on your children. My mind had been swirling with these thoughts for about eighteen straight months. Now, as our last tour was about to kick off, I was beginning to experience more moments of peace, and even a bit of optimism about the road ahead, so I decided I would reach out to someone who'd been through something similar.

Laura and Mark Bryan had finalized their divorce back in the summer of 2007, and Laura was now getting ready to move into a new place for her and the kids right across the street from Darius and his family. Laura and I had barely spoken since September 2007, both of us having been deeply entrenched in navigating the mayhem of ending marriages.

Talking that spring, we knew we had both survived the divorce tornado and could commiserate with one another over feelings of grief, defeat, and wounded pride, which are common after divorce. It wasn't all doom and gloom, though—we laughed about the divorce diets we'd been on, which had left us looking slim and trim thanks to the stress.

We had blazed similar paths of change from the end of 2004 up to the present, too, beginning with sobriety. Laura's last drink had been at Tiger Woods's wedding; mine just forty days later. As a result, we'd both backed away from the party-centric, rock 'n' roll lifestyle, too, and become more open to a spiritual path. Laura was leaps and bounds ahead of me in her knowledge of the Bible, and I held her in high regard for that, and she had even gifted me my first recovery Bible back in 2005.

This was a side of Laura I hadn't seen in the 1990s and early 2000s. Back then, she had simply been Mark's cute and fiery wife, someone I could identify with when it came to partying and have spirited debates with about race, religion, or whatever else. Now, she was more consumed with wrangling her three children into car seats and leading the Alpha Group at her neighborhood church. I swore she must have had a third arm hidden somewhere to deal with all the laundry, lifting, and love that Marlee, Kenny, and Madelynn required on a daily basis. I admired her fortitude.

With our lives seeming to run in parallel, maybe it wasn't that surprising when we started to feel a strong connection. Still, we were aware of the pitfalls. Though we got closer, we were not just *any* single parents. She was Laura Bryan, former wife of Mark Bryan, my guitarist and longtime friend; for my part, I was still a bandmate to the father of her three children.

Words couldn't begin to describe the complexity of it all.

As the band slipped into our final summer tour, and I officially finished my solo album *Snowman Melting* with Francis, Laura and I became willing to share our failures and imperfections with each other, without fear. Laura had witnessed or heard about many of my low points anyway, and she was open to sharing some of hers with me. Our two twisted and tangled paths seemed to fit together, but were we allowed to hang out with one another? To laugh, and have fun, and more? How was this supposed to work? Were there boundaries we should not cross?

In the end, Laura and I decided to take a chance, having lunch together at a restaurant in Columbia called California Dreaming that since the early 1980s had been the place to impress your date if you were a USC student with 30 bucks in your pocket.

It was July 15, 2008: our first date. In some ways we were like two college kids—nervous, and a bit giddy. Our attraction to one another was strong, as was our apprehension that this relationship would do more than just raise a few eyebrows. The two of us together (dating) was akin to a slap in the face to our exes, as Laura and I appeared to be breaking the "bro code," for whatever *that* is worth.

Besides that impact, the ripple would be felt by a much bigger group around us. The greater Hootie Family was a fully inter-twined, uniquely connected group of parents, siblings, cousins, and crew. My dad was friends with Mark's dad, who was close to my sister, who had married Mark's childhood friend, Kevin, who knew Dean's folks, who were friends with Laura, who'd had a close relationship with my mom. And that was just the tip of the iceberg. From nearly twenty years of touring, our crew knew all of the band's immediate and extended family, from Darius's family in the Southeast, to Deb's family in the Midwest, to Mark and Dean's scattered siblings. NO ONE in the massive, closely-linked Hootie family would look at Laura and Soni together and say, "Oh yeah, that's completely normal and acceptable, and I have no further questions or comments." It was comparable to ripping the lid off of Pandora's Box, imagining all the close friends and family who were going to have big opinions on the subject.

But, with all that in mind, still the date was splendid. We ate and laughed and peeked over the top of our booth to see if anyone noticed us.

Because Laura lived almost two hours away in Mount Pleasant and was the main caretaker for Marlee, Kenny, and Madelynn, and because we were in the middle of a summer tour, our opportunity for a second date would have to wait. We talked every day, and I found myself eagerly awaiting each conversation, wondering out loud what people would think if we announced we were dating.

Toward the end of his and Laura's divorce, Mark had brought up this very issue.

"Laura and I are about to be divorced, and it looks like you and Deb are headed in that same direction. And, I know you and Laura have a lot in common now with sobriety and church. But just do me a favor—if you and Laura ever end up dating one another down the road, would you tell me personally so I don't have to hear it from someone else?"

Back then, his request had caught me off guard.

"Sure, dude," I'd said. "I can do that."

Now sitting in Greenville, South Carolina, having our second official lunch date, I realized I'd need to have that conversation with Mark sooner rather than later, and it wasn't going to be easy.

~

On August 8, I took the long walk from inside the House of Blues through the noisy Showboat Casino in Atlantic City, New Jersey, out into the parking lot where I knew Mark was sitting alone on our tour bus. One person telling another about a few recent dates wouldn't normally be earth-shattering news, but this was no normal situation.

I cut right to the chase.

"Hey man, you mentioned something a while back that you would like me to tell you face-to-face if Laura and I ever went out on a date together, and that day has come. Recently we went on a lunch date, actually two lunch dates, and I just wanted to let you know, so you don't have to hear it from someone else."

Mark's head went down, but after a long pause and a sigh he looked at me and said with an air of hurt, "Seriously? Well, uh, thanks for letting me know."

I could tell from his quick departure from the bus, accompanied by a slamming door, that he wasn't at all thankful for my announcement. I was truly sorry this was painful for him, but the truth was I was not sorry for dating Laura.

In some ways, I had already willingly stepped out of our once-sacred partying fellowship by getting sober. Now, explaining to Mark I was dating his ex-wife, I knew I might well be creating an even bigger chasm between us.

We plodded through what would be our final two weeks of shows. After my very brief conversation on the bus with Mark, we didn't speak about it anymore, though I know there was plenty of whispering going on around us. But we continued to ride on the same bus together, and peace was maintained. Between the looming band dormancy, which left most of the crew nervous about whether their jobs would be spared, and the growing Soni/Laura soap opera, these were dark times at Club Hootie.

Speaking of clubs. Our final show of the tour, and for the unforeseen future, took place at The Canyon Club, in a strip mall off the 101 in Agoura Hills, California. Despite the small crowd, we made the best of it onstage, enjoying every chorus and every smiling face beaming back at us. We made no special announcement, no fanfare when the final note was played, no big farewells or hugs or tears, just the sound of a bunch of gear being transitioned off the stage into their empty cases.

Was this the way all bands fade into oblivion—back down the path to clubs where it all began, with a new question hanging in the air: "Where did everybody go?"

It was August 26, 2008.

thirty-two
KNEELING IN THE SAND

BY OCTOBER 2008, less than two months after the band's last show, two unlikely storylines were gaining traction in the Hootie world.

First, Darius's single, "Don't Think I Don't Think About It," which he'd released back in May, had made it all the way to #1. It was an astounding feat on several levels: to break through to the top of the charts going from rock to country was hard enough, but he also became the first Black solo artist to go to #1 on the country charts since Charley Pride way back in 1983. I was so proud of him, though also quite surprised. I couldn't believe Hootie & the Blowfish had spent the previous ten years being rejected by pop and rock radio programmers only to have Darius rise to the top of the *country* charts—at least now one of us could say we had broken through!

His accomplishment prompted two questions I would hear repeated about a thousand times in the upcoming months: "When did Darius go country?" and "When did Hootie & the Blowfish break up?" As far as the public knew we were still just some aging rock band plodding along into obscurity, and many had no idea

Darius had put out a country record. As annoying as it was to have to answer these two questions over and over again, I was happy to brag on my friend.

The second thing that happened was this: during the same week Darius was busy shocking the music business, Laura and I were sending another jolt through our group of family and friends by getting engaged. We'd done so under a sunny Carolina sky while wading through the still-warm Atlantic waters off Sullivan's Island. I had even gone down on one knee, trying not to let the coastal current ruin the moment by tipping me over.

It was proof that love does not always make sense, at least as viewed from the outside. The American poet Bayard Taylor wrote, "The loving are the daring," and we were certainly that. (Or insane, if you asked around for long enough.) In the past, Darius had accused me of being in love with love, so my claiming this new love story was somehow unique would be a hard sell to him and some of my closest friends. But, as crazy as the idea of Laura and me together may have seemed, nothing had ever felt so right in my heart.

All of that said, if dealing with fleeting fame, addiction, recovery, and divorce wasn't enough, I'd just added a whole new level of crazy to the story. For a start, we still lived 120 miles apart, and that roadway between us would get a lot of wear and tear from our respective car wheels in coming months.

And we were not just visiting each other. We were trying to explain to all of the five Bryan/Sonefeld kids that we would be marrying one another in the near future. Their ages back then were 4, 5, 8, 9, and 10. We tried to tell them that not only would they be gaining a stepdad or stepmom, but a whole bunch of step-siblings, too. As for me, well, I had to start transitioning from the silly uncle figure in Marlee, Kenny, and Madelynn's lives to something I would later discover was more serious and demanding: the role of stepfather. Laura was undergoing a similar transition with Cameron and Mason.

~

In December, the bizarre new world of Hootie & Blowfish continued. In one 24-hour period, Darius would have his big homecoming concert in Charleston, South Carolina, as a country star, and Laura and I would tie the knot in a poolside ceremony nearby. Many of the friends and family who gathered in front of Laura and me and the kids had attended either my first wedding, Laura's, or both. Some may have been wondering if this implausible partnership could ever survive, especially as we'd been dating for just five months. In fact, I think we both appreciated the fact that these people had had enough hope in us to bother showing up at all. Even my staunchly Catholic dad found something beautiful about seeing the son he raised Catholic being married by an Episcopal priest to a Methodist.

Not everyone blessed our union, of course, but we plowed forward anyway. This was uncharted territory, and by the middle of the summer of 2009, after eight months of marriage and going back and forth between Columbia and Charleston, we faced a difficult choice. The new school year was about to begin, and we thought it would be best to have our kids under one roof. We hoped a simple answer would fall into our laps that would make everyone happy and cause little or no upheaval, but that miracle never revealed itself. Laura ended up making the ultimate sacrifice by uprooting herself and the Bryan kids from the town they'd lived in the previous ten years, Mount Pleasant, and relocating to Columbia just in time for the 2009 school year to begin.

Besides having to get five kids quickly registered for fall classes, we faced the task of moving all seven of us into a new home three days before school started. We got lucky finding a house in a great location on Wyndham Road, with three upstairs bedrooms and a family room in the middle. I was overwhelmed with gratitude that

Laura and her kids were willing to make a major move so that we could have one place we could call our home.

What looked like utter chaos—bikes, bookcases, clothing, canines, all arriving from our two houses and being tossed into one—was actually an invigorating experience. The boys, now aged five and nine, shared a bedroom and didn't seem to mind that their bathroom was still painted pink from the girl who had previously lived there. With my help, we excitedly put up posters of the Washington Redskins, the South Carolina Gamecocks, and Liverpool Football Club. The three girls shared two bedrooms and one bathroom. Standing in the boys' room, I could hear the girls shrieking, "OMG I love those sandals! That top is *sooooo* cute! Do you like the store Justice?"

It was my fourth dwelling in an eighteen-month span and the beginning of an indefinite period of paying three mortgages, three electric bills, three water bills, three of everything, while we tried to sell the homes we'd just vacated.

"Unconventional" was a word we were becoming very familiar with, but nothing felt more unconventional than the new situation between Laura, Mark, and me. No one quite knew how to act. Though Laura and I felt legitimate in our marriage, we had barely begun to establish the exact roles the two of us would play as stepparents and partners, let alone how Mark (and Deb to a lesser degree) would fit into this arrangement. It was a tangle for sure. We had the two Sonefeld kids going back and forth on a weekly basis between Deb's house and ours (she lived about a mile away); and the Bryan kids spent roughly every other weekend with Mark.

There's no instruction manual that comes with becoming step-father to your bandmate's children. I'd known Mark Bryan since 1989. Ironically, Laura had met Mark and me on the exact same night back in 1991. So much history was behind us in friendship, marriage, traveling, partying, and music, yet suddenly we all had to discover new parts to play.

In the beginning, I found myself answering the door to see Mark standing tensely on my porch, ready to pick up the three Bryan children for a weekend. I didn't know if I needed to say something to clear the air. Weeks went by; months. Neither of us ever got the nerve up to address the weirdness. If there was a disagreement about when and where the Bryan kids would be coming or going, then it would be handled by Mark and Laura. I stood nearby within earshot, but if the discussion became serious, it would end up on the front porch with just the two of them. Any scheduling problems with the Sonefeld kids would be up to Debbie and me to solve, of course. I would email a suggested schedule for our two kids on a calendar from month to month. If she had any problems with it, she would usually just call me. What we were learning was divorce is not an event, at least when there are kids involved—it's a process. Finalizing your divorce on paper doesn't mean you no longer see the person you've just divorced. It doesn't mean you don't communicate with them. It just means you no longer live with them or have sex with them.

Laura and I tried our best to split life's daily challenges into two categories: first, identifying when it was our job to change or adjust our own attitudes and actions; and second, accepting the things we simply could not change, or that were not our job to change, in other people and circumstances. It didn't mean we were never wrong or always unselfish, but this purposeful thinking did give us a way of organizing the chaotic world we lived in.

~

"Wait, does Kenny like cheese on his sandwich?"

"Nope, that's Cameron. Kenny likes lettuce now," Laura says.

"Last week I swear I put cheese on Kenny's sandwich."

"Yes, you did. And that was a mistake. He's decided he's over cheese. It upsets his stomach. And actually, Cameron now says she doesn't want turkey sandwiches at all. She's switching back to PB and J for a while."

"Okay, got it. So I can make two PB and J's, then? One for her and one for Marlee?"

"Nope. Marlee says she no longer eats sandwiches."

"What? What does she eat, then?"

"Not sandwiches."

These morning conversations took me back to my childhood growing up in a bustling family of seven. There was something comforting about being part of such a big mix, then and now. Having Laura and me and all the kids eating dinner at our kitchen table was glorious, even if it at times it was frenzied. Our weekends were consumed by soccer matches, volleyball tournaments, and occasional trips to the mountains or beach. We had a garage full of bicycles and a soccer goal in the front yard.

During the first two years on Wyndham Road, the five kids were in three different schools, but then that became five kids in four schools, and eventually five kids in five schools for several years in a row. That was a lot of teachers and classes and counselors to keep up with, and our heads were spinning with pickups, drop-offs, and after-school activities. But we cherished every minute of it, knowing this stretch of their lives would not last forever.

One Christmas, while reminiscing about Mary Lou, Laura suggested we get out the recipe book Mom had put together while she was dying and celebrate her memory by baking. As each ingredient was added, memories of standing next to Mom at the kitchen island came flooding back. Baking her cookies again was like discovering a home movie of my childhood I'd never seen before. Laura and I unearthed the memories together; it was healing; we'd both loved her dearly.

School functions were a bit more challenging. Over time, our crew received lots of curious stares as bystanders tried to figure out who was married to whom and which child belonged to which adult. But we were hardly unique in blending a family. Sure, we would win the local award for the most uniquely blended family, with Mark and me still playing in a band together, but I learned when to stand proud and tall as a father and stepfather, and when to humble myself and take a backseat. Together, the four of us—Mark, Laura, Deb, and I—developed a decent understanding of how to do parent-teacher conferences, school plays, and sporting events.

One thing we quickly learned was not to have Mark and me sit next to each other. This limited the weird attention we received as once-famous musicians. "Isn't that half of Hootie & the Blowfish? What are they doing at a youth gymnastics event together?"

~

The seasons came and went, and when we thought we had figured how and why one of our children thought and acted the way they did, they would change and develop, mutating into another more grown-up version of themselves. Just when we would get comfortable with a seating pattern in Laura's truck for our next road trip, someone would grow three inches and be too long to fit in their normal seat. With five kids, there was always something, and it was that controlled chaos and constant buzzing of life that I thrived on. My heart pumped with joy, and I knew I was just where I was supposed to be.

thirty-three

FROM LOST TO FOUND

MY CREATIVE SPIRIT came alive again after settling into life on Wyndham Road, too.

I wanted to write something fresh and inspiring. I had no idea when Hootie would get back together, so I wrote music that matched my current life experience. The songs I had contributed to the later Hootie catalog were stories about my fears and relational difficulties anyway, and I just didn't have much of that in my life now. With some sobriety under my belt, and having been given a second chance in love, my life was now a celebration of renewal and restoration, not a struggle filled with heartache and confusion. Working closely with other recovering men, I continued to see hope, peace, and victory.

Laura suggested I write about that spiritual journey, and more specifically, about finding a higher power as a source of direction. So, I began writing, and eventually recorded a trilogy of original, contemporary Christian-themed EPs.

The first one, called *Found*, was released in 2012 and included titles such as "The Shelter Of Your Wings," "I Decree," and "Calling All Prayers." I'd spent more than a year writing the music and lyrics, and I self-funded a quality recording, utilizing the production skills of Stan Lynch (Tom Petty & The Heartbreakers) and Billy Chapin, along with the best Nashville musicians. Throughout the recording, I prayed that God would give me the boldness to sing it confidently. But, as I sat staring at the shiny, golden, finished CD in my hands, I realized I had put the cart before the horse. I had no real audience to speak of, no backing band, and basically no proven skills as a solo performer, let alone a destination I could envision. Where was I now?

Enter, Celebrate Recovery.

I was only vaguely familiar with Celebrate Recovery when I was invited to share my testimony and sing a few of my new songs on a Friday night at a local church.

Celebrate Recovery combined traditional 12-Step recovery with biblical scriptures and principles, and was helping Christians battle not only chemical addictions but problems with eating, gambling, sex, porn, and codependency. Sitting in the front row, I listened as the leader addressed the crowd of forty to fifty people: "This is a Christ-centered 12-Step recovery program for anyone struggling with hurt, pain, or addiction." A man next to me responded, "Amen, brother!"

"If you've got some hurts, hang-ups, or habits, you're in the right place!" From somewhere in the back of the room I heard a woman exclaim, "That's right, tell it!"

I was so nervous for my first appearance as a solo artist. The voices of self-doubt swirled in my head as the leader introduced me, and they did not shut up as I stepped up to the microphone. I guess I'd never truly appreciated what Darius does as a lead singer. I never knew what it was like to have *everyone* in a big room staring at you. I'd always assumed there wasn't much difference between sitting behind a drum kit on stage and standing in front of a lead vocal microphone. Now my heart raced, practically beating its way out of my chest. Reaching for my acoustic guitar, I was thankful for a prop to hold on to.

Besides my distress for singing, I had an underlying anxiety about standing before a group of total strangers and professing my love of Jesus Christ for the first time. I *felt* my love for him, and I'd sung it aloud at home and in the studio. I'd just never stood up and publicly *proclaimed* it. I sent up a last-minute, silent flare to God, "Lord, wherever you are, please lift me up so I can give these folks a sincere message and a solid performance."

I strummed my guitar once to make sure it was working, and I addressed the audience, "Hello everybody. I am so glad to be here with y'all tonight. I do have a brief disclaimer though." I paused for dramatic effect, "If you're looking for Hootie tonight, you're in the wrong place, 'cause he's not gonna be here. There's only one Blowfish in the neighborhood, and it's yours truly." The audience laughed. "Seriously though, I'm not a preacher, or a pastor, and frankly, just standing up here on an altar is making me a little sweaty. I'm not a trained or seasoned singer, and as some of you might know, I've spent the last twenty years on stage as a drummer." More laughs followed and suddenly I was breathing again. "But I do feel called tonight to sing a few worship songs I've written about my journey in sobriety, and my attempts to follow our Savior, Jesus Christ. The process has absolutely transformed my life."

I looked out to see a slew of engaging smiles, and the reception warmed me.

If my first night with Celebrate Recovery was any indication, it was going to be a fulfilling relationship going forward. The evening was filled with laughter, some teaching, some tears, and an occasional forgotten lyric, but all of these are ingredients of the recovery conversation.

I used my first Celebrate Recovery appearance as a foundation to start connecting with others around the state. I booked a date in Lexington, then Sumter, then Greenville, Greenwood, Union, Myrtle Beach, and Spartanburg, and onward. I decided no town or church should be considered too small to visit. I relished any opportunity to share my music and recovery experience with others. I knew God was doing a miraculous work in me by removing my obsession with worrying about how many people showed up at these occasions. So, each night, whether there were fifteen people in attendance or a hundred and fifty, the message remained the same.

At a small rural church where I played in 2013, I was in a conversation with the Celebrate Recovery leader to determine exactly where it was I would be plugging in and speaking.

"That's where the speaker usually stands," he said, pointing toward a beautiful ornate stage/altar. It loomed above the audience.

"Ya know, if it doesn't make a big difference to you, do you think it would be okay if I didn't stand all the way up there, and instead placed myself right down here on the floor in the center aisle, at eye level? I think I'd be more comfortable here," I said, gesturing to the seats surrounding us.

"Well," he replied, scratching his head, "I suppose that's okay. But don't you want to be up there under the stage lights, where everybody can see you?"

"Actually, what I'd really like is to be able to establish some eye contact and intimacy with the group, which is difficult when I'm thirty feet away and stuck up there in the glare of the lights. I know some folks seem to be impressed by my life in the limelight with Hootie & the Blowfish, but we'll all be better off if I'm not put up on any pedestal, physically *or* figuratively. I need to be part of this group, not set apart from it. I need the constant reminder that in most ways I'm no different in my suffering then they are in theirs. Does that make sense?"

"I never looked at it from that perspective, but it sure does," he said. And with that, we moved the microphone and music stand down to the floor.

Laura traveled along with me whenever she was able and not only was it reassuring to see her beautiful face in the crowd, but she also became a valuable part of my education in public speaking. I trusted her to offer insights that no first-time listener or general Hootie fan would be willing to offer.

Driving home after an event one night, I asked, "Did anything strike you tonight as noteworthy, or cringeworthy? I'm working out a couple of new ideas, as you may have noticed."

Laura responded, "Well, can I just tell you again that you are a very funny man? Your ability to give the audience a chance to laugh, even if *you* are often the brunt of the joke, is a real gift, so keep leaning into it!"

"Well, thank you, my love."

She then gently caressed my shoulder and I felt her eyes directly on me from the passenger seat. This typically signified she was about to deliver some delicate news. "Your back story about drinking and drugging needs to be shorter. I'm not saying it's unimportant, but it drags on too long, and I think it's stealing time away from the most important part of your story: your recovery."

I nodded my head in silent consideration.

"Maybe think about it this way for next time: a little less gory, a little more glory."

Truth and grace. One of the many reasons I married her.

~

The part of these gigs that always made them special was the con-nection I made with people. Sure, with Hootie gigs it was hard to miss the energy onstage during the show, but in sobriety I'd found it hard to fit in with the post-show party environment.

Things were different now. I cherished the post-show experience. Without fail, someone would approach me wanting to share how moved they were by my witness. They said my presence onstage, frankly confessing my missteps and emotional deformities and the solution to being freed from the bad thinking, was encouraging and valuable; it helped them to courageously face the same problems in their own lives. This was the connection I relished. Of course, I knew I was only sharing what others had freely given to me, but to be a link in the chain that brings the message of hope and love to others is an indescribable gift and privilege. I was seeing that no matter how far down the scale of integrity I had gone, honestly sharing my experience benefited others like I never could have imagined.

~

The summer of 2014 marked the twenty-year anniversary of the release of the record that had changed the lives of my bandmates and me forever, *Cracked Rear View*. Some of our crew and close friends wondered out loud if we would take advantage of the moment by rereleasing it or doing a special anniversary tour or something.

Though we looked seriously at the idea, ultimately only half of the band was interested in such an undertaking. I could not imagine jumping back into a big Hootie commitment, to be honest. We were knee-deep in the evolution of "The Bronefelds"—the name we used to refer to the melding of the Bryan and Sonefeld children. It was coined by a babysitter named Hannah—coincidentally the same Hannah after whom Darius named the first track on *Cracked Rear View*, Hannah Jane. Two of our kids were entering middle schools and three were now in high school. There was no part of me willing to pull away from this; I loved watching our kids perform in school plays and choral concerts, or experiencing those early adventures in their getting their first boyfriends or girlfriends, or teaching them to drive.

The summer of 2014 also ushered in a weightier milestone—July 20 would mark a decade since my mom had passed. I'd spent nearly half of this period tangled up, often having to remove myself from a crowd to wail in pain over the loss of a living mom. My tears also represented my shame and regret for not having dedicated more time to her during her final months. All of this was accompanied by a bitter taste of venom toward the local church for shutting their doors on her final wish of a musical send-off.

Eventually, to relieve the anguish, I was driven to my knees to spend time in prayer. I prayed my crying and breakdowns would diminish, even though I believed the tears represented a deep love. I prayed to stop the incessant what-ifs. "What if I'd cancelled the band tour to be with my sick mom? What if I'd at least stayed back from that final West Coast swing and been able to be with my brothers for her final breaths?" Strangely, I never once prayed for God to remove the ill will which I held toward the church. My still-twisted thinking relished the feeling of my blood boiling, looking down my nose at the church, and allowing anger to churn in me. Though it was unhealthy to hold onto this resentment, I went back to "re-feeling" it time and time again, the momentary self-pity and empowerment like a warm, comforting blanket.

Over time, the prayer and my surrendering to the things I could never go back and change helped to ease some of the tension. The biggest relief, though, came after Laura and I started making regular visits to Mom's gravesite, at Laura's suggestion.

Mom's ashes are interred in a Catholic columbarium less than a mile away from our front door. After propping our bikes against the entrance, I stood beside Laura in front of Mom's niche. I watched as Laura's fingers caressed the letters on the granite surface, M-a-r-y L-o-u-i-s-e S-o-n-e-f-e-l-d. She went slowly over each etching, as if there was a power in the connection. It gave me pause to reflect.

"I can't believe she's been gone ten years," I said, sitting on a bench.

"Yeah, it's crazy. So many good times to remember, the road trips, the dinners out. So many laughs, and that sweet, mischievous smile of hers."

"Yeah, she really could light up a room."

"You know, we really have an amazing gift here," Laura said, looking around us.

I too gazed around this peaceful outdoor space, sheltered on three sides by thick trees and protected on the other by the back of the tall stone church, both of which made me forget there was a noisy, fast-paced world just beyond this sanctuary. I took in the beauty of the dozen manicured rose bushes that formed a circle around a small fountain that trickled pleasantly in the middle. I really did find some connection with Mom here. Even though she was technically not here, there was still a peace I felt.

The irony is not lost on me that the church, the one I'd been so peeved at, gets credit for creating this wonderful spot—a spot that has provided me with so much healing. This tiny, hidden garden was the setting for my regrowth, a salve for my wounded heart, and the reason the once-sharpened edges of my psyche were now softening.

Darius's career was skyrocketing in 2014, too, and that impacted his vote to pass up a twentieth reunion tour. The night he picked up his Grammy for Best Country Solo Performance (for "Wagon Wheel" in 2013), I remember turning to Laura and putting my arm around her saying, "We are not gonna have to worry about Darius calling any time soon to book more Hootie gigs." Darius had already had a string of #1 singles off his first two CDs, but "Wagon Wheel" had been blowing up to staggering levels, and winning a Grammy award left no doubt he was a solidified country star in for the long haul. I breathed a sigh of relief.

There were brief moments during our dormant years when I would wonder why couldn't that be Hootie & the Blowfish up there, experiencing fame and fortune again? This was just my ego poking its head up, wanting to be fed. But it didn't take long for me to see that that was not my purpose. The universe had set me on a different path. Thankfully, it was a path that was authentic for *me*—that of being focused on the happenings on Wyndham Road.

The further Darius's star rose, the more affirmation I received that *home* was my home.

~

Our social life was limited, but we were fine with that. We were still sensitive to those occasional stares out in public, real or imagined, so we didn't spend much time out. The fact that neither of us drank also had affected things. After a few years of turning down most invitations to parties and alcohol-fueled gatherings, the invitations basically stopped coming. And, since we didn't keep alcohol in the house, our friends weren't exactly lining up to come over to hang out and drink by themselves.

Don't get me wrong—we cherished our lives free from the obstruction of mind-altering chemicals and the toxic aftermath they caused us. In fact, it suited us fine, as it meant more time with our ever-changing family.

~

And then, suddenly, we'd been married for five years.

We finally began to feel like a bona fide couple. The kids were now 9, 10, 13, 14, and 15. For two people who had felt like the odd couple for several years, it was nice to stand up and announce to nobody in particular, "See how almost normal we are!"

As Hootie & the Blowfish continued to play our three charity events each year in Charleston and North Myrtle Beach, I began feeling a freshness on stage again, too. I was no longer burned out or stressing about ticket sales, and it fulfilled me knowing we were using our time and talent to help raise millions of dollars for South Carolina charities. The music invigorated me, too—even the old stuff. I could appreciate our musical legacy after several years of having some breathing space away from touring. I began to wonder if maybe one day I would look forward to a band reunion that would take us out of our own backyard and across the country.

Though the experience on stage was positive, off-stage as a family at these Hootie events, we still walked with caution and humility. It was still awkward for some to see Laura and me leading our gaggle of kids, let alone the two of us holding hands or kissing. If you wanna feel left out of a party, just give up drinking and then marry your guitarist's ex-wife. Some former in-laws and former friends still stood at arm's length from us in the loud, drunken, backstage areas. I fought it for a time, forcing hugs on people who could not wholly accept our marriage, just to see them squirm.

There were victories, too, though. Occasionally someone would approach Laura and me at one of these events and, while warily looking over their shoulder, whisper, "Hey, I just want you to know *I* think you guys are doing a terrific job bringing up these kids." These comments held their weight in gold, but also confirmed something else: that while there were certainly people noticing the Bronefeld Family was functioning and beautiful on most levels, there must be another group of still-unconvinced folks out there if you have to whisper and look over your shoulder to give us a compliment. Moments like these were a chance to privately celebrate with Laura that at least a handful of people were willing to recognize we hadn't screwed up our kids with our unlikely marriage.

Mark and I continued to see each other on a regular basis with kids' drop-offs, pickups, and events. As we all grew more comfortable with our co-parenting roles, our living room became the hub we would all hang out in while the kids were in transition. Sometimes Deb and Mark's paths would cross at our house, and eventually even that didn't feel uncomfortable. It was always amicable, even if many of our conversations went only surface-deep. I had long since stopped either fearing a punch in the jaw from him or waiting for a "thank you for your efforts in helping raise my kids." We stuck to the safe middle ground.

Dean and I normally only saw each other at our three charity events each year, but when we did catch up, it was as if no time had passed. We were cheerful and comfortable, both happily engrossed in our family lives.

I saw Darius occasionally. Laura and the kids and I attended his nearby concerts when they fit into our crazy schedule. It was weird at first to conceive of Darius having another drummer, let alone another entire band. I had no major hang-ups with the idea, but it was certainly new territory watching Darius perform. The first time we went to see him was at the big amphitheater in Charlotte when he opened up for Rascal Flatts. Besides wanting to see his country set, I really wanted to experience him singing a Hootie song while I stood amidst the crowd. It turned out to be "Hold My Hand." They had a fresh new arrangement with a few subtle changes of tone and tempo, but I'm sure no one else in the audience could notice much difference. From the first note, the fans went absolutely wild for it. As I swung around doing a slow 360-degree turn I could see the huge audience swaying and singing to our song, and a big smile came over my face. It was beautiful. So fucking beautiful.

I would usually get in touch when one of Darius's singles reached #1, or if he had an awards show appearance, or for any one of the many accolades he was receiving. We were good friends, but we were living vastly different lives at the moment. He was enjoying his success and all the ups and downs that come with it. His insanely packed schedule and the sacrifices that come along with life in the spotlight made me tired watching from the outside. I didn't have to imagine what it was like, of course—I'd already lived it. It wore me out just thinking about logging hundreds of thousands of miles on airplanes and tour buses, hurrying to the next big gig, the next photo shoot, or the next TV opportunity. Darius, though, seemed to be handling it perfectly fine.

I was frequently asked if his making a great living playing the Hootie hits in his country set upset me. I couldn't have been happier, actually. He was singlehandedly keeping our Hootie name relevant by playing those songs and by mentioning our name in nearly every interview he did. He didn't have to mention Hootie & the Blowfish—he chose to do so. Sure, our songs enhanced his concerts, but he was the one out there working his ass off touring, not me. He deserved it, and he'd earned it.

thirty-four

CALIFORNIA DREAMIN'

UNSURE OF HOW many more opportunities we'd get, we took a family Spring Break trip to Southern California. Marlee was finishing high school in just over a year, and knowing that one of our kids was going off to college soon gave both Laura and me a queasy feeling. Kids moving out of our house? For college? It made us want to grab them and hold them tight, to selfishly tether them to our home so we could keep them in our sight forever.

Instead, the seven of us were relaxing, cruising around in the shiny Suburban we'd rented, staring through the tinted-glass windows across the hazy canyon outside. Eleven-year-old Mason was yelling, "I see it!" as we first set our eyes on the famous Hollywood sign in the distance. Next, we strolled down Rodeo Drive convincing ourselves we were seeing celebrities—"No, I swear that was Kanye in that Rolls-Royce that just went by," Marlee said. We cruised up to Malibu and gazed in amazement at the shoreline from a cliff high above. I took special note of the colorful misfits strolling by us in Venice Beach, a place where eleven years earlier you could have spotted me all coked-out, rollerblading by in my own freakish world.

Privately, Laura and I swapped memories, some fading and some crystal clear. The two of us had spent considerable time in Southern California, just not married to each other. The memories we had were a mixture of glories and regrets. We both laughed about the hideous mansion the band had rented on Sunset Boulevard while recording *Musical Chairs* in 1998, and the treadmill we both used there. We were all so young. I remembered Laura bringing baby Marlee out for a visit and my being envious that the Bryans were already starting a family.

This trip was a great break from carpools, parent meetings, and homework. The kids were all growing up quickly, and it was times like this that made us thankful I was not out touring or recording with the band . . . but it also spurred a conversation about *if* or *when* that might happen. What if the rest of the band wanted to go on tour now? What would I say? As the years passed by, every time Darius was asked about the band in the media, and he confirmed we hadn't broken up, it set off weeks of people asking me *when* we were coming back, as if it were suddenly right around the corner. Maybe that day was coming? Maybe it wouldn't be so bad to strap on my rock 'n' roll shoes one more time?

~

I celebrated a decade clean and sober in 2015, a feat I never dreamed possible.

I continued to grow my music and develop more confidence in telling my story of spiritual restoration. I booked my own gigs and funded my own records without the cumbersome strings of the music business attached. Marlee eventually graduated high school and left for the College of Charleston. Laura and I enjoyed an endless succession of days waking up early, groggy and grateful, and laying our heads back down each night together, gratified. We rarely spent a night apart from one another.

Time rolled on further, but I never felt it was *flying*. Rather, it was slow and purposeful. I cherished each and every day, taking time to notice just how beautiful it all was. 2015 became 2016, which turned into 2017, until somehow it was 2018. Our middle children Kenny and Cameron would be graduating high school and heading off to their respective destinations at Furman University and Wofford College. The two kids we'd been referring to as "the little ones"—Mason and Madelynn—were now so tall they stood practically eye-to-eye with us.

The twenty-fifth anniversary of the release of *Cracked Rear View*, which still sat in the top-10 list of bestselling albums of all time, would be in July 2019. I would be 54 years old. I knew if this Hootie reunion party was ever gonna happen, it would be *that* summer. And if it *was* going to happen, then the time to start planning was now.

thirty-five

GETTING THE BAND BACK TOGETHER

FOR THE PREVIOUS decade, the band had only gotten together for our charity events, and for a few days in 2017 to rerecord some of our early hits with Don Gehman.

It had felt good being together. We sat around the control room venting about our sports teams, griping about politics, and laughing about the old days. There was no weird drama amongst us. We got to go crazy together when the Gamecocks men's basketball team made it all the way to the Final Four for the first time, hugging and screaming and even shedding tears of joy together. The timing of our being together for this rare sporting success seemed serendipitous. It was a decent indication that we all still had enough in common to enjoy each other's company, and in the months that followed, we were able to agree in principle to tour in the summer of 2019, and to make a new record.

That was only eighteen months away, and we realized we needed more than just a casual verbal agreement, so in January 2018 we sat down with Clarence Spalding and Chris Parr—part of the Maverick group that was already managing Darius with such great success—and our longtime attorney, Gus Gusler.

The list of unanswered questions we now had was long.

Could the band's vision for 2019 become a reality? Could the four of us even agree on a vision? Was there a record company out there willing to put their efforts behind new Hootie music? Were there promoters prepared to take a chance on building a tour for us, a band that hadn't sold tickets outside of South Carolina in over a decade? We had no record deal, no publisher, no booking agent, just a glimmer of hope that Maverick would be motivated to step up.

Darius, too, had concerns, and he cut right to the chase.

"We can talk about this idea all day long, but the bottom line for me is if we can't go out and play amphitheaters or venues of that size, then I don't want to do this. If we're just gonna go out and play House of Blues or theaters, then I'm out."

He had said exactly what I was unwilling to say out loud. If we can't come back and make a big noise, then what's the point in making any noise at all?

In fact, all four of us agreed. We didn't think we deserved a certain level of acknowledgment for a comeback, and it wasn't as if we had total confidence that there were hordes of Hootie fans waiting to see us again, either. But we *did* hope this could be a big deal, rather than a brief glimmer of light. I admired Darius for putting his foot down and setting a firm boundary, something we didn't always do as a band. For all the spiritual or relational growth I could claim, it was Darius courageously saying exactly what he needed that helped propel us forward on a united front. It made standing up and speaking about other things I needed, or things I was unwilling to do, easier.

I had to be careful not to demand too much, as I was only one quarter of the group, but when my turn came I made it clear I wasn't willing to be away from my family for long stretches. I couldn't hide out for weeks at a time on the West Coast, or wherever, while we wrote songs and recorded. For that matter, I told them I was only willing to do a summer tour. I didn't want to be gone during big chunks of the school year in April, May, September, October, and beyond.

While the band was setting parameters on what we needed from Maverick, my bandmates and I were still setting some boundaries with each other. There would have to be some give and take from all of us. Sacrificing time and control was necessary to write and record a full-length album and go on tour. Thankfully, Maverick were interested. They showed us they were strong communicators and that this was not their first rodeo. They assured us they would use their connections and talk to their bookers and agents to put together a rough sketch of a tour. Meanwhile, it felt like the time to start working on new songs was already behind us.

~

We didn't wait for a full plan from Maverick before we started sharing songs with each other. I was anxious to break the ice as soon as possible, so I got together with Mark and Dean and our acoustic guitars. We all had heaps of songs we'd written while apart, and we needed to start sorting through them to see which of them might work for the band.

Quickly, the list grew to over twenty songs. Most of the songs I'd been writing at home over the past decade had lyrics that were overtly Christian, and I didn't think they would suit Hootie. I made a decision to edit all of the specific references to *God* and *Jesus* before offering them to the band. (All you evangelicals out there need not worry, though—you can still find my unabashedly nonsecular songs on my solo records, full of references to Jesus, crosses, praying, and the most important theme, love.)

The process was still complicated for me. On the early-morning, two-hour rides to the coast for our songwriting sessions, I would get all excited about the opportunity to make new music with my band.

With a hot coffee in one hand, steering wheel in the other, left foot tapping on the floorboard, I'd be humming great new choruses I'd proudly written, and imagining us singing them in front of amphitheaters packed full of screaming fans. But on the way home later that night, I was often demoralized, having let unfavorable reactions to my songs get the best of me. I just couldn't bear the rejection, though it's a natural component of writing as a group. When an idea of mine was not received well, or worse, if it was met with silence, I would absolutely crumble on the inside. In my youth, I would react to stress with a "fight or flight" response, either running away from my problems or duking it out in anger with my fists and mouth. Now, though, I used a better solution: *feel it*, and then *heal it*. I could not afford to stay emotionally tangled up, swinging like a pendulum from grandiosity to helplessness. I'd been working on this for years, but I was still at the beck and call of pessimism too much. I was never quite overwhelmed by it, and I'd never had to take meds for it, but those twenty-five years of alcohol were probably a way to self-medicate.

I tried to stay positive, even allowing myself to momentarily wonder if there could be space on the radio for one of our new songs, one that might usher in a *big* comeback. But the repeated insanity of hope followed by defeat that I went through during the years when our singles stopped charting had taught me it's better to just to be content making music for myself and my band, and not to rely on radio success as affirmation. I allowed myself to fall in love with a song, but I also knew it was dangerous to expect that it might be on the radio, or climbing up a chart. Those lean years had scarred me. And now, as I scanned the airwaves in 2019, it was hard to find a format that we could fit into anyway. We were not alternative, or cutting-edge, or hot, or new. We didn't look cool—hell, compared to a lot of bands, we were ancient.

And right before this doubt and negativity fully took over and forced me to wonder why we were bothering to write a bunch of new music in the first place, I remembered the most important thing.

Our fans.

I knew they had waited many years for new Hootie music and would relish this record. I recalled every conversation I'd had through our long dormancy when people politely asked when new music was coming. It's because of our fans that much of my life has been made possible. They've been there through the big hits, and through our dormancy.

That was enough motivation for me to keep going.

~

For most of the writing and preproduction, we ended up going back to Mark's house in Awendaw, which honestly was a place I was hoping to avoid. Though as a band we had some decent years of productivity there, I couldn't help but remember it as the place I used to ramp up my drug and alcohol consumption. I'd been out there a couple of times since Laura and I had been married—either to pick up the Bryan kids or to drop them off, and it was fine. I just didn't like the idea of trying to create new music there while looking over my shoulder for the ghosts of my addicted past. I decided to be positive about it, telling myself I would just have to make some new memories if I wanted to silence the echoes of the old ones.

Eventually, it became obvious we needed a producer on board to guide us. We had a lot of music piling up, but we needed to start thinning it out by deciding which songs were the best and which songs could be ditched.

With the help of Maverick, we were able to bring in the talented and highly respected producer/songwriter Jeff Trott, who'd worked with Sheryl Crow, Stevie Nicks, Aimee Mann, and a bunch of other top-flight acts, so we knew we were in good hands. He had the toughest job of anyone—to take our nostalgic feel and make it more contemporary, while at the same time navigating a band dynamic he knew little about.

As we wrapped up a steady period of writing, rehearsing, and preproduction toward the end of 2018, our first big test arrived: the official ticket on-sale date for the 2019 Group Therapy Tour. Maverick was optimistic, but made no promises. I was nervous, but tried not to show it. In any case, there was no turning back now.

thirty-six

ON THE ROAD AGAIN

MAVERICK AND OUR publicity team had set us up to make a big splash on national television to officially announce our 44-show comeback tour and plans for a new record.

Early on the morning of December 3, 2018, the four of us were seated anxiously in front of the cameras on the set of The Today Show. We were fidgety backstage, but easily fell into sync with the interview, keeping up with the high-energy hosts Kathie Lee and Hoda. Though we sounded the same as ever, we didn't all look how we had during our last appearance on this show fifteen years ago. I was wearing a long-sleeved, plaid, button-up shirt, and there was barely a hair left on my head. Dean had a slick zip-up jacket and now sported thick-rimmed glasses. Darius, well versed in doing interviews, was cool and calm discussing the upcoming tour. Mark was as outgoing as expected, bluntly admitting his feelings about the tour: "I'm really excited!" I tried my best to fill in the blank spaces with humor, as usual. Dean was quiet, unable to get in a word edgewise.

After a midday break, we headed over to our second stop, The Tonight Show, starring Jimmy Fallon. Sitting in the dressing room before the taping, our Maverick representative Chris Parr dipped his head in.

"Well, gents, you should be happy," Chris said. "Looking at the presale turnouts in a dozen different markets across the country, I'm seeing impressive numbers. Chicago—strong! LA—strong! New York—strong!" He sounded like a political analyst projecting voter turnout, and the good news was that the people had spoken. It was clear there was huge interest in a big Hootie tour. We all let out a collective sigh of relief.

The first week of sales after the presale were also solid, and that made everyone in Camp Hootie happy. It also helped fill that still needy place in my heart that desperately wanted the approval of others. Yes, I was struggling with my imperfections, but at least now I could admit it.

~

We headed into our first recording session at the prestigious Blackbird Studios in Nashville in late January 2019. Much had changed in the music world since our last time recording new material in 2004–05, but some things in our band dynamic remained consistent. Dean was still complex and introverted, and it sometimes took a crowbar to pull out his opinions and feelings. Mark was still teeming with energy to write more songs, play more gigs, and get back into action sooner than later. And Darius, whose gifted voice was as strong as ever, was still admittedly unwilling to trudge through the long, meticulous hours inside the studio. As he exited the control room heading for his tour bus parked in front of the studio, he'd say, "Just call me when you need me to sing."

Spending time in Nashville, and now officially back in the music business, I was cautiously optimistic. We'd been collaborating with other top-notch songwriters from Nashville, Los Angeles, and elsewhere, at the same time listening to hundreds of song pitches hoping to hear something that suited us. It was a treat working with most of the writers, but a lot of the song pitches were either too country, too hokey, or just didn't sound like anything Hootie & the Blowfish would ever sing.

I was conflicted with the songwriting we'd been doing. On the one hand, I saw the opportunity to collaborate with some great writers as just that, an opportunity. They worked fast, wrote catchy hooks, and there was an endless supply of them. On the other hand, I couldn't think of a less organic way of coming up with songs than shoving two or three artists who may or may not know each other into a small room, then setting a timer to three hours, and saying, "Now, write a song!" There's nothing inherently wrong with this design; it's extremely efficient, if nothing else. It's just not the way Hootie & the Blowfish wrote songs from the late '80s through 2004.

During this frustrating creative process, I sought enlightenment from a couple of my closest old songwriting friends who'd faced similar circumstances, Drew Copeland of Sister Hazel, and Edwin McCain. Drew reminded me, "Nobody ever said that being in a band would be easy. Fun, hell yeah! And silly, certainly. But not always easy." He was right. "Plus, it looks like your ticket sales are really solid for the summer. Just think, in a few months you'll be out there touring amphitheaters. You'll be part of something really important regardless of what happens with the album. Come on, how cool is that, dude?!"

Edwin, whom I'd stayed in touch with through our continued journey in sobriety, put it in perspective: "Man, we get to make a living writing and playing music, and that just blows my mind every time I think about it. I *never* thought that could happen!"

This bonding, venting, and laughing at ourselves helped remind me what the late Father Joseph Martin said in his talks on the 12 steps to recovery—gratitude is the hinge upon which a happy life swings.

We were trying to find our musical bearings, to discover what Hootie & the Blowfish were supposed to sound like, or look like, in the year 2019. We were fourteen years removed from our last studio record, and staring at the heels of Darius's decade-long country career. Should our new music be representative of the four guys in ragged Bermuda shorts, backward baseball caps, and t-shirts from 1994? Or should we lean into something more current, pick out some matching cowboy hats, and line up behind Darius? These were questions we had not yet answered.

~

We recorded. Our engineer Buckley Miller gave us a thumbs-up from behind the big double-paned window in the control room, suggesting the last take was a solid performance. The song was "Turn it Up," an idea Mark had brought in that we all loved from the first time we heard it. The mood was festive, as we'd added a horn section Mark recruited from back home in Charleston to play on the track. Jeff Trott happily suggested we should all come in from the big studio and give it a listen. In the control room, several managers who were watching and listening were now chatting. There were also some folks from the publishing company on their cell phones in the back of the room. Near the exit, a couple of record company executives were strategizing about not only how to promote us but how to protect the modern country brand Darius had spent years building.

The swarm of people made it feel like a kitchen with too many chefs. But like it or not, this was our reality, and there was no point in kicking everyone out just so we could have full control. What the hell would the four of us do with full control anyway? The fact is, we'd signed on with a major label that had many moving parts. It had a hierarchy and all of the politics that typify any big business. We were partners with *everyone* who was crowded into this large control room, whether they were holding a spreadsheet, a Stratocaster, or a spliff. This is the music business.

After a year of songwriting, hatching almost a hundred songs, I was still unsure how this project was going to turn out, but I knew we had enough quality material to fill a full-length album. We continued recording, popping out several overtly country-flavored songs, "Everybody But You" and "Lonely On A Saturday Night," but we made a decision not to add all the standard country flavorings like fiddle or pedal steel. We stuck to our rock roots on "New Year's Day" and "Half A Day Ahead," and as usual Mark stayed behind to layer in loads of guitar well after the rest of us left. The groovy feel of "Not Tonight," a song cowritten with David Ryan Harris, added a contemporary feel to the mix. And, though no one can describe exactly what category Mark's "We Are One" should go in, it has proven to be an undeniable favorite for everyone who hears it.

Luckily, we had Jeff Trott, and Jeff Trott wasn't going to let us make a bad record, no matter how many outside influences there may be. He had rock 'n' roll in his blood, but he was smart enough to allow the country music side to voice their opinions, too. He was not going to let them push the record too far away from our roots—not if he could help it.

We ended up landing somewhere in the middle ground between the mid-tempo, melodic, Hootie Rock, and the contemporary, soulful twang Darius had developed. I was okay with that.

On a Saturday morning we were gathered in the studio to record. Mark was in the big room, plugged in along with Dean. Darius was in his vocal isolation booth with his hot tea. And the talented Ian Fitchuk (who had played, written, and produced with Kacey Musgraves among others) was playing a grand piano in his keyboard room. I was pacing behind Trott, who sat at the giant mixing console, twisting knobs and staring off into space, ruminating. They were on their fifth or sixth take of "Change," a song I'd brought in at the very beginning of this year-long process. If I could have just one wish come true for this album, it was for this song to be on it. The lyrics summed up exactly where I thought we all were at this time of our lives and career: facing change. It spoke to the frustration of raising children, being a partner, and getting old. I thought of all we'd been through as a band: dreams built and then dashed. Marriages, births, death, divorce, dormancy, and it would continue to change for us, if we were lucky.

The irony was that I didn't even play on the song. Darius sang:

No matter how I plan, my world keeps shifting like the sand, when I try to hold on it all just slips away.

I pile my expectations, but winds of change come in and blow em' down. As I grow old, one thing stays the same . . . always waiting there to meet me is change.

Yes, if my life has shown me anything, it's that *change* is something I'd better get used to if I want to have peace. It's all happening right in front of me.

~

Ten consecutive summers had come and gone since Laura and I got married and blended our five children into one family. We'd spent summers going on beach trips and hiking in the mountains, sending kids to soccer camps, theater camps, and Young Life retreats. I'd finally learned how to fit five bikes on the back of our SUV, developed into a decent soccer coach, and gotten pretty good at patching up a scraped knee without too many tears (theirs, not mine).

Laura had been the glue that held all of this together. Simultaneously, she had been coordinating many of our activities, being a fabulous encourager and teacher of all five children and me, and taking the brunt of the more monotonous duties like washing endless loads of laundry, and cooking meal after tasty meal. We'd been away without our kids, too, to help keep our sanity. We'd camped; we'd been to hotels . . .

. . . but *never* could we have imagined the two of us, along with the five Bronefeld kids, packed up in a tour bus and traveling across the country together for a Hootie & the Blowfish summer tour.

The idea thrilled me, and petrified me. For a start, this was massively bigger than any other tour we'd created, in terms of infrastructure. We were carrying over seventy people with us from show to show. There were eight tour buses and ten semitrucks. Laura was aware that I'd never before integrated my immediate family into my touring life. I had no idea how any of them would react to being on a tour, or how I would feel living with my family on a bus. Would they get bored, miss home, the dogs, their own beds? If they didn't enjoy touring and bailed on it, would I be forced into the old routine of saying goodbye and hello over and over every week and heading back out on my own?

Then, of course, there was the question of how Laura and Mark and I would do while spending the entire summer together in an environment the three of us were unaccustomed to, since Laura and I had married.

So we talked and prayed about it—what else could we do? We found the Serenity Prayer to be very helpful. Above all else, we knew we needed grace, so we became willing to give it.

~

Ticket sales were solid, but we were still hoping for a strong walk-up business. I checked the ticket count regularly, worried about how the showing would be. We rehearsed diligently, harder than any other time in our careers, not wanting our reunion to come across as haphazard. This tour had to be memorable and well-thought-out, so we put in time working with our production manager Jason Parkin,

Special Events Services, and visual artists to create a vivid, fluid set. We even paid attention to our wardrobe (I know, it's hilarious to imagine) to make sure we looked snappy. We thought and rethought the set list and how it flowed along with the video messaging and lights and everything else.

There was only one thing left to do, and that was to make some damn music.

And then, just as suddenly, we were on stage at the Veterans United Home Loans Amphitheater in Virginia Beach, Virginia. It was Thursday, May 30—opening night of our "Group Therapy Tour." We were positioned behind the mammoth Hootie curtain, the letters reading backward for all of us on stage. My adrenaline surged, and I realized I couldn't wait for that curtain to fly up. The stage techs milled around making last-minute checks, giving fist bumps just like a sports team in their pregame routine. This was a tradition for Darius and his country band and stage crew, many of whom we had borrowed from him for this tour. Though we'd rehearsed this entire set on this very stage all week, it felt different now with the surge of enthusiasm reaching us from the other side of the curtain. I scanned my drums and cymbals, perfectly buffed and shined. I looked directly to my left at Peter Holsapple, our talented multi-instrumentalist and friend, who was stepping onto my drum riser from his. Peter had toured and recorded with us off and on for almost twenty-five years. We would normally use this brief time to acknowledge the momentous occasion with a simple hug or a genuine, "Have fun!" The two of us were now wondering if we needed to take part in this newfangled *fist-bump* routine. But as our fists got within inches of each other, we quickly pulled them back and laughed hysterically. We then exchanged a more conventional, "Have a great show, brother."

As the final note of our intro song "Lowrider" faded away, the house lights went down. An urgent cheer let out until the voice of Samuel L. Jackson filled the air and a hush fell over the crowd.

The path of the righteous band is beset on all sides by the iniquities of the selfish and the tyranny of evil bands. Blessed is the band, who in the name of righteousness and good will shepherds the weak through the valley of darkness, for they are truly their brother's keeper and the finder of lost musicians . . .

This was a bit Sam suggested to us years earlier, altering the lines of *Pulp Fiction* as a dynamic way to introduce us at one of our Monday After the Masters charity concerts. He and Darius were friends, and Sam was one of our celebrity guests at the fundraiser. Someone in our crew had the fortitude to record it live that night. It worked well to hype up the already hyped-up crowd, many of whom hadn't seen us in fifteen or twenty years, especially as he sold it with the religious fervor of a jacked-up evangelist in a revival tent.

Beyond the curtain, there were 16,000 screaming Hootie fans crammed into the amphitheater. I picked up my sticks as Sam's final proclamations rose up with intensity.

Jackson had one more pronouncement:

And I will STRIKE DOWN upon thee with great vengeance and fuuuurious anger those who attempt to poison and destroy my brothers! And you will know the band's name . . . is HOOTIE & THE BLOWFISH!

As the curtain moved skyward, I clicked my sticks four times and by the time the curtain was fully gone, we were off. The sonic force of all the guitars strumming a G chord was intense in my ears, but it had never felt so good to get walloped by something that was probably causing hearing loss. I quickly reached down to try to lower the volume level on my monitor pack in between drumbeats. I didn't know what was louder though, Mark and Peter's guitar amps ringing in my ears, or the awesome tidal wave of applause that washed over us. It was wonderful.

There were beaming faces everywhere. I knew what they were feeling, because I am a music *fan* as well as a musician. I have stood at my seat waiting for my favorite band to strike the first few notes, and I have felt that hysteria. People were dancing and all smiles as we shared this space for these few moments. It wasn't a band and their fans; it was one big *us*—one seamless group of music-lovers enjoying the same feeling.

I strived to take it all in. Out on the top of the lawn section, people were standing and singing along. They were spilling beer on their blankets and tarps. I wished my smile was big enough to reach them out there. This was the culmination of all the hours of rehearsing and preparation, all the years of waiting and wondering if I might get one more taste of glory, one more affirmation that it was all real.

Some days, I wondered if it was just a dream.

We plowed our way through the set. It was a thrill without equal—everyone was up for every song. We played "I Go Blind" and "Not Even the Trees" and "I Will Wait" and we hit a high moment with "Hold My Hand." Just when I thought we couldn't go higher, we played "Let Her Cry." During the third verse, Darius stood alone at the tip of the catwalk playing guitar and singing. As the audience's collective voice grew louder than his own, he sagely pointed the microphone to the crowd, letting them know it was just as much their song as it was his, and they finished out the verse. This was not the same Darius Rucker I had walked on stage with in 1995 when we saw 20,000 Hootie fans in front of us for the very first time. He had learned how to work a big crowd, and right now he had them in the palm of his hand.

There were questions (not from me) about whether or not we would incorporate songs from Darius's country career into our set. We ended up deciding to put "Alright," one of Darius's biggest country hits, in the middle of the set. By the second syllable of "Al-right," it was obvious we'd made a wise choice. With a bump in the energy level and an extra skip in their step, the audience confirmed that his modern country had a happy place in a Hootie set.

The crescendo that just about knocked the roof off the building, though, came near the end of the regular set. It was a song that almost didn't make it into the set list called "Wagon Wheel," written by the unpissed-on Bob Dylan, whom I was suddenly a little thankful for, and Ketch Secor of Old Crow Medicine Show. Problem was, the song was sooooo big and popular, it ended up annoying a large segment of the listening population, even part of our own band and crew. It had become so strangely divisive over the seven years since Darius had a #1 hit with it, that people were separating into two distinct groups: ardent, hand-clapping supporters or naysaying haters putting their finger down their throat, saying, "Gag me, already!"

When I write a new song I always hope people will like it, but once in a career, if you're lucky, you might write (or record) one that's somehow *too catchy* or becomes too commercial, if there's such a thing. "Wagon Wheel" is just such a song for Darius. Songs like these can change your life though. They can single-handedly put your kids through college, fund entire charities, or keep food on a songwriter's table for decades.

Well, love it or hate it, when that chorus of "Wagon Wheel" hit that night, every single person was thrust onto a higher plane. People who were walking to the restroom were now frantically racing back to their seats. Ushers who had been sitting the entire show, staring bored into the Hootie abyss, were suddenly in the aisles, *rocking me, mama, like a southbound train.* The elderly were tossing their walkers and wheelchairs aside like Jesus had just appeared and healed them! It was a cascade of ecstasy like I'd never witnessed in a concert before.

The lesson for "Wagon Wheel": you can love it or you can hate, but don't ever try to deny it.

As the fans screamed for an encore, our band and a few crew had gathered on the side stage and were passing around a bottle of Jim Beam (I passed) before we granted the audience their wish. We watched as a grand piano was being pushed out to center stage. Then, for the first time in our history as a band, Darius and I walked out together to perform the song "Goodbye." From a dank, little room where I had plunked the first notes of this song on an upright piano in the early 1990s, to the grandest stage in front of 16,000 screaming fans, the song had survived.

That's what music does—it survives. It will survive all of us, too.

~

Virginia Beach was only the beginning. The surge of excitement grew night after night. Seventeen thousand fans swarmed to see us in Denver, the same in Dallas. Nineteen thousand joined the party in Hershey, the same in Hartford. And a mind-blowing 20,000 supporters pressed through the gates in Cleveland, and the same in Camden.

I stopped worrying about ticket sales after that.

As the weeks flew by, my family and the bigger Hootie family found their rhythm and their routine. Darius and Mark golfed daily. Dean was stuck rehabbing his newly implanted hip—his appearance on stage every night a reminder of seeing Eddie Van Halen limping around back in the '90s, badly in need of a new hip himself. It was nothing short of a miracle to see Dean up there performing each night.

When drawing up the tour way back in 2018, we went round and round trying to find another act to add to the bill, one that would be a good musical fit, and help us sell more tickets. We considered every imaginable possibility from old friends like Cowboy Mouth or Sister Hazel, to something more contemporary like St. Paul and The Broken Bones. While there was no shortage of groups that we thought would have made a fabulous addition to the ticket, we finally took the advice of our well-informed management team when they suggested who they believed to be not only a *great band*, but *the right band* for the bill. Barenaked Ladies. They couldn't have been more correct.

Surprisingly, our paths had crossed only a few times in our careers, and I never had the opportunity to hang out with them, but after a month on the Group Therapy Tour together, being with Ed, Jim, Kevin, and Tyler felt like old friends. Eating meals with them daily, meeting their families, and learning about BNL's long journey in music and the music business was a joy and an education. They were gifted songwriters and performers, as funny as the day is long, and blended in perfectly with our Hootie touring mindset: have fun, put on a great show, and have fun!. Nightly, we experienced the thrill of sharing the stage with them during a mic-dropping version of "With A Little Help From My Friends" (the Joe Cocker version). The crowd salivated over the rollicking, eleven-man, rocking rendition.

I tried to stick to the same schedule as back in Columbia, rising early for coffee, brief meditation, writing, and a workout. But *early* was difficult to achieve with the nights being so much later than I was used to. You could find our family crammed into the front lounge of our tour bus around 12:30 a.m. each night, eating pizza or tacos or cold French fries, overly stimulated and giggling from the day's events.

Laura braved the unknown every day, proudly showing the Hootie band, staff, and crew our family's version of *normal*. From east to west, she corralled the kids to get out and do some local sightseeing while encouraging me to seek out my 12-Step meetings. She, too, relished the solitude of our morning ritual: coffee, writing, and a workout.

The kids loved it. Within the first few weeks, I knew to look for Laura and the girls dancing behind our sound man Billy as soon as our set started. I knew I could find Mason playing video games with Darius's son Jack in one of the dressing rooms afterward. I don't know how we would have handled this tour as a family during any other year. But now with the kids 21, 19, 18, and two 15-year-olds, it seemed just right.

Our bus became just a condensed version of home. We stumbled around in pajamas, with red eyes and messy hair. (Well, I suppose I was the only one without messy hair.) We reunited with old friends and family in nearly every town. Honestly, if it weren't for the band, I wouldn't know half my distant relatives. My career has been a glue for many layers of my extended family life, and that has been a gift to me. So many of the markers of my life were revisited each night we arrived in a new town.

~

Along the way, I got to celebrate the fortieth anniversary of finishing Catholic school with a group of about eight classmates. I hung out with groups of my high school friends in six different cities. My college soccer family was present in no fewer than a dozen markets. I saw my roommates from college, Cliff and Andy, and their families. I hung out with my bandmates from the Calvin and Tootie days—Francis Dunnery showed up, as did Don Gehman and John Nau and Don Dixon.

Many industry friends who had experienced the band's unlikely rise to fame in the mid-'90s came back out to celebrate, and their presence confirmed we hadn't burned many bridges on our journey. With some pride, I can honestly say we were *nice guys* on the way up the ladder *and* the way back down, even when we were jaded, tired, or being lied to.

As the tour rolled on, I ran across some reminders of the other rockers we shared the road with in the '90s. We saw Steven Tyler across a quiet street in Lake Sunapee, New Hampshire, where his band Aerosmith originally formed, while we were on a few days off from the tour. He was 71 years old and still sporting his groovy rock 'n' roll outfit. Rather than butt in on the conversation he was having, we continued on our way, but I was happy to discover he was celebrating almost a decade of sobriety.

I read that Bono and his U2 bandmates had just announced yet another leg of touring for the fall of 2019, while continuing to raise awareness and financial support for the global AIDS crisis (RED) and extreme poverty and preventable disease (ONE). Though he was still a relatively young buck at 59 years old, his heart for philanthropy continued to inspire me.

Eddie Van Halen was having a tougher go at life. Though finally finding sobriety, his ongoing battles with cancer, combined with being a heavy smoker throughout most of his life, were beating him down. He was the same age—64—as my mom was when she passed away.

~

The summer got crazier as momentum built through social media and word-of-mouth. Twenty-two thousand came out in Bristow, Virginia; twenty-*three* thousand in Indianapolis. My home crowd in Chicago came out to the tune of 24,000. We hadn't seen crowds this size since the summer of 1995 when our first few singles were exploding onto radio. Rather than feeling like the summer was winding *down*, it felt like it was still winding *up*.

But the end would indeed finally arrive. The city that birthed Hootie & the Blowfish—Columbia, South Carolina—would be our final order of business.

The fans in Columbia, it turns out, were especially hungry for us. After being starved for Hootie & the Blowfish for the better part of fifteen years, they showed us just how much they missed us by gobbling up more than 32,000 tickets for our three-night stand at the Colonial Life Arena. I felt deep satisfaction as a special banner was unfurled for this occasion. It looked just like one of the sports banners you see hanging from the rafters where a team plays hockey or basketball. It read, "Hootie & the Blowfish—Back to Back to Back Sellouts," with the dates of the shows listed.

Not bad, Columbia. Not bad, at all.

For posterity, we filmed the first two nights in Columbia, hoping to release the concert and a documentary down the road sometime. Seeing the cameras added stress and some nerves to our performances, and they were a distraction for the audience, who couldn't help but stare at the swinging camera crane flying over the tops of their heads. So, for the third and final night, it was a big relief to have no cameras and gear disturbing the symbiotic relationship between our fans and us.

I ate a wonderful catered meal before the last show with many of the crew who would be heading back to their homes after that night. I headed to the dressing room to pick out my final outfit. Like each of the previous forty-six nights on tour, we gathered for our preshow meet and greet, taking pictures with over a hundred fans, family, or friends who had patiently waited in line for the opportunity.

On stage, our performance on the last night was easily the strongest of all the Columbia shows, comfortable and confident, freed from the constraints of filming the first two nights. I'm man enough to confess that when the tears began welling up in my eyes during "Time," it wasn't the first time I felt those powerful emotions that summer. I am regularly overcome by this soft-heartedness during this song, thinking about *time*. I thought about my first drum set and my mom's beaming smile as she watched me sitting behind it for the first time. I thought about her natural way of singing high harmonies, so I always sing an extra high one for her, during the last chorus. I saw my family out behind the soundboard being goofy, and I was thankful to have seen them grow up right before my eyes. I saw Laura, smiling, dancing, in her element, loving and protecting the children like a proud mother hen. I thought of how little I struggled with everything around me, and myself, compared to some other years. Sitting there pounding away, I truly did not have a problem in the world. I couldn't have invented one if I tried.

~

It was a little strange coming back home now to play these shows in Columbia, after traveling from coast to coast all summer, being the center of attention for throngs of fanatical admirers. It's easier to feel and act like a *rock star* out there, as you ride off down the highway night after night in your luxury tour bus. But, in your hometown, and more specifically in your own home, the title "rock star" feels a bit silly. Especially when you remove the hype and hysteria that defines a rock 'n' roll road show and replace it with the more mundane conditions of regular at-home life.

Less than twelve hours removed from being Mr. *Blowfish*, strutting around in the spotlight in skinny jeans, I was in my gym shorts and slippers taking out the garbage on Wyndham Road, hoping the neighbor didn't notice me. After that, I quietly loaded up our two eager dogs, Lulu and Mackie, to let them get some exercise in the woods nearby. And after that it was frying a pound of bacon and scrambling a bunch of eggs next to Laura, who was making a large stack of pancakes. I was thankful I didn't have to take some rock 'n' roll persona home with me. It wouldn't have worked anyway.

There's no telling if a tour bus might be rolling to a stop at our address down the road in a few years. I'll have to wait and see if there is a desire, or a need. For now, I'm certainly content being a dad, a husband, and a reliable fixture in the Bronefeld family, one day at a time.

ACKNOWLEDGMENTS

ON THE MORNING of my fifty-third birthday, October 20, 2017, as I sat drinking coffee next to my wife Laura in our front room, a couple of random thoughts came into my head. "What would it be like to type out some of the most meaningful memories from my life and consolidate them into one big story? How cool would it be if I started it right now, on my birthday?" More surprising than the idea itself was my follow-through. On that day, I began typing.

I proceeded forward with naïve energy, but it was the love, honesty, wisdom, and encouragement of my beautiful wife that kept me going each day. I can't thank you enough, my love.

Eighteen months later, racked with self-doubt about my writing, and unable to see a clear goal line anywhere in sight, I successfully stalked the talented journalist/author, J. R. Moehringer who not only took my call but offered to read some of my work. On numerous occasions he inspired me to push forward. "Just keep writing," he said. "Keep writing." You owed me nothing, J. R., but you gave me an amazing gift, and I thank you for that.

I trudged on, continuing to write for another year, still mostly clueless about memoirs or publishing, and called my old drummer friend, Steve Gorman, who had just published a fabulous book about his former band, The Black Crowes. I said, "Steve, I have no idea how I'm doing with my manuscript and I don't really know where I'm going." Graciously, Steve proclaimed, "I got a guy." Steve, thank you for sharing "your guy" with me, and thank you for being the lovely, humorous rhythm-machine that you are. The world is a better place with you in it.

Steve's guy turned out to be CAA's Anthony Mattero. I would soon learn he was a bit of a Hootie fan, and though that certainly didn't hurt, it was his generosity and gentle guidance that benefited me the most. Thank you, Anthony, for not only showing me where I was on my journey and who I needed to connect with next, but giving me explicit directions on how to find that person.

My next connection was Luke Dempsey who was willing to look past our deep footballing conflict to keenly edit my manuscript into a form that, when returned to me, was something I could really take pride in. Thank you, Luke, for your brutal honesty, and your skill to see which parts of my story were treasures, and which were trash. YNWA!

I headed back to the all-knowing Anthony Mattero who said, "Start asking people on this long list I'm sending you if they'll read your manuscript and represent you." And you know who said "Yes"? Marc Gerald from Europa Content! While Marc wasn't expecting to see a manuscript from a Blowfish that day, he read it anyway. When he felt something special pounding in his heart for this book, even if it surprised him a little, he followed that feeling and called me immediately, saying, "This is terrific! Let's get this thing published!" Marc is great at what he does, I found out. After the rejections started flowing in, he lifted my spirits, stating, "The company to support this book IS out there, I know it is. I just gotta find them." Thank you dearly, good man, for working hard to connect me with my next thank you.

Keith Wallman at Diversion Books. Thank you, thank you, thank you, for seeing value in my work, and taking a chance on it. For seeing where it still needed to grow and then taking the time to work with me to make it happen. To Evan Phail at Diversion Books, thank you for your patience in working with a rookie like me. That is a special skill. Thank you to Shannon Donnelly and Alex Sprague for your marketing and publicity guidance to get the word out! And finally, special thanks to Scott Waxman for running the Diversion ship.

~

Aside from the professional help I received along the way, I wanted to thank those very special to me.

Mom, I thank you for your love, my life, and for constantly showing me the value of reading. You always had a book on your desk, or in your lap, and the hundreds of Erma Bombeck stories you read aloud impacted me in ways that I would not understand for years.

Dad, thanks for your vivid and sometimes still-evolving memories of our family. You continue to teach me and love me and I am so thankful you are here with us every day.

To my siblings, Dave, Mike, Steve, and Katie, thanks for helping me recall and reminisce our time together under the same roof during the 1960s, '70s, and '80s, even if the only conclusion we could all agree on was, "Yeah, that happened."

Darius, Dean, and Mark, you three deserve a lifetime of thanks for providing me the opportunity to display a few of my talents while looking past many of my flagrant flaws. You've shown me what being a great bandmate looks like.

To Deb, thanks for being the mother of our two wonderful children, and sharing in the sometimes difficult task of raising them in two different homes.

To my children Cameron and Mason, thanks for the joy you've given me, and for being the central characters in a story where I become the beneficiary of immense healing.

To my bonus children Marlee, Kenny, and Madelynn, thank you for the honor of being your stepdad. I know you didn't volunteer for your positions as stepkids when I married your mom, but you've opened your hearts in a way that has helped me to become a better man.

To our entire Hootie road crew and staff, who have taken such good care of my family and me, especially during our 2019 tour. Thank you for working hard on every important detail so I can concentrate on performing, and writing this book!

A special shoutout goes to Chris Carney and Jessica Snyder from our Fishco office. Your efforts behind the scene have been invaluable, especially sleuthing out the many band facts and historical details that I couldn't locate during the first three years of writing.

To Peter Holsapple, an early champion of my writing, thank you for your willingness to discuss the literary world with which I was so unfamiliar and for making me feel I could one day be part of that world. Thank you for encouraging me to write and "Just have fun!"

To all of our managers, past and present, thanks for trying to always lead the band and me in the right direction. I know it's not easy herding cats!

A special thank-you goes out to Gus Gusler, who continues to look over every business contract I sign. Gus, you've shown me ethics are not only important but that doing the "right thing" is always the "best thing."

To Chip Latham, my close friend and a great man of faith, you've supported me through this entire book-writing endeavor, always reminding me that an eager audience would one day be waiting at the finish line for me.

Though you will remain anonymous, I have immense gratitude for my recovery community here in Columbia, South Carolina, for the experience, strength, and hope you've shared with me. You showed me being honest with oneself can lead to deep discovery, and it was my self-discovery which became the basis for this book.

To the late, great Dr. Sandra Wertz, my mentor and professor in Media Arts at the University of South Carolina. Thanks for educating me in the classroom, giving me your advice outside of it, and for displaying your infectious passion for music, movies, and the arts. God's peace to you and your family.

To Sam Holland, thank you for your interest and patience while sifting through hundreds and hundreds of images of my life. Thank you for editing, filing, scanning, shooting, and instructing. Your help has been priceless!

To all the musical memoirists I've read, such as Ben Folds, Jeff Tweedy, Charlie Daniels, Flea, and many more, deepest thanks for paving a path I could follow. Your courage has been a shining light for me.

I must recognize the people that made, and still make, those "month-at-a-glance" paper calendars I've obsessively filled out and saved since the late '80s—the same kind I saw my mom always using to organize her life. I could never have put the events of this book in the correct order without over thirty years of my saved calendars at my fingertips, so, thank you.

INDEX

ABOUT THE AUTHOR

HOOTIE & THE BLOWFISH drummer Jim "Soni" Sonefeld dreamt more of being a professional soccer player than a successful musician. But with the unsuspected success of the band's 1994 debut release, *Cracked Rear View*, he and his bandmates found themselves traveling the world to support what would become the sixteenth bestselling album of all time in the United States. The band would record four more studio albums and receive numerous awards, among them two Grammys. During this era, Sonefeld's lines of truth became blurred, and his addictions began to take over his life as he relied heavily on drugs and alcohol to cope with the emptiness growing inside of him. He struggled to find peace and to hold his personal life together, and in 2004 Sonefeld finally accepted that he was powerless over drugs and alcohol and that his life had become entirely unmanageable. In sobriety, Sonefeld discovered there were parts of his life that had incurred damages beyond repair, but that God would heal him if he turned his life over to His care.

Since then, a full spiritual awakening led to a complete lifestyle change and inspired Sonefeld to follow a new path of clarity, and nothing was clearer to him than God's calling to recreate himself as a contemporary Christian artist. He also helps others in recovery by sharing his story and his music with Celebrate Recovery groups around the United States.